THE GATES OF NOVEMBER

THE GATES OF NOVEMBER

Chronicles of the Slepak Family

CHAIM POTOK

Secker & Warburg
London

Originally published in the United States in 1996
by Alfred A. Knopf, Inc.

First published in Great Britain by Secker & Warburg 1997

1 3 5 7 9 10 8 6 4 2

Copyright © 1996 by Chaim Potok, Leonid Slepak,
Vladimir Slepak, Maria Slepak and Alexander Slepak

The authors have asserted their right
under the Copyright, Designs and Patents Act 1988
to be identified as the authors of this work

First published in the United Kingdom in 1997 by
Secker & Warburg,
Random House, 20 Vauxhall Bridge Road,
London SW1V 2SA

Random House Australia (Pty) Limited
20 Alfred Street, Milsons Point, Sydney,
New South Wales 2061, Australia

Random House New Zealand Limited
18 Poland Road, Glenfield,
Auckland 10, New Zealand

Random House South Africa (Pty) Limited
Endulini, 5A Jubilee Road, Parktown 2193, South Africa

Random House UK Limited Reg. No. 954009

A CIP catalogue record for this book is available from the British Library

ISBN 0-436-20440-1

Papers used by Random House UK Limited are natural,
recyclable products made from wood grown in sustainable forests.
The manufacturing processes conform to the environmental
regulations of the country of origin.

Printed and bound in Great Britain
by Creative Print and Design (Ebbw Vale) Wales

The story of the dissidents in the former Soviet Union is one of the few truly noble astonishments of the twentieth century. Some, like Andrei Sakharov, were of heroic stature even before they chose the path of opposition. Others, like Volodya and Masha Slepak, came to greatness only after they stepped forward. Clearly, all the dissidents could not be present in these pages. It is to each and every one of them that I dedicate this book.

A tedious season they await
Who hear November at the gate.

—Alexander Pushkin

Contents

History brought together on the same soil two vigorous peoples, Russians and Jews, whose bitter destiny it was to be ruinously at each other's throats.

Present-day Russia had its origins in unruly Slavic and Finnish tribes who migrated southward sometime in the eighth century of the Common Era, agreed among themselves to be ruled by a northern tribe known as the Scandinavian Rus (some claim the Rus came as conquerors), and created a state known as Kievan Russia, with Kiev on the Dnieper River as its leading city.

As for the Jews—tombstone inscriptions indicate that there were Jewish communities on the shores of the Black Sea as far back as the third century before the Common Era. In the early centuries of the Common Era, Jews began to flee toward what are now Georgia and Armenia from the persecutions of the Greek Orthodox Church of Byzantium. And there appears to be some truth to the legend that around 740 the pagan kingdom of the Khazars, an Asiatic tribe situated on the shores of the Caspian Sea, converted en masse to Judaism.

Shortly before the year 1000, the Kievan ruler Vladimir formed an alliance with Byzantium and adopted Greek Orthodox Christianity as the official religion of his state. Together, they crushed the Jewish kingdom of the Khazars, whose populace was absorbed into the world of the Kievan Rus.

Along with Greek Orthodoxy, there arrived from Byzantium a new

architecture, music, art, churches, a clergy, laws, an educational system—and a hatred of and contempt for the Jew. It was a loathing pure
and unmitigated; it suffused the entire Kievan polity, ruler and clergy-
man and nobleman and serf. It continued for centuries, from the height
of Kievan Russia's power to its disintegration in civil wars and final conquest by Mongols in 1240; then, untouched by the softening admixture
of Renaissance and Reformationist ideas which swept through Europe
but barely engaged Russia, it persisted into the Muscovite state, which
began its expansion under Ivan III and Ivan IV in the fifteenth and sixteenth centuries, and finally into the dynasty of the Romanovs, founded
in 1613.

Demon, ogre, heathen, and killer of Christ—that was how the Russian saw the Jew. The Orthodox empire of Muscovite Russia remained
virtually without Jews—until 1772.

In the reign of Catherine II, Poland fell to the three powers surrounding it: Germany, Austria, and Russia. Jews had been living in
Poland since the Middle Ages, at the invitation and under the protection
of Polish kings and nobles. By 1795 the portions of Poland procured by
the distant progeny of the Kievan Rus had brought under the dominion
of Muscovite Russia the largest Jewish population in the world.

It is estimated that in 1850 there were about 2,350,000 Jews in Russia.
They lived in a restricted region known as the Pale of Settlement: almost
a million square miles from the Baltic to the Black Sea; two thousand
townlets and cities in twenty-five provinces, the Jews one-ninth of the
population. By the close of the nineteenth century Jews in the empire of
Russia numbered around 5,000,000.

Official policies toward them vacillated from seeming benevolence to
outright cruelty, one tsar granting them rights which the next tsar would
withdraw. In essence, the Russians would have preferred that they simply vanish. Tsarist policy was tersely stated in 1895 by Konstantin
Pobedonostsev, head of the Holy Synod, the governing body of the
Russian Orthodox Church, under Alexander III (reigned 1881–1894),
and the tutor of Nicholas II (reigned 1894–1917): "One-third will die
out, one-third will flee the country, and one-third will dissolve into the
surrounding population"—by which he meant, will convert.

The response of the Jews to tsarist persecution ran the gamut from an
intensification of separateness by religionists to attempts at participation
in Russian culture by assimilationists to the joining of the ranks of socialists and revolutionaries by increasingly disenchanted and enraged
youth. The government-organized pogroms following the assassination
of Alexander II in 1881 bitterly disillusioned many Jews who had chosen

the path of assimilation. They began to turn their energies inward—to the revival of Jewish nationalism; to a culture of their own in a Jewish homeland; to the creation of a new literature in Yiddish and in a miraculously reborn and modernized Hebrew.

The rule of the tsars came to an end early in 1917 with the abdication of Nicholas II. Quiescent for three decades following the November 1917 Bolshevik Revolution (October according to the old Julian calendar then still in use in Russia), the rooted Russian hatred of the Jew surfaced in an especially insidious form during Stalin's final years and led, ultimately, to the turbulent and fateful events that befell the individuals whose lives are in the pages of this book.

History also brought me into the Russian world of Volodya Slepak and his wife, Masha.

Russia was very much a part of my family's life during my early New York years: detested by my parents in the 1930s; a needed ally during the Second World War; a sudden enemy once again afterward. Russian literature, art, music—intoxicating. Russian power—reptilian. It seemed a vast and sealed dark land, the Soviet Union, and it was only after the death of Stalin and in the aftermath of the Khrushchev years that there began to be heard the thin, small voices of Jews who were still alive behind the Iron Curtain. From books like *The Jews of Silence* by Elie Wiesel and *Between Hammer and Sickle* by Ben Ami (pseudonym of Lova Eliav); from the occasional visitor to the Soviet Union; from the diplomats who talked off the record; from the reports of perceptive journalists—from those sources and others came news of a nascent dissident movement inside one of the most repressive of modern states. Certain names began to move into prominence, among them that of the Slepaks. They had applied for exit visas from the Soviet Union in April 1970, had been repeatedly refused, and stood during the seventies at the center of an increasingly vocal and visible dissident movement.

In the early 1970s I lived in Philadelphia, which had become a major center of activity in the struggle to free Soviet Jews. By the late 1970s the rescue of Soviet Jewry was very high on the agenda of world Jewry. What the KGB and the Politburo regarded as a well-organized, sophisticated international network of Jewish smugglers and spies intent upon the destruction of the Soviet Union, Jews knew to be a fragile lifeline made up mostly of ordinary men and women determined to aid a suffering branch of their people.

From time to time I would hear about the Slepaks. It seemed that the constant refusal to grant them exit visas was connected to some kind of secret work in which Volodya Slepak, a highly trained electronics engineer, had once been engaged. There were also rumors that he was being deliberately held back by his father, who, it turned out, had once been high in the ranks of those legendary Bolsheviks who had fathered the Russian Revolution. An Old Bolshevik in the Slepak family! How had he survived the Stalinist purges of the thirties that had cut like scythes through Old Bolshevik ranks?

Then, in mid-1978, Volodya and Masha Slepak were suddenly arrested by the KGB and brought to trial. Five years later, released from Siberian exile, they returned to Moscow, where they resumed their bleak lives.

My wife said to me then that we ought to visit the Soviet Union and meet some of the people who were risking their lives by their open defiance of that regime. Most of all, she wanted us to meet Volodya and Masha Slepak.

ΩΩΩ

This book is about the Slepak family. It seeks to answer two questions. First: What conditions will drive individuals living in comfort at the very summit of a political system, suddenly to turn against that system and bring ruin down on their lives? And second: Can a single family serve as a microcosm that might shed light on what ultimately happened to all the peoples of the Soviet Union? That was once a land so filled with hope; then a slowly growing skepticism, and a slide into cynicism, disillusionment, alienation, rage, separation, and, in the end, a general disintegration.

What went wrong? Might there be a lesson in that for us all?

I should point out that nothing in this book is invented, save perhaps the configuration we all give to raw facts when we shape them into a narrative. The conversations in these pages have been set down precisely as they were imparted to me by the Slepaks, with only the very lightest of occasional touches for purposes of style and clarity. Throughout, the intent has been to present true events, to add them to the record of this century, for the future to ponder.

I wish to express my thanks to Leonard Gold and Ruth A. Carr of the New York Public Library for their help, as well as to Theodore Comet of the Joint Distribution Committee, Bert Siegel of the Philadelphia Jewish Community Relations Council, and the staff of Gratz College Library in Philadelphia. Thanks also to Owen Laster, my agent, and David Schlossberg, who were the first to suggest that I might be interested in this story, and to Dan and Sheila Segal, Eileen Sussman, and Connie and Joseph Smukler, whose early involvement with many of the Russians in this book edged me into the world of the Soviet Union and its Jews.

Thanks are also due the students in my 1992 Benjamin Franklin Honors Seminar at the University of Pennsylvania. Their keen minds and respectful interest—the awe on their faces the day they met Volodya Slepak in my home!—helped me realize the significance of this subject even to the young and gave me the impetus to move this book along at a crucial period in its development.

To my wife, Adena, I owe boundless gratitude. This was an especially difficult work: the volatile course of events in Russia has resulted in a dramatic lowering of the temperature on the subject of Russian Jewry. Was there anything about the Slepak story that was still worth telling? Her gentle persuasions, perceptive reading, and patient listening helped immeasurably to bring the book to life. And I conclude with words of deepest appreciation to my editor and friend Robert Gottlieb. For decades he has given me the keenest of readerly eyes, the most perceptive of editorial judgments. I am fortunate, indeed, to have Adena and Bob as an intrinsic part of my life.

THE GATES OF NOVEMBER

A Meeting in Moscow

On a Thursday evening in the first week of January 1985, Adena and I landed in a snowstorm at Sheremetevo Airport in Moscow. Early the next morning we left the humid warmth of our hotel and Adena slipped into a telephone booth on the street and dialed a number, while I waited outside in the bitter cold. After a moment or two I heard her say, "Hello, my husband and I are from Philadelphia. We're in Moscow, and we'd like to meet you."

She did not give our names. She said only, "My husband and I . . ."

The man at the other end told her briefly which Metro to take, how long the ride would last, and where he would meet us.

Adena and I do not idly travel about on the Jewish Sabbath, which begins on Friday at sundown. But before setting out on our journey to the Soviet Union, we had resolved that we would behave there as if we had entered a zone of emergency, a landscape of combat; whenever necessary, we would transgress religious laws. In wintry Moscow, daylight arrived around nine in the morning and was entirely gone by about three in the afternoon. Volodya Slepak worked and would be unable to see us until after six o'clock. And that Friday night was the only time we could meet with him and his wife, for there were many others to see, and our remaining nights in Moscow were accounted for. That was our choice: Keep the Sabbath and miss the Slepaks, or break the Sabbath and meet the Slepaks.

That evening we left the hotel and walked on snow and ice past St.

Basil's Cathedral and the Kremlin Passage. A street or so beyond Lenin's Tomb, we turned into the Marx Prospekt Metro station. The train was quiet, clean, crowded. In our gray down coats, insulated boots, and colored scarves, we were clearly Americans. This was the Reagan era; the wild American cowboy president was threatening the world with nuclear war. Passengers glared at us with unconcealed hostility.

We traveled for about a half hour.

The train pulled into our station. We walked with others along the platform and began to hang back, letting the crowd move past us. Soon we were the only ones there.

The well-lighted station had cream-colored tile walls, bright and clean. The air, smelling of cold, damp earth, echoed with vague and distant sounds: an eerie pinging of metal, the skitterings of unseen creatures.

Up ahead Volodya Slepak suddenly stepped out from behind a pillar and moved slowly toward us, his face familiar from the many photographs we had seen of him. The bright lights of the Metro revealed his sharp eyes and large nose and broad smile and graying Amish-style beard. He wore a dark coat and a fur cap with earflaps. Bearded, stocky, of medium height. He said in a deep, throaty voice, "Shalom aleichem," the traditional Hebrew greeting, meaning "Peace be with you." Startling to hear Hebrew in the Moscow Metro.

Adena and I gave the traditional response: "Aleichem shalom."

We shook hands.

"Please come with me."

We followed him through the station and up a stairway and out into the cold night.

Snow blew in waves through the streets. Beads of frozen moisture formed on my beard. I could barely see through my glasses.

He walked between us along the shoveled paths and plowed streets.

"Probably you do not like our Russian weather," he said.

"Is this your usual winter?" Adena asked.

"Perhaps not so usual," he said. "But it is not so very bad in Moscow. Other places it is terrible."

I told him the only time I'd ever felt this cold was during my sixteen months with the American Army in Korea.

"Ah, you were a soldier in Korea?"

"We got the winds from Siberia."

"Ah, yes. I know very well those winds."

We walked on in silence, carefully navigating tall banks of snow. He was taking us to the apartment of his wife's brother and sister-in-law. Not a soul visible anywhere in the white windblown night. Massive apartment houses on both sides of the street. Soft yellow lights in windows. The dry, squeaking sounds of our boots on the wind-scoured snow. Vague lights approaching slowly and then a car gliding past us, no headlights, only its dims glowing, the only car we'd seen since leaving the Metro.

I asked, "Why do they drive without headlights?"

"To save batteries."

"Isn't it dangerous?"

"Of course."

I asked what the accident rate was in Russia.

"The same as in America, about fifty thousand fatalities a year—but we have one-tenth your number of vehicles. Now, please, we go this way."

We turned onto a shoveled path, a murky whitish corridor between heaped-up mounds of snow. Ahead stood a towering apartment building.

"I must now ask you," he said, "let us not speak anymore until we are inside the apartment."

He unlocked the front door. We entered a dark foyer and began to climb barely visible stairs. The place had the air of an old New York tenement, but with no vivid sounds of life drifting out from behind closed doors. Here you wanted to walk on tiptoe, expecting a sudden leap out of the violet shadows by figures demanding to know what you were doing there.

At the top of the staircase, a corridor. We walked toward a door—which, a scant moment before we reached it, opened to us suddenly and mysteriously.

In the doorway stood a woman of early middle age. Without a sound, she beckoned us inside and as soon as we'd entered, closed and locked the door.

We were in a narrow hallway. Coat pegs protruded from the wall, a small mirror hung nearby, and close to the wall stood a bench around which were shoes and house slippers, all neatly arranged in pairs.

Volodya Slepak and the woman exchanged some words in Russian. I assumed she was Masha Slepak's sister-in-law. She pointed silently to the house slippers and then went down the hallway and into a room.

We removed our coats and hats and hung them on the pegs. Everything we wore dripped melting snow. Puddles formed on the hallway

linoleum floor. Adena and I proceeded to unlace and remove our wet
boots, and put on the slippers we had brought with us. Mine I carried
in my camera bag.

Standing in a gray woolen sweater and dark trousers and slippers, his
thick graying hair uncombed, his beard still wet with snow, Volodya
Slepak watched as we got into our house slippers, and flashed us an appealing smile.

"Ah, you come prepared. Very good. Now come with me, please. You
will meet everyone."

We followed him through the hallway into the main room of the
apartment.

It was a fair-sized room that served as both a living room and a dining room, the air warm and stuffy, the floor covered by a rug, the slightly
shabby genteel look not unlike that of the rooms in which I grew up in
middle-class neighborhoods of New York. In front of the couch stood a
table with seven place settings. Bookcases jammed with volumes and periodicals took up the entire wall to the right of the couch. The curtains
had been drawn over the windows on the other side of the room. Near
the windows stood a small desk on which were a telephone and a vase
filled with flowers. During the day I had seen elderly women bundled
against the cold, standing in the snow, peddling flowers from little
stands.

A few feet from the couch stood the dark-haired woman who had
opened the door for us and a middle-aged man I took to be Masha
Slepak's brother. Next to him was a stocky, pale-faced young man of
about eighteen, no doubt their son, Masha's nephew, about the same
height as his father, with thick dark hair and a bit of a stoop, and wearing on his sallow features an expression of deep melancholy.

Masha Slepak sat on the couch. She was a small, plump, shy-looking
woman, with pallid, roundish features and short reddish hair, her eyes
brown and alert behind thick glasses. She gazed at us with a wan, my-
opic look and a distant smile.

Our formal introduction to the family was brief.

"Here are people from America come to visit us," was all Volodya
Slepak said. There were polite handshakes. No one asked our names.

The atmosphere in the room was disquieting; it seemed to quiver
with barely suppressed apprehension. Someone once said that the only
true question we ought to ask one another is: "What are you going
through?" Probably in the course of this evening the question would be
answered without ever being asked. It was a desperate way for people like

these to sustain life and hope: through strangers dropping in from the sky.

Masha Slepak's brother and sister-in-law went into the kitchen. Her nephew retreated into a room off the hallway near the door to the apartment.

Earlier that day Adena and I had purchased a bottle of Stolichnaya vodka. This Adena now removed from her bag and presented to Volodya, who broke into an exuberant smile.

"Aha, that's good, that's good," he boomed, looking thoroughly delighted. "Thank you very much."

The room was sultry with radiator heat. No doubt the windows were fogged over behind the heavy curtains.

Adena went to the telephone to arrange our meetings for the next day. Volodya and I sat on chairs near the table.

"So," Volodya Slepak said, "you are from America."

His eyes, I noticed, were grayish green, mischievous and shrewd. Beneath the folds of his loose-fitting woolen sweater was the clear outline of a paunch.

I said, "Yes, from Philadelphia."

"Do you know many Jews in Philadelphia?"

"We bring greetings from lots of friends."

I mentioned the names of some people who had asked us to convey their good wishes to the Slepaks. He acknowledged the names with a hearty "Yes, of course, we know them."

The conversation, slowly warming, still carried a measure of awkwardness, the quality of a hospital or prison visit, where the knowledge that one of the parties will sooner or later get up and leave while the other must remain behind chills the air and brings to all the talk an undercurrent of melancholy. Volodya Slepak's English, with its heavy Russian accents, was fluent. And there was something beguiling about his eyes and expressive mouth and deep-throated nasal voice, a compelling, robust force that radiated energy.

All the time we talked, Masha Slepak sat quietly, her eyes watchful behind her thick glasses.

Volodya Slepak rubbed his beard and said, "If you permit me, I must ask you something."

"Please," I said.

"There is a man who lives in Philadelphia. The writer Chaim Potok. Do you perhaps know him?"

I said, trying to conceal my surprise, "Well, yes . . ."

"You do?" His face lit up.

I said, "I'm Chaim Potok."

His eyes narrowed. He looked confused.

Masha Slepak said something to him in Russian, the first time she had entered the conversation, and he responded to her quietly in Russian while still looking at me.

Both of them gazed at me with some unease.

"No, excuse me," Volodya Slepak said. "Perhaps you did not understand. My English is not always so good. I asked if you knew the American writer Chaim Potok."

I glanced at Adena—she was still talking on the phone at the other end of the room—and said slowly, "Yes, I know Chaim Potok. I *am* Chaim Potok." And I reached into a pocket and drew out one of the calling cards I had been advised to have printed for the trip. In a Russian home, I'd been told, they served as a kind of genteel announcement of one's identity, a bourgeois emblem of individuality amid the ideological leveling of personality purportedly characteristic of the Soviet world.

Volodya Slepak took the card, lifted the bottom of his sweater, removed a pair of reading glasses from his shirt pocket, slipped them on, raised the card to his eyes, and peered at it. I thought I could see the skin above the line of his beard and along his broad forehead turn crimson. He took off his glasses and stared at me in astonishment and then uttered a sudden loud "Whooo!" that resounded through the apartment.

Adena turned and looked at Volodya.

Masha Slepak, seeming confused, spoke rapidly in Russian, and Volodya replied. I heard my name in his cascade of words. She said, "Oh!" and put both her hands to her mouth and stared at me.

Her brother and sister-in-law came in from the kitchen, and a moment later the pale-looking nephew burst from his room and rushed to the side of his alarmed parents.

"You are Chaim Potok?" Volodya Slepak said, grasping my hand with both of his and pumping it. He got to his feet and I stood as well, and he embraced me. I felt entirely swallowed up by his hard, muscular frame and his ebullience, by the strength I sensed in his arms. And I experienced no small astonishment of my own at that moment and a sensation of profound pleasure that my work had somehow reached and touched this admirable man.

He boomed to those who had just entered the room, "This is the writer Chaim Potok!" and his voice rang in my ears.

The brother and sister-in-law nodded courteously, with no sign of recognition. The young man responded with a vacant stare. Adena hung up the telephone and joined us.

"What a surprise!" Volodya said. "We must make a toast!"

He said something in Russian, reached for the bottle of vodka we had brought, and began to open it, while Masha's sister-in-law hurried into the kitchen and returned with a tray of small glasses. Volodya poured drinks. We raised our glasses.

"To our friends from Philadelphia," he said. "And to freedom."

"To my first meeting with people I feel I've known for a long time," I said.

"To new friends," said Adena.

Masha Slepak held her glass, looking intently at Adena and at me. There was something about the way she was watching us, as if her eyes were categorizing, filing, storing things away. Her brother and sister-in-law, who apparently knew no more English than Masha, stood with their drinks, bewildered and somewhat apprehensive over Volodya's exuberance. And the nephew seemed utterly confounded by the glass of vodka thrust into his hand.

The seven of us emptied our glasses to seal our moment of meeting, and returned them to the tray. The brother and sister-in-law returned to the kitchen, and the nephew started down the hallway to his room. Volodya Slepak watched him go and waited until he had closed the door to the room. "There is a big problem with him," he said.

"What's that?" I asked.

"He is of an age when he can be taken into the army. If they take him, Masha's brother and sister-in-law will not leave even if they are given exit visas."

"Have they applied for visas?"

"Oh, yes. And they have been refused. They will not apply again if their son is in the army."

"I understand."

"And later the authorities will use his having been in the army as a reason not to give him an exit visa. They will say because he was a soldier, he knows state secrets." He was silent a moment. "It is a big problem. They might send him to the war in Afghanistan." He paused. "Maybe you or your wife know an American girl he might marry."

His words were an appeal to save a life.

Adena and I exchanged glances and shook our heads.

The subject of this doleful solicitation was called back into the room by his mother a few minutes later, and we took our places around the table. It was Shabbat, but there were no candles, or wine, or braided bread. A consuming desolation lay upon the room. All sat very still looking down at the table, and I sensed that they were waiting for me to do something.

I poured some vodka into my water glass, indicated that they should do the same with their glasses, and rose to my feet. They stood. I chanted the Shabbat Kiddush blessing—normally performed with sacramental wine—over the vodka. Even in Korea, in the worst of times, there had always been wine for Kiddush. I chanted slowly, glancing at the faces of the Russians. No embarrassment there, and no apparent discomfort. Solemn and respectful. I finished the Kiddush, and we drank the vodka. Then, over a loaf of dark bread, I recited the blessing for bread and sliced the loaf and passed it around. We sat down.

The aura of sanctity given the table by the blessings left everyone wordless for a moment. A Shabbat meal was clearly not a commonplace occurrence in the lives of these Soviet Jews. The dinner, I remember, consisted of a salad of cooked beets, potatoes and onions, and steamed white fish with cabbage and carrots. And small poppyseed cinnamon cookies. And tea. And much conversation.

Adena and I talked about the origins of our families in Russia. Escape had been the theme of their lives: my great-grandfather and his flight to Poland to avoid conscription and twenty-five years of army service under Nicholas I; Adena's father and his flight from Nicholas II to elude arrest for participating in Zionist activities. Breaking out, bribing one's way across closed borders, getting as far as possible from that oppressive land—that was the legacy they left us. We had come to the Soviet Union, Adena said, to meet with dissidents, to express solidarity with them, to tell them they were not forgotten. All the time we talked, Volodya quietly translated our words to Masha and the others.

A warm intimacy settled upon the room, a quality of familiarity and closeness brought on by a shared table. The conversation with Volodya meandered into tributaries: Stalin, the Second World War, Cold War politics, the present Soviet regime, the dissidents, and the petitions, letters, headlines, demonstrations. The talk grew animated, and even Masha began to join in, expressing herself in halting Yiddish and English. From time to time her brother and sister-in-law ventured a few words. Only the young man sat in silence, lost, it seemed to me, in a miasma of sadness.

Slipping from one subject to another, we arrived somehow at the matter of Volodya's health, and Masha suddenly turned to me and, pointing to my midsection, said with a sober look, "Small." For a moment, I didn't understand. Then she directed a finger at Volodya's prominent paunch and said, "Not small," and I sensed the weight of her admonishment.

Volodya's voice, normally loud, bellowed forth in laughter. His face beamed; his eyes flashed. He patted his belly, said, "Masha wishes me to lose weight," and laughed again.

Masha said something in Russian. Volodya translated. "Masha wishes to know how you stay so thin."

I explained in simple English the normal and healthful way I ate. Volodya listened and translated. Masha grew increasingly absorbed. Her face grew animated; her eyes brightened. Of all things to excite her so— a modest, studied style of eating. Perhaps her husband was in ill health and needed some rules to rein in his appetite.

When I was done, Masha spoke briefly in Russian to Volodya. He rose from the table, left the room, and returned a moment later with a pad and a pencil. "Say again how you eat, and I will write it down. We will make Masha happy."

Later we all helped clear the table, and as we moved about, a perceptible tension returned to the air. I noticed that Masha's sister-in-law was glancing repeatedly at the kitchen clock. Finally, they all went to the telephone.

Volodya explained to us that his in-laws were about to make their fortnightly call to their daughter and son-in-law, who had a newborn child and lived in Beersheba, Israel. The call, which had been prearranged, went through with no difficulty.

Mother and father and son took turns talking into the telephone. They talked loudly, as if they had little faith in the instrument's mysterious power and thought they had to propel their voices through the hidden wires that stretched across land and sea. Responding voices crackled from the black receiver. Volodya translated quietly. The baby was well. His name was Daniel. The daughter was very happy. She sent her love to her parents and brother and aunt and uncle. She was eagerly awaiting the day when they all would be given permission to emigrate.

Masha spoke on the telephone. Then Volodya. The call came to an end.

Masha turned away from the telephone, her face ashen, her lips tight. All the early self-restraint seemed to have drained from her. She said to Adena in hesitant and broken English, "I never again to see my children. I never to see my new grandchild in America." Suddenly impatient with the language, she lapsed into Russian, and Volodya translated. "Our two sons received their visas to Israel years ago, and now they live in the United States. The wife of the son who lives in Philadelphia is pregnant and will soon give birth. We will never again be a family. This is our bitter lot. We are doomed to live out our lives in the Soviet Union. At least we succeeded in getting the children out. Not for a moment do we regret what we did."

She stopped, and Volodya added, "There is reason to hope that Masha's brother and sister-in-law will be able to leave if we can keep their son out of the army." The young man said something in Russian and returned to his room. His parents went into the kitchen. Masha and Adena sat for a while on the couch, talking quietly together.

Sometime later we said good-bye to Masha's brother and sister-in-law and nephew and started back. The snow was still falling. Volodya and Masha said they would accompany us to the hotel.

The Metro was nearly deserted. Volodya and I sat on one side of the car, and opposite us were Masha and Adena. Adena told me later that Masha talked mostly about the years she and Volodya had spent in Siberia. Her legs, badly frostbitten, were not as painful now as they had once been, though she couldn't stand for very long. Glancing at Masha from time to time, I caught an occasional flash of fire from the eyes behind the thick glasses. It occurred to me that there was probably a good deal more to her than she had revealed tonight, and it saddened me that I would never have the opportunity to know her better.

We emerged from the Metro station into the snow. It was quite late. I put my scarf over my face, a feeble defense against the wind. Near the steps outside the hotel we stood a few minutes longer, still talking.

"I have read two of your books in English," Volodya said. "And now, here we are together, speaking as friends."

We stood there some while longer, reluctant to part. Finally, we shook hands and embraced and said to one another, "Lehitraot," which is Hebrew for "until we meet again," though none of us really believed that was remotely probable. Adena and I watched them walk slowly away and vanish into the snow-shrouded Russian night.

In the months that followed, I would remember the Slepaks at odd moments: staring out a window at a snowstorm; reciting the blessing over a cup of wine before a Shabbat dinner; on a subway train; reading news from the Soviet Union. I followed with admiration and heartache their

strife-filled lives. Then, in October 1987, with a suddenness that was stupefying, they received their exit visas and were out of the Soviet Union
and on their way to Israel!

One winter evening not long afterward, in a restaurant in New York,
my agent, Owen Laster, asked me and Adena if we knew the Slepaks. We
said yes, we knew them. He told me that Volodya had made tapes in
Russian of their story and the tapes had been translated into English by
one of the sons. Would I be interested in listening to the tapes and writing about the Slepaks?

The Jewish dissident struggle was then at its height. I thought: Listen
to the tapes, see if they're worthwhile, and maybe join the effort to free
the Russian Jews.

I agreed to listen to the tapes. In due course, book contracts were
signed. I began the necessary research. Adena and I flew to Israel, met
with the Slepaks, and returned with nearly forty hours of video and audiotapes, which were later augmented by more than twenty additional
hours of audiotapes, many dozens of handwritten faxes, and countless
telephone calls concerning details large and small.

All the material in my possession—tapes, faxes, records of face-to-face
conversations, and telephone calls—constituted the chronicles of a family that was in many ways an extreme example of the perennial Jewish
plight in Russia, the plight of a deviant people against whom the Russians had unceasingly defined themselves. But as I went through those
chronicles again and again, a very particular family drama began to surface, and I came slowly to realize that what I had in my possession was
not only the classic tale of Russians and Jews at each other's throats but
also a tangled and singular human story about a father and a son—with
a baffling mystery at its core.

THE FATHER

The Fire Bringer

S hortly after the turn of the century, a thirteen-year-old boy in a
small town in White Russia fled from the impoverished home of
his mother, his father having died five years earlier. In the years
that followed, he went on moving, across oceans and continents. By the
time he reached the mainland of Asia nearly two decades later, he had
been remarkably metamorphosed from a harmless small-town Russian
Jewish boy into a cultured and dedicated Bolshevik killer.

The small town was Kopys, about fifteen kilometers from the town of
his birth, Dubrovno, on the Dnieper River.

In 1766 there were 801 Jewish taxpayers in Dubrovno and its environs.
One hundred years later it had become the center of a textile industry
that manufactured and distributed prayer shawls throughout Russia and
Europe and as far away as America. By the end of the eighteenth century
Dubrovno also had a tile factory and a community of religious scribes,
who wrote phylacteries, Torah scrolls, and mezuzahs, the little contain-
ers with passages of the Torah that Jews affix to the doorposts of their
homes.

The weavers of Dubrovno labored on antiquated handlooms and
were brutally exploited by the merchants, who sold them yarn at high
profit and purchased finished products at low prices. During the latter
half of the nineteenth century, big-city competition from machine-
woven prayer shawls crippled the textile industry of Dubrovno. The
weavers began to leave. In 1897, four years after Solomon Slepak was

born, there were 4,364 Jews in Dubrovno, constituting about 57 percent of the total population. The town was so inconsequential that it did not even have its own railway station.

Photographs offer us images of Jewish life in Dubrovno.

A portrait of Solomon Slepak's father shows a man with a long black beard and a tall dark skullcap. He had migrated to Dubrovno from somewhere in the Ukraine. Family lore relates that he was physically very strong; that his life's dream was to send his son, Solomon, to a yeshiva, an academy of higher Jewish learning, where he would study for the rabbinate; and that in a certain Ukrainian town about one-third of the Jews were named Slepak, which in Ukrainian means "blind."

There is a full-length photograph of an elderly man named Munya, who was a sexton in a Dubrovno synagogue. He also wears a tall dark skullcap and a long dark coat that hangs slightly open, revealing knee-high boots and ritual fringes. He stares at us through shadowed, melancholy eyes. His lips are thin, unsmiling. A flowing white beard reaches nearly to his chest. There is a stoic grace about his poverty, a quiet dignity to his burdened life. Though there is no evidence that he was related to the Slepaks, it takes no prodigious leap of the imagination to envision him as similar in look and garb to Solomon Slepak's father, who was a *melamed*, a poor teacher of children.

And there is a photograph of a synagogue celebration in Dubrovno. An extraordinary occasion, one of enormous joy: A scribe has completed the writing of a Torah scroll, a lengthy and demanding sacred enterprise, a year or more of the most painstaking labor. In the photograph we see the Holy Ark, which is richly ornamented with a bevy of animals and birds and a delicately filigreed facade. A crowd of about sixty men, women, and children stand in a loose semicircle behind a bearded man in a cap, knee breeches, and boots, who appears to be doing some sort of dance. Two young-looking men, a fiddler and a clarinetist, play their instruments. The clarinetist has no beard and is wearing a derby; perhaps he is a professional musician, an outsider, hired for the occasion. A bearded elder carries the Torah scroll, which is suitably adorned with a silver crown. In the background, near the Ark and the wall of the synagogue, stand women and children in neatly arranged rows. In the foreground are men and boys. And once again it is no great feat of the imagination to envision one of those boys as young Solomon Slepak, who was a student in his father's little school and certainly attended synagogue.

No face in that photograph wears a smile. This was, after all, a picture for posterity, marking a high moment of public celebration.

Other photographs mark suffering and death. There is an intriguing photograph that invites us to contemplate the miracle of a pogrom mysteriously averted: The synagogue in Mstislavl, built in the first half of the seventeenth century, stands tall and boldly peaked against a whitish sky, its destruction suddenly halted by Tsar Peter the Great, who, on entering the city with troops in 1708, visited the synagogue and mysteriously and abruptly ordered his soldiers to cease their plundering and killing of Jews. "Only with the help of God did the tsar save us," comments the record book of that Jewish community. But the hand of God seemed unable to save others. And so we have photographs of a different sort: pogroms consummated with singular barbarousness.

Pictures of pogroms are difficult to bear. The head wounds are what shock one most. The Russians, wielding sabers and axes, seemed to go for the Jewish head. One photograph of the wounded shows nearly every head bandaged, thirty or so heads, assembled to record and display the event to the world, most of them the heads of elderly men and women. And there are photographs of rows and rows of bodies with heads fearsome to behold. City after city in Russia, from 1881 to 1917, witnessed fractured Jewish heads and rows of Jewish bodies: Mogilev, Minsk, Gomel, Bialystok, Lodz, Kiev, Zhitomir, Vologda, Simbirsk, Balta, Smela, Odessa. And Kishinev.

Solomon Slepak was about three years old when his family moved from Dubrovno to nearby Kopys. They lived with a family of rabbis friendly to Solomon's father. The Jews in and near Dubrovno would certainly have heard of the 1903 pogrom in Kishinev, a city not far from Odessa near the Black Sea; it attracted the attention of the world. More than three hundred dead, thousands wounded, six hundred children orphaned, fifteen hundred homes and shops plundered, forty thousand people left without property or means of work. The Kishinev pogrom occurred when Solomon Slepak was ten years old. His father had been dead about two years.

In October 1905, there was one week in which three hundred pogroms took place in cities throughout Russia. Five months later young Solomon Slepak became a bar mitzvah and entered adulthood. Soon afterward he was told by his mother, Basheva, that she wished him to enter an academy of traditional Jewish learning, become a rabbi, and carry on the tradition of his late father, Israel, by linking his fate to the generations of rabbis and teachers in the father's family. Either that or—the implied threat, though unstated, was quite clear—leave the house. Slepak family history reverberates with echoes of furious quarrels between mother and son, the mother defending her dead husband's dream, the son weighing his own future.

The chronicles tell us that at the age of thirteen, Solomon Slepak left home.

Other young Jews were leaving then, too, fleeing from their religious homes, living with fellow runaways in vile rooms, sharing food and clothes, attending or waiting to be accepted into Russian schools, barely eking out livelihoods by tutoring the children of well-to-do Jewish families or working at odd jobs. Many died of hunger and disease.

Solomon Slepak fled to his older brother, Aaron, who still lived in nearby Dubrovno and worked in the textile factory. Aaron was then twenty-seven, devout, married, and with children. Solomon sought his brother's support, but his brother thought it a fine idea that Solomon become a rabbi and urged him to return home.

Solomon moved on once again, to the town of Orsha, some twenty kilometers north of Dubrovno, to the home of a Dr. Zarkhi, an old friend of his family's. The doctor, who was not an observant Jew, took the boy in and gave him a room in the attic.

No one seems to know why this Dr. Zarkhi accepted the thirteen-year-old Solomon into his home and what his precise connection was to the Slepak family. But it was not uncommon in those days for people to take in the runaway children of friends rather than abandon them to a bed in a reeking cellar or tenement, to streets and hooligans and the specter of disease, starvation, death.

Solomon Slepak intended to enter a technical school, but he was too young and unprepared for the qualifying entrance examinations. He helped himself by getting his date of birth changed on his official documents from March 6, 1893, to March 6, 1892—no details are available as to how that feat was accomplished; probably a small bribe was slipped to some low-level official—making himself a year older and, he hoped, thereby gaining earlier admission to the school. He began to study for the examinations.

About ten thousand Jews lived in Orsha; they were a little over 50 percent of the total population. Like Dubrovno, Orsha was situated on the

Dnieper River; unlike Dubrovno, it had a railroad station. More than thirty Orsha Jews lost their lives in the pogroms that swept through the cities of Russia in October 1905.

That was a time of upheaval not only for Jews but also for Russians. In January 1905 workers had demonstrated in the streets of St. Petersburg, urged on by an Orthodox priest, Father Georgy Gapon. They asked to meet with their beloved tsar in the Winter Palace and present him with a petition of grievances; they were met instead by a hail of bullets from the tsar's troops. Estimates of the slain ran from 130 to nearly 1,000. Regarded until then with profound reverence by most Russians, the tsar now became an object of loathing and fury. "Nicholas the Bloody," the Russians began to call him.

It is hardly likely that Solomon Slepak was unaware of the events then taking place in Russia. The sophisticated, secularist family of Dr. Zarkhi no doubt contained avid readers. More than two thousand periodicals of all opinions were being published in Russia in those years; tsarist censorship of the press was lax. Between 1906 and 1914 the different factions of the Social Democratic Party that were calling for revolution published legally more than three thousand titles. Surely some of those publications found their way into Dr. Zarkhi's home and were read by Solomon Slepak.

After passing his entrance examinations, Solomon entered the technical school, where he studied mathematics, physics, accounting, German, and French, among other subjects. Not part of the curriculum was the everyday talk among students about contemporary events: the tsar's reluctant agreement to transform the country into a constitutional monarchy; the election of the first parliament in 1906, its dissolution by the tsar, and the three parliamentary elections that followed; the more than forty political parties that were represented, including delegates from Jewish parties; the stratagems and maneuverings of the revolutionaries. In the corridors and classrooms of the school, and while swimming in the waters of the Dnieper and lounging along the riverbank, older students quickly radicalized younger ones.

The family chronicles tell us that Solomon was introduced to radical ideas during his years in the technical school, and attended meetings of the Social Democratic Party. But there is no indication that he had yet turned into a revolutionary.

He was graduated in 1913, intending to continue his studies in a university. He was twenty, short, stocky, with thick, curly hair black like the wing of a crow, a somewhat too-large nose, thickish lips, and slanted dark brown eyes that gave him a slightly Mongol look. He had short arms and legs, was broad-shouldered, very strong, and in excellent health. Splendid material for the army of Tsar Nicholas II.

בבב

Solomon Slepak completed his studies in a year rife with rumors of impending war. He applied to the High Technological Institute in Moscow and was rejected; the institute's quota system admitted a low and fixed number of Jews. The rage in the hearts of young Russian Jews because of that quota system!

The country was preparing for war. Solomon Slepak, now supporting himself by tutoring, was a relative newcomer to Orsha and still unmarried. And regarded as somewhat unstable politically, not an actual member of a revolutionary party, to be sure, but a participant in meetings of a suspicious nature. The police seemed to be watching him. His name was near the top in the recruitment lists the Orsha community was required to submit to the army. But he had no intention of joining the army of Russia. Instead he fled, crossing the border on foot into Russian Poland. It is not known if he had somehow obtained the necessary passport from local officials or if he crossed illegally; the only document it is certain he had with him was his school diploma. Carrying few clothes and very little money, he made his way across Poland into Germany, somehow avoiding the numerous control points along Germany's eastern border. For a while he worked at odd jobs, fixing this, lugging that, accumulating the necessary thirty dollars—about one hundred rubles, a great deal of money in those days—for his travel ticket and the additional thirty dollars he would need to show the American immigration officials at Ellis Island in order to be admitted into the country.

In Hamburg he obtained a United States visa from the consular office and boarded a ship that sailed to England and America. He traveled steerage class in one of the three enclosed lower decks of the ship with more than a thousand other passengers, in a crowded room that was about seven feet high and extended the entire breadth of the ship and to about one-third its length. The air was unutterably foul, reeking of dirty bodies, tobacco, garlic, disinfectants, and the stench of the nearby toilet rooms; the floor slippery with the vomit of the seasick.

One sailed in steerage—so named because it was originally located near the rudder—to the noise of the stirring screws, the roll and thud of waves, the staccato of hawsers, and the trembling of steel railings. At times, when the weather grew calm, there might be cardplaying and even

music and dancing on the decks, but nearly always the journey, lasting
about ten days, was a hell that some thought cleansed them of sins and
prepared them as if newly born for the land of Columbus.

At the end of that dreadful voyage, as the ship made its way through
the Narrows between Brooklyn and Staten Island, Solomon Slepak
gazed spellbound at the Statue of Liberty, utterly mesmerized by the
sight of the tip of Manhattan Island. And when the ship docked at one
of the piers on the New York shore, he watched as those who had sailed
in first and second class disembarked and entered customs directly to
have their papers and baggage checked; then he and all the others who
had traveled in steerage, save American citizens, left by walking down a
gangplank at the stern and assembled on the pier in groups of thirty.
From there they were loaded onto barges, together with their baggage,
for the brief journey across the water to the red buildings on Ellis Island.

In 1913, the year Solomon Slepak arrived in the United States, nearly
nine hundred thousand immigrants came through Ellis Island. The immigration procedures on the island were a fearful experience. Faces in
photographs reveal the fright in immigrant hearts.

Solomon passed through the preliminary medical inspection in the
second-floor registry room—no hernia, no TB, no heart ailments, no
mental defects—and then stood on numerous lines and sat on clean
wooden benches and went through further examinations: the genitalia
for venereal disease, the skin for a "loathsome or dangerous contagious
disease." Light streamed into the vast room from tall side windows, and
the air was fresh. One doctor examined his scalp, another his fingernails;
a third painfully probed his eyes. He was asked his age, his destination.
Was he an anarchist, a polygamist, had he ever been in prison, who had
paid his passage, could he read and write, did he have a job waiting for
him? To the last question he replied that he did not have a job, and displayed his school diploma to verify his employability and usefulness to
America. An interpreter translated his responses to the examiners and
the immigration inspector. To the inspector's final query, "Do you have
thirty dollars? If less, how much?" he responded by showing the equivalent of thirty dollars in foreign money he had earned as an itinerant fixer
in Poland and Germany and received his "Admitted" card. Together with
other new immigrants he left the building and walked to the ferry.

A mile-long ride over the waters of Upper New York Bay brought him
to the terminal at the Battery. Behind the wire netting that entirely en-

capsulated the walk from the boats waited the anxious and eager crowd of relatives and friends. He looked around for his older sister, Bayla.

Bayla was an outcast, a virtual excommunicate from her family, a daughter whose name was never spoken by her mother. Before departing for America some years earlier, she had committed a heinous act. One of her children, a daughter, had been born retarded. As conditions in Russia worsened into deepening nightmare, Bayla became determined to take her family to America. Aware that the retarded child would be turned away by the immigration authorities and thereby jeopardize the entry of the entire family, she did the unspeakable: She decided to deliver the child into the care of her grandmother, Bayla's mother.

Violent quarrels rocked the family over that decision. It was unheard of, scandalous, to leave behind forever one child while taking the others. What kind of mother did such a thing—deserted a disabled child? One had to have a heart of stone! And what would happen to the poor creature when her grandmother passed on to the True World? Who would care for her then?

Bayla turned away from her child and left her mother and older brother and sailed with her family to America, and was waiting on the dock when her younger brother disembarked from the ferry with his few belongings, his thirty dollars, and his diploma. They took the subway to her family in Brooklyn.

It was during his years in New York that Solomon Slepak became a revolutionary. He lived with his sister's family on Division Avenue in the Williamsburg section of Brooklyn. The streets were a mix of Jews from Eastern Europe, Italians from Sicily and the region around Naples, and Ukrainians and Poles. Dirty, noisy, crowded streets. Old nineteenth-century brownstones with bay windows and ironwork fences; and walk-up apartments; and wood-frame row houses later to become firetraps and slums. A steel bridge, completed in 1903, spanned the East River. It became known as the Jews' Bridge; the *New York Herald* called it "the Jews' Highway." It linked the newly arrived immigrant Jews on the once-elegant streets of Williamsburg to the Jews who lived on Delancey Street in the heart of the teeming Lower East Side of Manhattan, the "miserably darkened Hebrews" with whom "the thoroughly acclimated American Jew . . . has no religious, social or intellectual ties," in the words of the *Hebrew Standard* in 1894. Riding or walking across the bridge on a warm, clear day, one could see the Manhattan skyline, gaze into the heart of capitalism. Did Solomon Slepak, recently come to Marxism and the Social Democratic Party, marvel at the power of this purported enemy of the proletariat? Did he see class struggle in the swarm and crush of people on the streets, the Jews pushing their carts, the filthy sidewalks, the dark tenements; or in his first job in a factory that made men's and women's belts, wallets, and purses, where he labored at a hot press stamping out leather patterns? In capitalist fashion, the leather company soon went broke, there being scant demand for its goods. He took a job selling dishes, peddling his wares before the Passover festival, when dishes used all year long must be stored away and dishes used only for the festival brought out or acquired. And he caught on to a common scam: Start across the street with your cart of dishes, step into the path of an oncoming truck, and then jump adroitly out of the way while letting the truck smash into and destroy the dishes. And claim the insurance. Learning quickly the seamy side of America.

About his sister, Bayla, there are no further details in the chronicles, and nothing at all about her husband. But a fascinating tableau has been handed down through the years: The four children and their uncle are seated on the floor around a daily English newspaper; the uncle reads, and the children correct him. Month after month he sat on the floor with the children and the newspapers, reading aloud and being corrected. He was learning English.

And, at the same time, reading about sweatshop bosses exploiting workers; about the efforts to pass child labor laws; about new laws governing factory safety, workmen's compensation, maximum hours for women. And he would surely have read accounts of the assassinations of Archduke Franz Ferdinand and his wife, Sophie, and the editorial surmise that the archduke's removal would probably make for greater tranquillity in Europe.

And he must have read about the war and the slaughter that began in Europe in August 1914. And about the Battle of Tannenberg, fought by German and Russian troops in the last days of August at a cost of thirteen thousand German and thirty thousand Russian dead. On the western front, the Germans advanced toward Paris. During the early days of September, French and British troops halted the Germans at the Marne in a series of battles that cost each side about a quarter of a million casualties and forever changed the nature of war. In mid-September the first trenches of the war were dug, and the nightmare of deadlocked warfare began.

All this Solomon read in English on the floor with his sister Bayla's children, and certainly a good deal more on his own in Yiddish. And doubtless discussed at length with his newfound friend, a man named Gregory Zarkhin, about whom the family chronicles tell us little: a Jew from a small town in White Russia, tall, blond-haired, chiseled face, aquiline nose. The chronicles do note that it was Gregory Zarkhin who introduced Solomon Slepak into New York's revolutionary circles. But how and where they met; the precise nature of their relationship; the ideas they embraced, the conversations they shared, the strategies planned and the dreams held in common—not a word.

There was no American Communist movement in the United States until September 1919, when the first manifesto of the Communist Party of America prematurely proclaimed the demise of capitalism. But there were circles where one could talk about the war and the tsar, about capitalism and Marxism, about the bourgeoisie and the proletariat, about the strikes of previous years—cloakmakers' strikes, cigar makers' and hatmakers' strikes, children's strikes, bakery strikes, meat and rent strikes—and engage in heated debates with anarchists and socialists, plan a union meeting, a demonstration, a strike, a parade, and anticipate the revolution in America. Persuasive to many in those troubled days were Karl Marx's theory of surplus value and forms of production and his iron conviction of the inevitability of communism, as if ordained by inexorable laws of history.

What goes into the making of a revolutionary, a man or woman who breaks with the legal systems and protocols of his or her world, renounces past ties of friendship and blood, becomes contemptuous of the society in which he or she lives, showing it no mercy and expecting no mercy from it in return, and sets out to intensify the suffering of people by any means available so as to accelerate the coming of revolution? Surely one begins by being partial to revolution, accepting of its consequences, perhaps because of a deep initial disillusionment with the codes of one's own people or class. Appalled by social injustice. A growing awareness of the illusory nature of genteel surface appearances; certainty that beneath the civilized facade lay the real world of power, money, and greed. Rage at the insurmountable obstacles put in the path of one's career and dreams by the entrenched laws of the powers-that-be. Years of recurrent anger and hate, which finally begin to burn with a steady flame. One becomes obsessed by a single goal: Redeem the despicable past with blood; cleanse away its evils; create the world anew. No more theorizing, no more observing as a bystander. The weak talked, dreamed, idealized. The strong accepted the bitter realities of life, and acted.

The chronicles contain no record of the growth of Solomon Slepak's political consciousness during those wartime years in New York. One imagines a dedicated revolutionary traveling from one clandestine meeting to another, carrying messages through all sorts of weather, passed from comrade to comrade, fed behind counters in railway eating houses and the kitchens of union halls, arrested, thrown into jail. But Solomon took a job as a window washer on skyscrapers during the day, and in the evenings he began to attend medical school. Which leads one to believe that he was precariously balanced between two different futures: full-time dedicated revolutionary or member of the bourgeoisie.

Imperial Russia, too, seemed suspended between futures.

For the tsar and his armies, the war went disastrously in 1915. There were rumors that the Russian Army had run out of ammunition and weapons and that one-fourth of its soldiers were being sent to the front lines unarmed and with orders to pick up the weapons of the dead. A bungling bureaucracy; a policy of oppression against religious and ethnic minorities; shortsighted ministers; the vast territorial losses and casualties of the war; a tsar who would not cooperate with even the most moderate of progressive groups and was too often dependent upon his witless wife, Alexandra, and her adviser, the bizarre and depraved holy man Gregory Rasputin: that was Russia in 1915 and 1916.

Acting against the advice of most of his ministers, the tsar took personal command of the armed forces and left for the front. Empress Alexandra, politically a reactionary, emotionally a near-hysteric, remained in the capital (its name now changed to Petrograd from the original German, Petersburg, because of the war with Germany). Together with her Siberian peasant, Rasputin, she virtually controlled the capital. She began to change ministers repeatedly, often on the advice of Rasputin. The two of them, a half-mad empress and a diabolic holy man, held in their hands the fate of Russia.

On the night of December 17, 1916, a member of the royal family, along with an aristocrat related to the family by marriage, carried out a messy murder of Rasputin; he proved difficult to kill and had to be shot a number of times. His body was thrown off a bridge into the water and was not found until the following day. It was a desperate attempt to save imperial Russia and the Romanov dynasty.

On March 8 (February 23 by the old Russian calendar), word spread that there was not enough bread in the city. Housewives and women factory workers took to the streets in demonstrations. By evening one hundred thousand workers were on strike. Lines of hungry people began to form outside the bakeries. Riots broke out. A bakery was looted, and Cossack troops were called in, but they refused to fire on the people and instead drove the police away. Then the Petrograd military garrison, made up of pensioned peasant conscripts, mutinied. Crowds surged through the city, shouting, "Long live the republic!"

The tsar wrote in his diary: "Riots began in Petrograd several days ago. To my regret, troops have begun to take part in them. It is a hateful feeling to be so far away and receive such poor, fragmentary news!" And he added, "In the afternoon took a walk down the road to Orsha. . . ."

One day in March 1917, Solomon Slepak opened his New York newspaper and read that the monarch of his native land, Tsar Nicholas II, had abdicated the throne.

There is a photograph of the parlor car on the imperial train where the tsar signed the instrument of abdication. A sofa, an easy chair, a coffee table, sconces, a wooden side bar with an unclear framed photograph—of the empress, very likely—and a round clock on the silk-covered walls, with one hand on the eight and the other on the twelve. He had abdicated in favor of his brother: "We transfer our legacy to our brother Grand Duke Michael Alexandrovich and bless him on his ascension to the Throne of the Russian State."

But the next day, after being told by Alexander Kerensky, a member of the Socialist Revolutionary Party and the only socialist in the cabinet, that he could not conceal from the new tsar "the dangers that taking power would subject you to personally," Michael, in tears, abdicated in favor of the Provisional Government.

The regime of the Romanovs was over.

Almost immediately the state bureaucracy disintegrated.

The tsar and his family were arrested.

Workers roamed about Petrograd in a delirium of joy. The centuries under the tsarist yoke had crumbled astonishingly in only a few days.

Factory laborers, clerks, drivers, peasants with red armbands walked the streets, assembled to hear speeches, and thought themselves the freest citizens in the world.

The crowd had been victorious; now it wanted to rule.

Moderate socialist members of the parliament found it necessary to negotiate with members of the soviets, councils of workers' and soldiers' deputies run by radical socialist intellectuals. It was a shaky arrangement.

The Provisional Government chose to ignore the prevailing pacifist atmosphere and to continue the war against Germany. It made all citizens equal before the law; it granted freedom of religion, speech, press, assembly; it proclaimed strikes to be permissible. It officially abolished the Jewish Pale of Settlement—though in actuality, the Pale had already ceased to exist because hundreds of thousands of Jews had been driven into the heartland of Russia before the advancing German and Austrian armies. But the government was helpless before an upward-spiraling inflation; it could not increase industrial production or halt the disintegration of the economy. Peasants were appropriating land; ethnic minorities began to assert their rights to self-rule; workers' committees controlled factory management; debating committees ran the army's chain of command. Incompetent intellectuals stepped into the vacuum left by the vanished bureaucracy. Alexander Kerensky, now the prime minister, proved powerless in his attempts to maneuver between the moderates and the radicals. By the early fall of 1917 Russia was on the brink of anarchy.

In Petrograd and Moscow waited the leaders of the Bolsheviks, once the majority wing of the Russian Social Democratic Workers' Party—the Mensheviks had constituted the minority wing—for the appropriate moment to overthrow the Provisional Government.

The Bolshevik Party was a unique organization directed from above by an intellectual elite and created for the explicit goals of conspiracy, taking power, and launching a revolution. It is estimated that it had in its ranks about two hundred thousand members, of whom five to ten thousand constituted a highly disciplined core, one-third of them intellectuals. Motivated by ideology and the realization that failure meant, at best, their return to an underground existence and, at worst, their annihilation, they composed a substantial force in a country approaching anarchy.

Vladimir Lenin, leader of the party, intended to seize power in Russia, reconquer the borderlands that had declared their independence, as well as Siberia, and make the party the master not only of Russia but of all the world.

ᒧᒧᒧ

In New York, Solomon Slepak washed skyscraper windows and studied medicine.

It requires little effort of the imagination to conjure the elation, debates, speeches, and general tumult among the New York revolutionaries at their meetings during the period of the Kerensky government. Friction between radicals and liberals; concern over every bit of news from Petrograd and Moscow—and the Russian Army: Would it continue to support Kerensky or stand aside, thereby enabling the Bolsheviks to make their move?

There is no way of knowing if it was Gregory Zarkhin or Solomon Slepak who came up with the idea that they return to Russia and take part in the coming struggle. It was unusual at that time for immigrant Jews to leave America and go back to their country of origin, though many had left earlier. Applying for visas, Solomon and Zarkhin were closely questioned by Russian consular officials in New York: the Provisional Government saw it as not in its best interest to augment the domestic ranks of the Bolsheviks. Because the two men were suspected of revolutionary sympathies, their request for visas was turned down.

It is not at all clear why they did not then attempt to enter Russia illegally. In New York at that time were the Bolshevik Nicholas Bukharin and the soon-to-be Bolsheviks Leon Trotsky and Volodarsky. All quickly returned to Russia via England and the North Atlantic. Then, on November 7 of that year, by the Western world's Gregorian calendar, which the Bolsheviks adopted in 1918—October 25, according to Russia's old Julian calendar—the benign revolution of March was taken over by Lenin, and Russia set out upon the path of international revolution. It appeared that a quarrel had erupted between the head of the army and Kerensky, a jockeying for power, and now the army stood aside as the Bolsheviks took control.

It was, at first, the most bloodless of revolutions. Hardly a weapon was fired in the Winter Palace, and Petrograd fell into Bolshevik hands, so inept was the Provisional Government. "We found the power lying in the streets," Lenin later said, "and we picked it up."

In New York, Solomon Slepak quit his window-washing job, dropped out of medical school, and began making arrangements to return to Russia by way of the Far East. Gregory Zarkhin had left for Canada shortly after their requests for Russian visas had been refused, and Solomon planned to meet him there. Together they would take a cargo ship to Vladivostok, which was then under anti-Bolshevik control. As soon as they arrived, they would contact the Bolshevik underground.

Solomon rode by train to the American-Canadian border and was stopped by the Canadians because his documents were not in order: He was not an American citizen and had no entry visa for Canada. The Canadians did not especially want to admit anyone who was a recent immigrant to the United States from Russia, which was then in an increasingly violent revolution. They sent Solomon back to New York by train, and to make certain he got there, they transported him in the custody of an immigration officer, who gave him a dollar bill when they arrived and let him go. Solomon promptly took the next train back to Canada, this time disembarking before he reached the border and crossing on foot through fields. In the distance stood a farmhouse. He knocked on the door. French Canadians. He had not forgotten the French he had learned in the technical school in Orsha. He spent some weeks on the farm as a seasonal laborer.

Then he began ·to travel westward through Canada, working on farms, fixing this, hauling that. His English was good enough to get him by. No one asked for his identity papers. He worked; he was paid; he left. Accumulating travel money.

He met Gregory Zarkhin in Vancouver, which at the time had a fairly sizable Russian immigrant population. And a Russian dockworkers' trade union of about a thousand men, organized and led by Zarkhin, who was chairman of the union. Solomon Slepak began to work on the docks and was soon the deputy chairman. Awhile later Zarkhin left for Vladivostok alone; they had decided it was unwise to travel and arrive together. With Zarkhin gone, Solomon Slepak assumed leadership of the union.

While the young revolutionary labored on the docks of Vancouver, Lenin set about organizing a Communist state. One of his earliest acts, in December 1917, was the creation of a political secret police force, the Cheka—the Extraordinary Commission for the Struggle against Counterrevolution, Sabotage, and Speculation—under the leadership of a Polish nobleman turned Bolshevik, Felix Dzerzhinsky.

In January 1918, aided by sailors from the Baltic Fleet, Lenin dispersed the legitimately elected Constituent Assembly which had assembled in

Petrograd. The Bolsheviks had only 24 percent of the vote, but Lenin argued that a soviet democracy of the working class was a higher principle than a bourgeois democracy of one man, one vote. The Assembly had no soldiery it could rally to its side. That single act by Lenin was the death of the parliamentary democracy that had been evolving in Russia over the previous twelve years.

After the dissolution of the Constituent Assembly, the process began of seeking out the Socialist Revolutionaries, Constitutional Democrats, and Mensheviks—all who had opposed the new regime and were still unwilling to repent and join the Bolshevik cause. Those arrested were exiled to prison camps or executed. In addition, Lenin soon permitted peasants to seize land, gave over control of many factories to committees of workers, nationalized all the banks, impounded private bank accounts, made foreign trade a state monopoly, abolished the judicial system and replaced it with people's courts and revolutionary tribunals. Members of the upper and middle classes lost their property. Religious education was ended, church property appropriated. All titles and ranks vanished.

On March 3, 1918, the Germans and Bolsheviks signed the Treaty of Brest-Litovsk. By then civil war had broken out in the cities and industrial regions of central Russia.

That same March, Solomon Slepak left Vancouver and began his journey across the Pacific to Vladivostok. He was twenty-five years old, and about to enter an Asian world of extreme political complexity and conflict, a landscape with a tortured history.

In 1858 a nearly prostrate China, beset by rebellion and at war with Britain and France, had yielded to Russia the left bank of the Amur River, a region rich in coal, tin, iron, and gold. Two years later the hapless Chinese ceded to the Russians the region of the Ussuri River on the Pacific coast: wild and wooded country; towering, round-shouldered hills and deep shadowy valleys dense with undergrowth and ribboned with torrential streams.

The town of Vladivostok was established by the Russians in 1860; it lay about five hundred miles southeast of the city of Harbin, and was Russia's gateway to the Pacific. In 1875 Russia transferred the Kurile Islands to Japan in exchange for the southern half of Sakhalin Island, which the Japanese took back and annexed in 1905. That entire region, from Lake Baikal to Vladivostok—more than twelve hundred miles from east to west, and at one point eight hundred miles and at another, four hundred miles, from north to south—was occupied after the 1917 revolution by various armed forces, all enemies of the Bolsheviks: 72,000 Japanese, 7,000 Americans, 6,400 British, 4,400 Canadians. It had a population of more than 1,500,000 Russians, 300,000 Japanese and Chinese, 250,000 Mongols, and 25,000 Jews.

The region was governed by an administration headed by Admiral Alexander Kolchak, commander of the White armies in the east. ("White" was the term of opprobrium which the Bolsheviks applied to their opponents, white having been the emblematic color of nineteenth-century French monarchists.) Kolchak was a taciturn man, given to dark moods and politically naïve. His favorite reading was, reportedly, the *Protocols of the Elders of Zion*, a document forged by Russian secret police during the reign of Tsar Nicholas II, which purports to be the secret plans for the takeover of the world by the Jews.

Sometime in April 1918 Solomon Slepak sailed into Vladivostok on board a cargo ship. He saw the ships of many nations—Japanese, British, American, French—at anchor in the bay. The city had a broad, partly paved main street, was thronged with office buildings, hotels, stores. On some streets he saw all manner of livestock; on others, soldiers from France, Italy, Japan, Canada, Great Britain, America. The harbor, calm as a lake, sat locked in by gently rolling hills. The population—Russians, Cossacks, Chinese, Koreans—numbered around 50,000; in a year it would surge to 180,000: refugees from the raging Civil War, hungry and dirty, many sick with typhus.

The city was suffering a shortage of living space; there seemed to be no vacant rooms anywhere. Still, Solomon Slepak found a place to stay and managed to locate his friend Zarkhin. Quickly they organized an underground council and set up a Bolshevik press, which they operated in the very heart of the city, printing pamphlets, broadsides, newsletters for the cause of the revolution. One of Solomon's main tasks was to translate the material into English so it could be read by the American troops, who seemed not as averse to the Bolsheviks as were the British and the French. After some months, they were discovered by the police, arrested, tried, convicted as revolutionaries, and sentenced to death.

They spent two weeks in prison, waiting to be executed. A cellmate went mad and hanged himself. Solomon was told he had one day to live.

It was now one year after the November 1917 Revolution. In mid-1918 the Bolsheviks had changed their name to the Communist Party and moved the capital of Russia from Petrograd to Moscow. During those first years of the Civil War, 1917–1918, the cities and industrial regions of central Russia had been won over to the Revolution, through propaganda, terror, and blood. But the Bolshevik armies were hastily organized and made up largely of ill-trained peasants and the urban underclass. Battles were still being fought all along the periphery of central Russia, and the borderlands, including Siberia and the Far Eastern Province, had set themselves on a course of separation and independence, and would have to be reconquered.

The Civil War lasted three years, from the end of 1917 to the end of 1920. Millions perished from combat, famine, and disease, including Tsar Nicholas II and his family, executed in July 1918 on the orders of Lenin himself, who wished no tsar or would-be tsar left alive around whom monarchists might rally.

In the fall of 1918, in his cell in Vladivostok, Solomon Slepak awaited execution.

Something then occurred in the Siberian city of Omsk—an event connected with Admiral Kolchak—that saved Solomon's life. As a result of that event, an amnesty was declared, and the death sentences of political prisoners were commuted to life imprisonment at hard labor on Sakhalin Island.

The family chronicles are at a loss to explain the sudden amnesty. But because it coincides with the period in November 1918 when the Council of Ministers of Russia's Far Eastern Province granted Kolchak dictatorial powers, it is possible that it was he who declared the amnesty to mark his assumption of the office of Supreme Ruler of Eastern Russia and Siberia. "I shall take neither the path of reaction nor the ruinous course of party politics," he stated on the day he took power. "My principal objective is to create an army capable of combat, victory over Bolshevism, and the introduction of legality and the rule of law. . . ."

Whatever the reasons for the amnesty, Solomon Slepak was abruptly spared on the day of his appointed death. Together with his friend Zarkhin and the other political prisoners, he began the long trek to Sakhalin Island.

They went on foot to the city of Nikolayevsk, some 750 miles to the north. It was winter. Sakhalin Island lay north of Hokkaido, the northernmost island of Japan. Fierce Siberian winds blew across the seas. The

Tatar Strait between the mainland and Sakhalin Island was frozen. They crossed to the island over the ice.

The island, bitter-cold and damp, had dense forests and steep mountain ranges, was rich in coal and iron deposits, and was originally barren of people. The region south of the fiftieth parallel belonged to Japan. The Russians populated their part of the island with convicts and exiles.

There is a photograph, taken in 1915, of a Jewish woman thief being placed in irons on Sakhalin. Three guards and two leather-aproned smiths stand, all stiffly posing. The woman appears to be in her forties— hands shackled, features rigid, defiant. "Sonka of the Golden Hands" she was called. The building in the background is made of logs; one of the windows lies awkwardly off its frame. From the visible presence of the ground and the obvious absence of winter garb—no fur caps, no gloves, no coats—the photograph appears to have been taken in weather a good deal warmer than that which greeted Solomon Slepak when, early in 1919, he stepped onto the island where the anti-Bolshevik Kolchak regime intended him to spend the rest of his life at hard labor.

The labor camp was in the town of Aleksandrovsk some thirty miles north of the fiftieth parallel. Camp and town seethed with Bolshevik activity. The political prisoners lived apart from the criminals, the thieves and murderers, an arrangement that made it easier for Gregory Zarkhin and Solomon Slepak to smuggle letters out to the Bolsheviks in Aleksandrovsk and Nikolayevsk, to continue to direct underground activities on the mainland from their cells on Sakhalin, and ultimately to stage their own revolution. They organized the Bolshevik prisoners, about two hundred men, into a tightly disciplined fighting unit, and in April 1919 they rose up against the guards and gained control of the labor camp and the town of Aleksandrovsk. Solomon and Zarkhin ordered the release of the criminals in the camp. The fact that they were criminals was not their fault, Solomon and Zarkhin declared at a meeting of the prisoners; the blame lay with the tsarist society that had forced them into an outlaw life by not providing them with a decent education and the economic means to fulfill their goals. They were not criminals in their hearts. They should help overthrow the regime that turned good men into criminals. Most of the criminals joined them.

Gregory Zarkhin now decided to leave Sakhalin and return to the mainland; he vanishes from this narrative until his abrupt reappearance some years later. Solomon remained and was elected first chairman of the Soviet of People's Commissars of Sakhalin. He was now the head Bolshevik on the Russian part of the island.

In the south, the Japanese, who had no love for Russians and ab-

horred Bolsheviks, advanced on Aleksandrovsk, with the intention of
taking the entire island.

Solomon organized his men, the original two hundred political prisoners and the many criminals who had joined them, into a small army.
(Where had the son of a small-town Russian Jewish teacher learned the
skills of weapons and war? The chronicles are silent on that.) But,
though disciplined and dedicated, Solomon's force knew itself to be out-
numbered and outgunned by the Japanese, whose rapid advance into the
north it could not hope to stop. Solomon decided to move his men to
the mainland and link up with Bolshevik partisans operating there
under the command of a man named Nicholas Triapitsin. By now, however, the ice had thawed, and there were no boats large enough to take
all his men across the Tatar Strait, some fifteen miles at the narrowest
point.

He crossed to the mainland with three other men in a small boat and
found the captain of a large boat, who refused to help. Solomon put a
gun to the captain's head and commandeered both him and his boat. It
took several back-and-forth crossings to bring all his men to the mainland. They managed somehow to avoid the patrolling Japanese warships.
On the mainland they began to make their way to the partisan army led
by Triapitsin. Solomon Slepak's army now numbered close to three
thousand men.

Nicholas Triapitsin commanded a division of partisans. In those chaotic
years of the Russian Civil War, a division meant anything from five
thousand to fifteen thousand men. Bands of brigands and partisans
roamed everywhere, taking advantage of the absence of order to loot and
kill. Whites plundered and killed Reds and Red sympathizers; Reds
plundered and killed Whites and White sympathizers.

The seven-month period between May and November 1919 was the
bloodiest time of the Civil War; the fiercest and most decisive battles, re-
sulting in the final defeat of the Whites, were fought then by a newly organized Red Army of three million men. Its field units were commanded
by tens of thousands of former tsarist officers: men who had once been
hunted and imprisoned pariahs, but whom the Bolsheviks had reluctantly, out of dire need, rehabilitated and recruited. Anti-Bolshevik foreign troops on Russian soil—the hesitant British, French, and American
forces who failed to engage in any consequential combat, and even the
more aggressive Czechoslovak Legion, made up of soldiers who had been
captured by the tsar's army during the war, and who had subsequently

broken out and taken up arms against the Reds—played no significant role in the outcome of the Civil War.

Somewhere on the mainland of Asia, between the Sea of Okhotsk and Lake Baikal, Solomon Slepak and his army linked up with the partisan division of Nicholas Triapitsin. It was the spring of 1919. Triapitsin had heard of the deeds of Solomon Slepak on Sakhalin Island and greeted him warmly as "Sam," the name by which the latter was then popularly known. He welcomed "Sam" and his men into the ranks of the partisans. There would be a party that night, he said, to celebrate the birthday of the woman he loved.

There was a party that night, but not the one planned by Triapitsin.

Once again the family chronicles blur and details become unclear, perhaps because of what is about to ensue. Triapitsin and his lover, a woman known only as Sonya, became drunk, as did many of his officers. Possibly they spoke too boldly in their drunkenness, began to make anarchist noises. Doubts about the Revolution? Slurs against Trotsky, who was then organizing the new Red Army into a fighting machine that would bring an end to any need for partisan forces? An unwillingness to accept the verbal orders "Sam" claimed he brought from the Bolshevik center in Russia? What seems clear is that Solomon Slepak ordered his core of two hundred loyal men to surround the building where the party was taking place, drew his gun, and arrested an astonished Triapitsin and his staff officers. There then followed a swift trial, with no defense and no appeal, before a military troika, a court of three men appointed by Solomon Slepak. All the defendants, including Triapitsin's lover, were found guilty of counterrevolutionary activities—and shot. Their bodies were thrown into a nearby river.

Solomon contacted the Bolshevik political head of the Far Eastern Province and informed him of the executions. He received in response the gratitude of the official and an immediate appointment to the positions of deputy minister of the Far Eastern Province, commander of the Bolshevik Far Eastern Army, and head of the Amur-Argun front, the region where the Shilka and Argun rivers join to form the Amur River. His orders were to suppress the Ussuri Cossacks, who were rampaging in the region between Lake Baikal and the city of Khabarovsk, hijacking trains, plundering, killing. And to halt the advance of the Japanese Army in Siberia.

Solomon Slepak now had under his command an army of about ten thousand men.

Decades later, in Moscow, in the presence of his son, Volodya, he would meet an Old Bolshevik named Abram Kamzel, a lean gray-haired man in his early eighties, tall, with blue eyes. Solomon was then in his seventies.

"Slepak?" said the Old Bolshevik in astonishment. "You are still alive?"

"You see I am alive," said Solomon.

Kamzel stared at Solomon in disbelief. Then, recovering himself, he said, "You murdered so many of Triapitsin's partisans with your troika courts. Do you remember how Sonya begged you to spare her and her lover? Triapitsin was a good Bolshevik. Did you think he was an anarchist? Do you remember his last words? 'It's a pity to die on such a beautiful morning.' Did you kill him so you could take over his command?"

Solomon's face turned to stone.

The old man went on talking, as if to himself. "Whenever people heard the name Sam, they thought only about cruelty to the enemies of the Revolution, about wiping out opponents without mercy. The waters of the river turned red from the blood of the corpses. . . ."

Solomon Slepak. Fiery convert to a new faith. Bringer of fire and death to the enemies of Bolshevik Russia and the Communist Party.

The Russian Jews who gave themselves heart and mind to the Bolshevik cause were, like Solomon Slepak, men and women who inhabited a cruel between-world: no longer part of the world of their Jewish beginnings, which they had long since abandoned, and not yet fully a part of the world of Russia, which loathed and feared Jews. During the Civil War, anti-Semitism was so rife among Russians of all ages, parties, classes, and nationalities as virtually to border on national psychosis. Reinforcing the traditional picture of the Jews promulgated by church and state for a thousand years was the fact of their sudden appearance throughout Russia. The Pale of Settlement, where Jews had been forced to live under the tsars, had virtually emptied of Jews during the war, and now they were to be found in cities in the very heart of the country. Their presence at the highest levels of government and in places where Jews had never before been seen came at the same time as the Revolution: Leon Trotsky, second only to Lenin; Yakov Sverdlov, who ran the day-to-day affairs of the Communist Party; Kamenev, Zinoviev, Radek; so many others—all of Jewish descent, all unable to return to their own people, all loathing the monarchist and anti-Semitic ranks of the Whites. The Communist Party, a seeming haven for the radical intelligentsia and apparently uninterested in the ethnic and religious origins of its members, became the sole refuge of certain marginal Jews, who believed it would bring a great and true salvation to the world, a revolutionary universalism in which the destructive differences that divided humankind would once and for all be forever dissolved. It mattered little to most Russians that these Jews were no more Jewish than their non-Jewish atheist party comrades; that they did not speak for or identify with Jews, and indeed were often the enemies of Jews. Further, because many Jews stepped into the vacuum created by the disintegration of the tsarist bureaucracy, it now seemed to many Russians that Jewish government officials were everywhere. Their sudden appearance, concurrent as it was with the Revolution and the Civil War, forever linked those events in the minds of Russians, for whom the Jew now became the evil cause of the Fatherland's unutterable misery.

Not since the massacres during the Cossack uprising against Poland in the middle of the seventeenth century was the slaughter of Jews on so vast a scale. Prelates of the Orthodox Church saw the Civil War as a struggle of biblical proportions against godless Jews who were attempting to conquer Holy Russia. White and Red armies, bands of brigands, marauding Cossacks, roaming gangs of thieves—everyone plundered and killed Jews in obscene and brutal ways, though the Red Army officially forbade its troops from staging pogroms and at times punished the perpetrators. Photographs of pogrom victims show hideous head and face wounds, amputees, corpses, children weeping over the bodies of parents. About 150,000 Jews died in the pogroms of the Russian Civil War.

Small wonder the dread of the Jews and the reaction by the chief rabbi of Moscow, Jacob Mazeh, who, hearing Trotsky say that he was not a Jew and would not help Jews, stated that it was the Trotskys who made the Revolution and the Bronsteins—Trotsky's original Jewish name—who paid the bills for it. Small wonder the story about the Jewish Red Army soldier who, half crazed, ran about executing wounded Ukrainians abandoned by the retreating Whites. "He would wipe his bayonet in the grass to remove the blood," relates the chronicle of that event, "and with every head he cut off he screamed, 'This is my payment for my murdered sister, this is my retribution for my murdered mother!' The Jewish crowd," concludes the story, "held its breath and kept silent."

And in the Far East, Solomon Slepak headed a division of partisans that fought Japanese troops and anarchic Cossack bands and moved to link up with the Red Army's advance upon the city of Omsk, where Admiral

Kolchak ruled as head of the Whites of Siberia and the Far Eastern Province.

There were about twenty-five thousand Jews in the Far Eastern Province at that time. The family chronicles are silent about whether or not Solomon Slepak, as commanding officer of a Red partisan division, attempted to establish any sort of contact with that community. It is known that he had a Jewish girlfriend named Zlata.

In November 1919 the Red Army defeated the army of Admiral Kolchak, and shortly afterward the city of Omsk fell without a battle. Accounts of the flight of Whites eastward describe a nightmare of typhus and death. Kolchak was taken by the Bolsheviks, who executed him in February 1920 on the orders of Lenin.

Some while later Solomon linked up with the Red Army and turned over to it command of his division. The Civil War dragged on some additional months; the last effective White army, fighting in the Crimea under the command of Peter Wrangel, was evacuated in November by British, French, and Russian ships. The Whites not captured by the Reds slipped out of the country and vanished.

Then came famine. Twenty million Russians died in the years that followed the Revolution. The Russian economy was in utter ruins. Still, Lenin and his band of revolutionaries had triumphed.

But Lenin did not regard the success of the Revolution as his only goal; it was, rather, a means to the more essential end of world revolution. All of Russia was to serve as a wedge into the West and global capitalism. His program was to divide existing Social Democratic parties, separate and organize their most radical members, and wherever possible, incite revolution.

To these ends, Lenin created in March 1919 the First Communist International, known as the Comintern or the Third International. And in the midst of the Civil War there took place the First Congress of the Comintern, a gathering of foreign revolutionary socialists, most of them in Moscow by chance and with no authority from their home parties to represent them. "Our task," Trotsky announced at that milestone event, "is to generalize the revolutionary experience of the working class . . . and hasten the victory of the Communist Revolution throughout the world."

The Second Congress of the Comintern opened in Petrograd in July 1920, with everyone sensing that the end of the Civil War was near.

There was some concern about a threat against the life of Lenin; hence the location of the Congress in Petrograd rather than Moscow. Indeed, Lenin had nearly lost his life on August 30, 1918, when, after addressing an assembly of factory workers in Moscow, he was shot twice by a Right Social Revolutionary named Fanny Kaplan (some think she took the blame to shield someone else). One bullet broke his left shoulder and wounded his left arm; the other pierced his left lung. Had the second bullet penetrated one millimeter to the right or left, Lenin would have died.

Attending the Second Congress were 217 delegates from thirty-six countries. The Russians had 69 delegates, one of whom was Solomon Slepak, who lived then in the Siberian city of Chita and was editor in chief of the Far Eastern *Pravda*, a position given to him because he was educated, had spent four years in America, knew English, and was deemed reliable. The role of editor was one of considerable importance, because Bolsheviks regarded their newspapers and propaganda activity as the very heart of revolutionary organizations; Molotov would serve as the editor of *Pravda*, as would Bukharin. Solomon attended the Congress as the deputy from Sakhalin Island.

Four days after it opened in Petrograd, the congress moved to Moscow, where it remained until early August. Deputy Solomon Slepak attended its sessions in the city whose High Technological Institute had rejected him seven years earlier because he was a Jew.

The Wildcat in the Garden

What a triumphant time, that summer of 1920 in Petrograd and Moscow, when the Comintern convened to plan the conquest of the world! Solomon Slepak voted eagerly with the others in favor of the twenty-one points set down by Lenin, among which were: Enter no alliances anywhere with reformists and centrists; propagandize the armed forces of all nations so they will in due course join the side of revolutionaries; take over trade unions; organize Communist cells everywhere; follow strict party discipline; stage armed insurrections. . . . Never mind the war cripples on Moscow's streets, the grimy look of the city, its horrendous living conditions, the famine raging in the countryside, the people standing on line for potatoes and bread, the streets virtually empty of traffic save for the long black cars of the secret police. Never mind all that! The Civil War was nearly over. And the Red Army, engaged in a border war with Poland, was rapidly approaching Warsaw, its advances posted daily on the large map in the main hall in full view of the deputies. "The struggle for Communism shall be transferred to America, and perhaps also to Asia and other parts of the world," Gregory Zinoviev, who had been appointed chairman of the Comintern by Lenin, had written during the summer of 1919 before the First Congress. Many in that Second Congress were certain that at the third anniversary of the Revolution, all in the Comintern would celebrate the worldwide triumph of communism.

To his surprise and delight, Solomon Slepak ran across his old friend

Gregory Zarkhin at the Congress. The tall blond Bolshevik from White Russia was now head of the Press Department of the Comintern. Zarkhin—who had changed his name to Voitinsky when he became involved with the Bolshevik underground in Vladivostok and retained that name the rest of his life—invited Solomon to remain in Moscow as deputy head of the Press Department. Making the necessary official inquiries, Solomon was advised to vacate the editorship of the Far Eastern *Pravda* and accept the position with the Comintern. An astonishing rise into the heart of Moscow, into the very center of power.

He lived on Tverskaya Street, in the Hotel Lux (now the Hotel Tsentralnaya), which had been commandeered by the Comintern for its members. Two blocks away stood the site of the future statue of the founder of Moscow, Yuri Dolgoruky, erected in 1948 as part of the 800th-anniversary celebration of the city. Directly across the street from the statue was the Moscow Soviet, the municipal building. Less than a mile away was the Kremlin.

The family chronicles are without information regarding Solomon Slepak's daily activities. There are no details as to what crossed his desk; nor do we know to whom he reported, his contacts with the Central Committee, the Politburo, the Cheka, the Communist parties throughout the world.

With unrest everywhere following the end of World War I, much of the world appeared to be on the brink of revolution and class war. The abdication of the kaiser in Germany and the takeover of power by a shaky Social Democratic government was seen by Lenin as a repetition of the same events that had brought the Bolsheviks to power in Russia. In Britain—labor unrest and a weak government. In France, Italy, Hungary—demonstrations, strikes. In America—near national hysteria over the Reds; strikes in major industries; even the police force of Boston out on strike. All over the world—new Communist parties of greater or lesser strength, splitting away from or capturing existing Socialist parties. Western intellectuals and liberals thrilled to the vision of power— armies, police, hosts of bureaucrats—in the hands of Russian intellectuals, and were enchanted by the prospect of a new social order and the destruction of the abhorrent bourgeois class. The Communists in America, Britain, Sweden, Australia remained small splinter organizations, but in France, Italy, Germany they became major parties. Nearly everywhere in the world, it seemed, Communists craved to join the

Comintern, accept subservience to Lenin, participate in the coming world revolution.

But during the years that immediately followed the Third International, not a single trade union in the Western world fell to the Communists. The Communist putsch in Germany was smashed by the German government. The war with Poland ended soon after the close of the Second Congress with an astounding defeat suffered by the Red Army and with a treaty, signed in March 1921, that cost the Bolsheviks much coveted territory. Inside Russia there was domestic unrest: peasant uprisings, a stunning mutiny at the naval base in Kronstadt by sailors once fiercely loyal to the Bolsheviks, continuing economic collapse, agrarian failure, starvation. The labor strikes in Europe and America were broken or settled. The dream of world revolution, the very essence and postulate of Communism, had to be rethought. Lenin now needed to concern himself with the consolidation of socialism in his own country.

The Far East, though, appeared for a while a rich field for Bolshevik harvesting. Applying pure ideology to practical necessity in a region virtually empty of industrial workers or Communists, Lenin, during the Second Congress, had urged the formation of temporary working alliances of Communist parties and their erstwhile enemies, bourgeois national liberation movements. And evaluating the Politburo's Far East strategy, he remarked, "The road to Paris lies through Peking."

Gregory Voitinsky had earlier entered China in the spring of 1920, about two months before the convening of the Second Congress. Together with a Chinese named Yang Wing-chai, he traveled first to Peking and then to Shanghai, looking for Communists, and found a tiny leftist enclave in each city. He then returned to Russia.

In July 1921 thirteen young Chinese men, meeting first in a girls' school in the French Concession in Shanghai and then on an excursion boat—secret police had been spotted near the school—founded the Communist Party of China. One of those present was a twenty-seven-year-old named Mao Tse-tung.

Later that year the Comintern sent Voitinsky back into China. His task: to establish contact with the new Chinese Communist Party and open communications between Lenin and Sun Yat-sen, the president of China, who had headed the revolutionary movement that, in February 1912, had brought about the abdication of the last Manchu emperor.

Earlier in 1921, as director of the Kuomintang, the Nationalist People's Party, Sun had organized a revolt against the government in Peking headed by Yüan Shih-kai, the increasingly dictatorial president of China, and set himself up as president of a self-proclaimed national government in Canton. He would need allies in his effort to liberate northern China. The Comintern had ordered Voitinsky to explore the feasibility of joining the Communists to the Kuomintang, a union of Russian-style Communism and Chinese-style nationalism. After all, hadn't Sun Yat-sen sent a telegram of congratulations to Lenin soon after the Revolution?

According to the family chronicles, Voitinsky arrived in China—and shortly thereafter disappeared.

Word came back some while later: He had been arrested and imprisoned, probably by Whites still operating in Manchuria. The Comintern then resolved to send Solomon Slepak into China. He was to ransom Voitinsky, get him out of China, and complete his mission. Solomon traveled with a false American passport and a great deal of money to use for bribes, money probably acquired through the sale abroad of tsarist jewels, a method employed by Lenin to finance covert operations of Communist cells and newspapers.

The family chronicles tell us nothing of his travels. But there were no choices then in the way one journeyed from Russia to China. One took the two-week journey across Russia on the Trans-Siberian Railroad. From the Manchuria station on the border one traveled to Harbin via the Chinese Eastern Railroad, which was still held by White Russians. Then from Harbin on the South Manchurian Railroad, which was operated by the Japanese, to Mukden. From there one journeyed to Peking on the railroad run by the British. Then the Chinese Railroad to Shanghai and the boat to Swatow and by foot into Kwangtung Province and by train to Canton, where lived Sun Yat-sen.

This was a period of appalling turmoil in China. The imperial regime was dead, along with the idea of a constitutional monarchy. Educated Chinese, many of whom had studied in universities in Japan and Europe, sought to establish some kind of republican government to unify the land and build a nation. In the meantime, the land lay in fragments, ruled by militarist regimes, feuding warlords, a half dozen or so predatory foreign armies, and missionaries.

Somehow, in this roiling land, Solomon Slepak found and rescued his friend Gregory Voitinsky. And made contact with Sun Yat-sen. Strangely, in none of the books I have read on this period in Chinese history is there any mention of Sun Yat-sen in connection with a mysteri-

ous Russian bearing an American name and passport. Indeed, it is
Voitinsky who is credited with making the first contact with Sun Yat-
sen. And mention is often made of two important Comintern agents of
that period in China: S. A. Dalin and Michael Borodin. But there is the
evidence of a photograph of Sun Yat-sen that bears his signature beneath
these words in Russian: "To dear Comrade Slepak, in memory of our
meeting." The Slepak family chronicles insist that it was Solomon who
persuaded Sun Yat-sen to admit Communists into the Kuomintang, a
fateful decision taken in August 1922, while Solomon Slepak was still in
China. Opening the Kuomintang to the Communists also opened
China to Michael Borodin, the Comintern agent who arrived in Canton
in October 1923 to aid in the creation of a Chinese Communist Party
along the lines of the party in the Soviet Union. That first success of
Solomon Slepak's, if the chronicles are correct, dramatically altered
human history.

Why is there no mention of Slepak in the numerous books I've
combed on this period of Russian-Chinese history? Was he only a low-
echelon bureaucrat? But would Zinoviev and the Central Committee of
the Comintern have sent a minor figure on a major mission to rescue a
Comintern agent and open relations with Sun Yat-sen, who held the future of China in his hands? And would they have let him return later to
China for two more years? Not very likely. Was Solomon Slepak, then,
a full-fledged Comintern agent? With Cheka connections? Surely he was
being kept up-to-date by Cheka agents on events in China.

These are not the only questions left us by the family chronicles.

Shortly after he returned from China, Slepak was called to the office
of Georgi Chicherin, the people's commissar of foreign affairs. There he
met with Deputy Commissar Maxim Litvinov, who informed him that
the Foreign Ministry had decided to send him to Japan as the correspondent for Rosta, the Russian Telegraphic Agency, founded in 1918
and forerunner of Tass, the telegraphic agency of the Soviet Union.

The Japanese had no diplomatic relations with Bolshevik Russia.
Solomon Slepak would be the first Russian in any official capacity in
Japan since the Revolution. It would be a mission of some delicacy, having to do with a good deal more than journalism, and involving meetings with ministers of state, perhaps with the emperor himself.

He would need to change his obviously Jewish name. After all, he was
now representing the new Russia. "In all the world they are saying the
Jews have taken power in Russia," Litvinov remarked. "It's not good for
you to go as Solomon Izrailevich Slepak. Change your name to Semion

Ignatievich. A good Russian name." Litvinov himself was of Jewish origin.

And as it was against the policy of the Foreign Ministry to send on an extended foreign diplomatic mission anyone who was unmarried, he would need to find a wife, and quickly.

Solomon Slepak remembered a girl he had known during his childhood and made immediate arrangements to visit his mother, who had survived the war and the Revolution. He had not been home since he had run away seventeen years before. His mother still lived in Kopys, some miles from Dubrovno, the small town of his Jewish beginnings.

Nothing of that journey home is recorded in the family chronicles: no conversations, no memories, no account of who was alive and who dead, of conditions in little Dubrovno and larger Kopys, about three miles away, of the consequences of the war and the Revolution on the region. And not a word about his mother.

All we are told is that he found the girl who had been his childhood friend. Black hair, brown eyes, and half a head taller than the short, stocky Solomon Slepak. She could read, was notably talkative, had no formal advanced education. Her name was Fanya. He asked her to marry him, and she accepted.

He returned with her to Moscow.

Meanwhile, the Soviet Foreign Ministry, while trying to obtain the required diplomatic documents for Solomon Slepak's—or, more accurately, Semion Ignatievich's—entry into Japan, had run into unexpected difficulties.

The Japanese, it turned out, knew precisely who he was and were decidedly unhappy about his coming. They had not forgotten the Bolshevik known as Sam, who had organized the uprising on Sakhalin Island and commanded the Red partisans on the mainland and slaughtered Ussuri Cossacks, allies of the Japanese in Siberia during the Russian Civil War. Clearly, the Japanese would not welcome a man who had been responsible for the defeat of their former allies and the deaths of so many of their own soldiers.

The Office of the People's Commissar of Foreign Affairs informed the Japanese Foreign Ministry that if the journalist Semion Ignatievich was not given proper credentials to enter Japan as a foreign correspondent, the three Japanese foreign correspondents then in Russia would be expelled immediately. The Japanese yielded.

Solomon Slepak and his wife traveled to Japan and arrived in Tokyo in late 1922. At first they lived in a hotel in Tokyo; then they moved to an apartment. As the sole representative in Japan of Soviet Russia, Solomon Slepak was treated as a quasi ambassador of the new Bolshevik country and invited to diplomatic functions. He received an audience with the emperor. Though ostensibly a journalist, he was nevertheless being accorded high diplomatic status. Was he permitted to transmit coded messages to Chicherin and Litvinov? Could he send and receive sealed mail?

The following year Fanya Slepak gave birth to a girl in a Japanese hospital. A difficult forceps delivery. The child was born dead.

On Monday, January 21, 1924, Vladimir Lenin died after the last of a series of strokes, without designating a successor. Trotsky had refused Lenin's earlier offer of deputyship, in part out of concern that his taking such a high position would give the Soviet Union's enemies a final justification for claiming that the country was controlled by Jews.

A war of succession broke out among Stalin, Trotsky, and others in the Politburo. At Stalin's initiative, Lenin was embalmed and placed on permanent public display in a mausoleum on Red Square, an echo of the Russian Orthodox folk belief that the bodies of saints never decay, and a sign of proper continuity between Lenin and those who would succeed him in governing the Soviet state he had founded.

A small number of specialists in the art of embalming were formed into a group named the Immortalization Commission and given the task of preserving the mummified corpse. The city of Petrograd, once St. Petersburg, was renamed Leningrad.

That same year, 1924, Fanya Slepak gave birth to a second baby girl, whom the Slepaks named Rosa, after the German Communist leader Rosa Luxemburg. The delivery, which took place in a Japanese hospital, was again by forceps, marks of which the child bore until the age of three. The following year Fanya gave birth to twin boys. Both were delivered by forceps and born dead. Fanya told her husband that she thought the Japanese had tried to kill their second child and had successfully murdered the first child and the twins because of what Solomon and his army of partisans had done to them during the Civil War. When she became pregnant again, she insisted that the baby be born in the Soviet Union.

Solomon and Fanya Slepak and their little daughter, Rosa, returned to Moscow, where, on October 29, 1927, Fanya gave birth to a healthy boy, without the aid of forceps. They named the child Vladimir, after Vladimir Lenin, and called him Volodya.

Two months later, on December 27, 1927, the Fifteenth All-Union Congress of the Communist Party, meeting in Moscow, condemned deviation from the party line and removed Trotsky and his supporters from positions of importance—its way of acknowledging the power of a unified party and stifling all opposition to Stalin. Stalin's rivals quickly recanted.

Solomon Slepak, living in Moscow at the time of the Fifteenth Congress and still working as a correspondent for Rosta, attended the sessions and witnessed Stalin's ascent to power.

Some while later he was reassigned to China, again as a foreign correspondent. In mid-January 1928 the Slepak family boarded a train for the long journey from Moscow to Peking. And during that trip, little Volodya, two and a half months old, saved their lives.

It was a journey of nearly five thousand miles along the sweep of the Trans-Siberian Railroad, running from Moscow to Vladivostok. South of Chita the railway branched into two lines. Travelers could continue north and east through Russian territory to the city of Khabarovsk and then south on the single-track railbed to Vladivostok, or take the Russian-run Eastern Chinese Railroad through Manchuria east to Harbin and south to Peking.

Solomon and Fanya Slepak, with their little daughter and infant son, were taking the train through thousands of miles of snow-covered wasteland and winter forests and isolated villages to Harbin and Peking.

Harbin lay in the midst of vast swamps and grasslands—a grant of Manchurian land ceded by the Chinese to the Russians in 1896. Many who lived there had come from Russia to work on the railroad. Its population increased after the Revolution and in the twenties numbered about one hundred thousand. Relations between the Kremlin and Chiang Kai-shek were bad. Russian Whites and Chinese bands roamed the steppes, looting Soviet trains.

The train in which the Slepaks were riding came to a sudden stop some miles before Harbin. Armed Whites went through the cars, ordering everyone off. The passengers—Russians, Europeans, Chinese—stood in the cold, waiting for their papers to be checked. Bolsheviks and Jews were told to stand aside. Solomon Slepak, traveling under the name of Semion Ignatievich and carrying a Soviet passport and Tass credentials, was informed by the officer in command that he was a filthy Bolshevik whose party had brought ruin to Russia and was now trying to destroy China. The commander then ordered a young officer to take this Bolshevik filth and his family a distance from the train and shoot them.

The Slepaks began to move past the crowd of passengers, followed by the officer. The infant Volodya started crying. Fanya held him to her, keeping him warm, but his crying grew shrill, piercing. Some of the women among the passengers murmured at the officer. What sort of human being was he, killing an infant in the arms of its mother? Would such an inhuman act advance their cause and the nationalist cause of China? The murmurings grew louder, as did the shrill screams of the infant. The officer, some distance now from his commander, looked distraught. Somewhere weapons were fired: executions, no doubt. Near the Slepak family the crowd was turning restless, its murmurings louder, menacing. Abruptly the officer holstered his weapon, pushed Solomon Slepak and his wife and children into the crowd, and walked away. The crowd swallowed them, and soon they were back aboard the train and traveled without further incident to Harbin and Peking.

In Peking they lived in a brick cottage behind the brick walls of the Soviet compound, a large parklike area of private houses and office buildings set among trees and bushes. Near their cottage was a pavilion with Ping-Pong tables, a short distance behind the pavilion lay the tennis court, and not far from the front of the cottage were the gates to the compound. At the far end of the compound near the wall opposite those gates stood the main building containing the embassy offices and the apartments of the ambassador and other diplomats.

Front stairs brought one up to the veranda of the Slepak home; it in turn led to the living room into which opened the bedroom of Solomon and Fanya, as well as Solomon's study. Each of the children had a private bedroom, and their two nannies slept in a room nearby. The staff, all Chinese, consisted of a cook, a maid, Solomon's secretary-translator, whose Russian was perfect, and a courier. The courier rode a bicycle to deliver press releases from Solomon to Chinese and foreign press bureaus and to pick up newspapers and releases for Solomon. A stairway led from the rear hallway off the living room down to the basement, where there were storage rooms, the kitchen, and a room that contained a rotary press.

The apparent serenity inside the Soviet compound was a false mirror of events outside. China was experiencing its own savage civil war. Sun Yat-

sen had died in 1925, his dream of a united and Westernized China un-
fulfilled. Chiang Kai-shek, appointed by Sun to head the new Wham-
poa Military Academy set up to train the officer corps of the
Kuomintang army, was now commander in chief of a military force that
had begun to move north from Canton, subduing the countryside and
predatory private armies. Chiang's initial goals were the reunification of
China and the birth of a new Western-oriented government led by the
Kuomintang Party, which was at the time still dominated by Chinese
Communists whose instructions issued from agents of the Comintern—
Borodin and Dalin, among others.

Early in April 1927, about ten months before the arrival of the Slepak
family, police had forcibly entered the Soviet Embassy in Peking and discovered documents that revealed the degree of Soviet infiltration into
Chinese affairs under Borodin's direction. Arrested on the premises were
nineteen Chinese Communists, all of them later strangled to death for
treason.

Some days later Chiang Kai-shek set out to break the hold of the Chinese Communists on the Kuomintang Party through a series of anti-
Communist actions in many cities and a coup in Shanghai, where the
first revolutionary Marxist cell—the nucleus of the future Chinese
Communist Party—had been organized in May 1920. Chiang's loyalties
lay not with the Kremlin but with the bankers, merchants, and landlord
families whose loans and revenue he needed. Communist unions and
organizations were outlawed, hundreds of Chinese Communist leaders
executed.

Among the Kremlin's Chinese followers shot during this period of purg-
ing was Solomon Slepak's personal secretary, the husband of Volodya's
nanny. That nanny saved Volodya from serious injury—indeed may
have saved his life.

That is Volodya Slepak's earliest memory: his life being saved. He is
not quite three years old. His nanny is walking down the wooden stairs
from the veranda of the cottage with little Volodya in her arms, he prat-
tling in Chinese, when one of the steps suddenly gives way beneath her
feet. She begins to tumble forward. Instinctively she raises the child over
her head and plunges her foot deep into the splintering wood to steady
herself and keep the child from falling headlong down the stairs to the
ground. Her leg snaps.

His very first clear memory: swaying precariously in the air over the
head of his Chinese nanny, and her muted cry.

The fabric of the years that follow is woven from little clues, from flashes of remembrance. Soon after the incident on the veranda, the family moved to the city of Mukden, some 350 miles northeast of Peking, where they lived in a large house with a flat roof inside a walled compound amid an expanse of flowers and trees. There were many servants. And Volodya's nanny had come with them from Peking.

A community of Jews, dating from the twelfth century and made up mostly of merchants from Iran, had once existed in the Chinese city of K'ai-feng. The Chinese, lacking Christendom's perception of the Jew as the killer of Christ and the servant of Satan, lived on cordial terms with the Jews of K'ai-feng, whom they regarded as belonging to "the religion that extracts the sinews"—an allusion to one of the Jewish dietary laws which requires the removal of the network of blood vessels from the thigh of an animal before its meat may be eaten. Jews served in the Ming and Ch'ing dynasties as physicians, officials, and army officers, but in time they vanished, and by the end of the nineteenth century there were virtually none in China save for the small community in Shanghai led by the prosperous Sassoon and Hardoon and Kadoorie families, who made fortunes in transportation, construction, and banking. Then a new migration commenced after the 1904–1905 Russo-Japanese War. Many Jewish soldiers mustering out of the Russian Army chose to live in Harbin rather than return to tsarist Russia. The Chinese Eastern Railroad, built by the Russians, brought to Harbin European and Russian Jews as well as Jews from Siberia who had engaged in dairy production and cattle raising.

About ten thousand Jews lived in Harbin after 1917, and there were significant numbers of Jews in Tientsin, Mukden, and Shanghai. In photographs, we can see the staff of Bernstein and Sons in Tientsin, a company which exported furs from China to Europe and the United States; and teachers and students in the Skidelsky Talmud Torah in Harbin: skullcapped children, bearded elders, and on the blackboard, in Hebrew, the words "The study of Torah is good when accompanied by civility."

The kindergarten Volodya attended in Mukden had probably been established by Russian Jews who had fled pogroms and the Revolution. Volodya recalls a Purim party he attended; the holiday celebrates the foiling of an ancient persecution of Jews planned by a Persian minister of state. An intriguing image: a Bolshevik sending his son to a Jewish kindergarten's Purim revelry. Hadn't Solomon Slepak left religion behind in Dubrovno and Kopys when he fled from home nearly thirty years before? Perhaps it was simply a good school for little children, and he regarded Purim as emblematic of his Bolshevik vision of universal equality and the end to bigotry.

One day in Mukden, Fanya Slepak and her children climbed to the roof of their house and stood looking out over the city. For a long time the streets were eerily silent and empty. Suddenly khaki-uniformed troops appeared everywhere and military police were directing army vehicles. In the distance a shell exploded, and there came the firecracker sounds of shooting. Bullets whistled past their heads. Fanya scooped up the children and ran with them down into the cellar of the house.

It was September 1931. On the pretext of protecting the tracks of their South Manchurian Railroad, the Japanese had invaded Manchuria and seized Mukden. They proclaimed the new state of Manchukuo in February 1932, and one month later, Solomon Slepak traveled to Harbin as a correspondent for Tass to attend the installation, as regent, of the last remaining member of the Manchu dynasty, Henry Pu Yi, a puppet of the Japanese. And that December, Solomon returned to Moscow to make his required two-year report to his chiefs. He visited his mother and remained in Russia through the following summer while his family enjoyed the beach at Pey-Tay-Ho near Port Arthur. The fair-skinned little Volodya came down with a bad case of sun poisoning. When Solomon returned to Mukden after the summer, he told the children he had been away so long because his mother had been ill and died and he had attended her funeral. Shortly after his return he and his family were ordered back to Peking, where they moved into the same house they had lived in before. At that time the Communists in China were being relentlessly rooted out and exterminated by Chiang Kai-shek. Young Volodya, attentive to his surroundings now, was aware of odd goings-on in the house: night meetings in his father's study; doors and windows closed; hushed voices.

His nanny taught him Chinese songs. His sister, three years older than he, with curly brown hair and brown eyes, had her own circle of friends and saw little of her brother. He had a tricycle. In the pavilion were tables, chairs, a pool table, and he would watch the adults play. There were mulberry trees in the compound, and he would gather the berries and eat them. How his mother scolded him once when he smeared his shirt blue with berries! One day a wildcat got into the garden, and that evening he and his sister, while strolling through the compound, suddenly spotted it and watched with spine-tingling fear its swift leapings and glidings through the shadows. They raced back into the house. A wildcat in their garden! The thrill and dread of sharing a frightful secret.

His father enrolled Volodya in the American school for the children of diplomats, which his sister attended. There were some Chinese students in the school, but most were American. It was a good school, his father said. The best.

Volodya, who spoke Chinese as well as Russian, now began to learn English. And arithmetic. In school all morning. Home for lunch. More school in the afternoon. Classes, sports. Happy days.

In the spring of 1934 he suddenly fell ill. The doctors in the German hospital in Peking diagnosed the illness as amoebic dysentery. A swastika flew from the hospital flagpole, and a picture of Adolf Hitler hung on the wall behind the desk of the head nurse. The doctors spoke German.

Frightened by the hospital, Volodya told his father, "I don't want to be here with fascists!"

His father said it was the best hospital in China.

That summer Solomon Slepak returned to Moscow. Volodya was in and out of the hospital, the German doctors unable to cure him. One of the doctors, Professor Krieg, a tall, grayish-blond man, with blue eyes behind gilded-frame glasses, told Fanya there was something in the food or water that was affecting the boy. He said he did not think the child would live and suggested that they consider leaving China.

In his hospital room, the seven-year-old Volodya lay very ill: diarrhea, blood and mucus in his feces, exhaustion. His nanny slept next to him on a narrow bed.

Fanya Slepak cabled her husband to inform him of Professor Krieg's advice. After a few days, Solomon cabled back: They were being transferred to Moscow.

Fanya cabled that she would not travel by train alone with the children through China. Solomon cabled that they were to go by boat to Kobe in Japan and from there by train to Tsuruga. A boat would then take them to Vladivostok, where they were to take the train to Moscow. The train traveled only through Russian territory. He would meet them when they arrived in Moscow.

Volodya vaguely recalls his parents' large trunks filled with ivory sculptures, paintings, silks, Chinese kimonos, books. The trunks were sealed. In Kobe, Fanya Slepak, claiming diplomatic immunity, refused to open them for the Japanese customs inspectors. The stevedores dropped the trunks into the water and then fished them out. Still Fanya Slepak would not open them. As they left Kobe, the ship's captain offered to clear a deck of all passengers so she could spread out the objects and let them dry. Politely she refused—embarrassed, perhaps, by the number of objects inside, their immense worth. The trunks traveled wet all the way to the Soviet Union. Many of the objects bore water marks all the years afterward.

After sailing from Japan, the boat docked in Vladivostok, where Volodya said good-bye to his Chinese nanny. Decades later he wrote: "My nanny was with me all my life in China—in Peking, Mukden, once more in Peking, at all seashores where we went every summer. She accompanied us on our way home to Russia through Japan, until we came to Vladivostok. We parted with her in Vladivostok. From there we went to Moscow and she went back to Peking. From that moment, I never heard from her or about her."

Many years later Volodya asked his father why he had always been given diplomatic status in Asia when all the while he was only a correspondent. His father turned away and would not respond.

In Moscow, they moved into two rooms in a rented communal apartment on Petrovka Street, not far from the Hotel Lux. Four other families lived in the apartment. All shared a bathroom, kitchen, toilet. In the communal kitchen there were frequent quarrels among the women. Slowly, over the course of the next year, Volodya's health improved.

Solomon Slepak, who had reclaimed his original name and was no longer Semion Ignatievich, was now working at Tass.

The agency had two departments: International Tass and Internal Tass. The former, the larger of the two, dealt with news and information concerning countries outside the Soviet Union; the latter, with domestic matters.

Solomon Slepak was deputy chief of International Tass. In 1936 Beriozov, the head of that department, was arrested by the secret police. Solomon became acting head. Beriozov was later shot.

The office had to be covered around the clock. Solomon worked twelve-hour shifts, alternating with his deputy, Kotsin, and reporting to the head of the Press Department of the Central Committee. Soon after Solomon became acting head, Daletsky, the director of Tass, who was a Jew, learned from his close friend Karakhan, also a Jew and a deputy minister of foreign affairs, that they were both about to be arrested. Daletsky shot himself in his office. Karakhan too committed suicide. The great purge had begun.

Decades later Solomon told Volodya that three years after the family left Peking, members of the Russian diplomatic staff who had served there began to be ordered back to Moscow. One by one, summoned for reassignment; and once back in Moscow, all were arrested, including Ambassador Bogomolov. Prolonged contact with foreigners, for whatever reason, had by then been made to carry an automatic presumption of guilt. Accused of counterrevolutionary activity and of spying for the Japanese, they were all shot.

That might have been the fate of Solomon Slepak as well had he and his family remained in Peking. But now, in Moscow, he went on working as acting head of International Tass, his many years in China inexplicably overlooked by Stalin and the secret police.

Cutting Down the Forest

There were uprisings in Spanish Morocco and parts of Spain in 1936, and the British Labour Party expressed its support of the faltering Spanish Republic while the British government remained uncommitted. With Hitler's approval, twenty German transport planes flew to Spanish Morocco to airlift General Franco's Army of Africa into Seville. It had been Franco's idea, the first such use of aircraft in history. Granada fell to Franco, and the Comintern agreed to help the Republic. The Spanish Civil War began in earnest.

That summer a Spanish soccer team arrived in Moscow to play a Russian team called Spartak. Solomon Slepak took nine-year-old Volodya to the game. In the stadium before the start of the game, a party leader spoke of the menace of fascism and General Franco, and a worker representative praised the courage of the Republican forces. The Soviet team won. That was the only time Solomon Slepak took his son to a sports event.

The Slepak family lived then on Petroverigsky Pereulok, having moved in the spring of 1935 from their rooms on Petrovka Street. The city still bore a gray and grimy look; many of its buildings stood half crumbled. There were few automobiles on the streets; people traveled mostly by tram. Many streets were being paved over with asphalt. The first line of the Metro had been completed the previous year. Only in the center of the city was there electricity. Most people cooked their food on kerosene stoves. Many homes were heated with firewood taken from torn-down wooden houses, but the apartments in which the Slepak family lived had central heating and hot water. There were no landlords in the Soviet Union; one obtained an apartment from the government and paid rent to the government. The Slepaks occupied rooms assigned to people who were working abroad for Tass for a year or two. Thus they moved five times during the decade of the thirties until, in 1940, they settled into an apartment on Gorky Street—as of 1936, the new name of Tverskaya Street. (In 1992 it again became Tverskaya.) There they lived until 1986.

The family often went to the movies. Volodya remembers seeing, among numerous other films, *Zlatie Gory* ("Golden Mountains"), *Tzirk* ("Circus"), *Iskateli Shastia* ("Seekers of Good Luck"), *Vratar* ("Goalkeeper"). They attended the Bolshoi Theater. Bolshoi tickets were difficult to obtain, but Solomon Slepak had connections and tickets were somehow always available to him, and the family saw with much pleasure the operas *Carmen, Rigoletto, Eugene Onegin*, and *Snow Maiden* and the ballets *Swan Lake* and *Nutcracker*. They visited the city zoo and went several times to the Moscow Circus, where they delighted in the clowns, gymnasts, jugglers, lions, tigers, elephants, and Russian bears.

From the time he became acting head of International Tass and began to work twelve-hour days, Solomon Slepak seldom saw his family on weekdays. He and his wife woke around six-thirty in the morning; Volodya and his sister, Rosa, a half hour later. Breakfast consisted of eggs or porridge, on occasion sausages, cheese, salad, tea. Solomon especially liked wild strawberry jam. Volodya and Rosa ate lunch in school, where they bought salad and tea and ate the sandwiches they brought from home. For dinner Fanya served soup and then meat or fish with potatoes and cooked grains. Food rationing had ended in 1934, but there was barely enough food in the regular city shops; people were happy to obtain bread and potatoes. The Slepaks ate better than most Russians did because they had returned from China with American dollars. Soviet citizens who worked abroad in the 1930s received part of their salary in rubles, deposited to their savings accounts in Russia, and part in American dollars, which they used abroad; they were permitted to bring back their savings in American dollars and shop in special stores that sold food to foreigners and Russians for hard currency. On most weekdays Solomon ate supper in the Tass cafeteria. "Your father is very busy," Fanya told the children. "He is doing important work."

Even in the summers he was busy. But sometimes the family rented a dacha outside Moscow, and Volodya and Rosa would swim in a nearby lake and walk through the forests of pines, firs, birches, and mountain ashes and pick berries with their parents. Solomon would swim, too, and take long walks alone in the forests and fields. Sometimes after a meal he relaxed in an armchair with a book. At times friends would visit.

For two years they rented a dacha very close to the dacha of Gregory Voitinsky and his family, whom they saw every day. Two middle-aged Bolsheviks talking quietly about—what? Old times in China? And guardedly, and only when absolutely certain they were alone, about the current nightmarish time in their homeland? Voitinsky was teaching then in the Department of Far Eastern Studies at Moscow University. Good memories, those weeks of summer in the dachas away from Moscow.

In the fall of 1936 the Slepaks moved to Neopalimovsky Pereulok, and a year later they moved again, to Bolshaya Serpukhovskaya Street. One of the apartments in which they rented rooms was occupied by two women who, because their husbands had been arrested, were suddenly bereft of all economic support; their own incomes left them with far less than they needed to survive. They had decided to rent part of their apartment, and the Slepaks were their first tenants. The women could often be heard crying in their room.

Volodya's first school was on Starosadsky Pereulok, not far from where he lived on Petroverigsky Pereulok. Schools had no names, only numbers: his was number 329. Because of a citywide shortage of school buildings, there were two shifts for the school's total student body of about eight hundred. When a school building was completed nearby, half the students of school 329, including Volodya but not his sister, were sent to the new building, number 617. It was a four-story brick building located on Spasoglinishchevsky Pereulok (now Arkhipova Street) opposite the Moscow synagogue, the city's only remaining Jewish house of worship. For Volodya the synagogue was connected "not with Jewishness but with religion," and as he had no interest at the time in anything religious, he has no recollection of ever seeing anyone entering or leaving it. Today school 617 is a hospital.

Most of the teachers in the schools Volodya attended were the sons and daughters of illiterate peasants, the very first educated peasant generation. He studied arithmetic, Russian language, Russian literature, geography, natural science, history. There were about thirty to forty students in each classroom. The walls were painted a light color; a blackboard covered the wall behind the teacher's chair and table. In almost every room there was a photograph of Stalin above the blackboard, and in some rooms, of Lenin too. Every student was required to join the Young Pioneers at the age of ten. They wore red ties and marched with red flags and attended meetings at which one of the teachers, a party member, spoke about events in the Soviet Union; about the international bourgeoisie who were the enemies of the people; about the fascists in Hitler's Germany who persecuted the Communists, arrested them, sent them off to concentration camps, shot them. No one ever mentioned the Jews.

Two of the apartments into which the Slepaks moved—on Neopalimovsky Pereulok and Bolshaya Serpukhovskaya Street—were quite far from the schools Volodya and Rosa attended. Solomon Slepak took them along every day in the Tass car that brought him to and from his office, at that time on Armiansky Pereulok. From there the children would walk the rest of the way to school so no one would spot them using the car. Solomon insisted that they continue to attend those schools despite their distance from where the family now lived; they were among the best schools in Moscow, he said.

On occasion Volodya caught the word *zhid* directed at him by certain students, and ignored it. The first time he had heard the word, he asked his father what it meant, and his father explained that it was a bad word used by ignorant and misguided persons as a nasty and crude description of the Jews, an ancient and honorable Mediterranean people who had been persecuted all through history and to whom their family belonged, and, his father went on, when the dream of a perfect Communist state came true, that persecution would end and all the peoples of the Soviet Union would live in harmony as one great nation and as a sign to the entire world that Comrade Stalin and the Communist Party had finally put an end to religious hatred and bigotry.

Volodya was about eight or nine at the time. A Jew! He was a Jew! Apparently he had forgotten the Purim celebration he had attended in Mukden years before. Then again, perhaps there was nothing especially Jewish about that event; it may have been merely another party, unremarkable save for the costumes and the clamor.

There was no organized Jewish community in Moscow when Volodya discovered that he was a Jew.

Lenin had detested anti-Semitism. He thought it contrary to the socialist ideal of equality and believed, with Karl Marx, that the Jews would have assimilated and disappeared long since had it not been for the persecutions to which they were endlessly subjected. Indeed, he had approved the decree of the July 1918 Council of People's Commissars condemning anti-Semitism as "fatal to the interests of the workers' and the peasants' revolution" and instructing all Soviet deputies "to take uncompromising measures to tear the anti-Semitic movement out by the roots."

But Jewish Communists had other notions about the future of Judaism in revolutionary Russia. At the June 1918 Second Conference of the Jewish Communist Sections, the Evsektsia, in Moscow, they resolved that the "Zionist Party plays a counterrevolutionary role" by hindering the penetration of Communist ideas among the toiling Jewish masses. They urged "the promulgation of a decree suspending all activities of the Zionist Party" and concluded that the "communal organs, which are the mainstay of all reactionary forces within the Jewish people, must be suppressed."

Lenin's government immediately adopted the resolution. Two leaders of the Jewish Commissariat, Simon Dimanstein and Samuel Agursky—the former a onetime yeshiva student, rabbi, and Lubavitcher Hasid—were appointed to the task of tearing down the Jewish community.

In June 1919 the government issued a decree closing all Jewish establishments. The decree carried the signatures of Samuel Agursky and Joseph Stalin. Most synagogues were padlocked or turned into Communist clubs, schools, dining halls; their possessions became the property of the Soviet state. There is a photograph of a pile of Torah scrolls from desecrated Russian synagogues, and it is difficult not to wonder if somewhere in that heap there might be the scroll whose completion was once celebrated with music and recorded in the photograph of Dubrovno Jews assembled before the Ark in their synagogue. Youngsters under the age of eighteen were forbidden to receive religious education outside their homes and required to attend classes in which communism would be taught. The Zionist movement, which had once numbered about three hundred thousand Jews, was banned. Religious officials—now regarded as "declassed members of society," individuals without civil rights—found it difficult to secure housing, jobs, food rations, and the admission of their children to schools. Circumcision—illegal. Marriage and divorce laws—repealed. The Hebrew language—suppressed. Jews were even warned against kissing the Torah; it was unhygienic. A secular Yiddish culture was what the Jewish Communists wanted for the Jews of Soviet Russia. Yiddish elementary schools; Yiddish newspapers and journals; Yiddish to be spoken at the meetings of the Jewish soviets.

The Jews were to be a nationality culture, with Yiddish as their language, socialism as their secular religion.

The campaign to cripple Judaism and assimilate the Jews into Communist culture was waged by Communist Jews; non-Jews did not participate in it. It was a Jewish civil war, brutal and unrelenting.

Hastening the process of assimilation was the breakup of cohesive Jewish townlets and the displacement of Jews into Moscow and Leningrad as a result of the World War, the Civil War, and the pogroms in the Ukraine and White Russia. It is estimated that in the 1930s more than 3 percent of Moscow's population of four to five million people was Jewish. To accelerate the process even further, Lenin urged the Jews to colonize certain areas of Russia, and thousands went. Some of the colonies were funded in part by the American Joint Distribution Committee, which had been established during World War I to bring aid to distressed European Jews. There are many photographs of Jews in those agricultural colonies: They shear sheep near Odessa; they eat breakfast in the fields of the Ukraine; they are on their way to a meeting in the Crimea; they live in temporary barracks; they raise pigs, as a way of demonstrating their rupture with the Jewish religion; they drive a John Deere tractor; they celebrate May Day.

But few Jews seemed interested in becoming part of a Yiddish-speaking nationality or in colonizing Russian land. Most secular Jews preferred assimilation into Russian high culture. In only a few years the intermarriage rate of Jews in the heart of the Soviet Union reached 25 percent. Zionists and religious Jews quickly came to regard Communist rule as a grim continuation of the repressive regime of the tsars. Indeed, many Jews believed themselves worse off under the Communists than they had been under the cruelest of the tsars.

Economic conditions had improved somewhat in the years after the emergency period known as War Communism and the devastating famine of the early 1920s. When the guns of the Civil War finally went silent at the end of 1920, Lenin had gazed upon widespread rebellions, strikes, hunger, and the shambles of the Soviet economy—a declining harvest, rampant inflation, industrial production at 13 percent of the prewar level—and had begun a reluctant retreat from pure ideological communism. In the spring of 1921, after a number of stumbling moves, he instituted his New Economic Policy: Peasants were now subject to standard taxes rather than to cruel outright requisitions; small businessmen could hire workers and freely trade the goods they produced; one could buy and sell urban property, enter the field of publishing, establish and take part in privatized retail trade. Gradually rationing was abolished, and the economy began to recover. A photograph of an open market during the period of the New Economic Policy, from 1921 to 1928, shows stalls bulging with produce. Most Soviet citizens—workers, peasants, small businessmen—seemed to benefit from the new policy. Jews, about one-third of them "declassed" because they had been artisans, small merchants, and craftsmen, found the policy a boon to their broken lives. But Bolsheviks like Zinoviev worried that the reappearance of private enterprise might destabilize political control and made a point of declaring that the New Economic Policy was nothing more than "a temporary deviation, a tactical retreat."

Lenin's policy regarding the Jews—the destruction of their institutions and their total assimilation—was followed and intensified by Stalin. The Comintern's failure to incite revolution throughout the capitalist world led Stalin to a new interpretation of communism: the continuing development of socialism in one country, the Soviet Union. Those who opposed him in his clash with the internationalist-minded Trotsky—Kamenev, Zinoviev, and others—he took to calling "rootless cosmopolitans"—that is, party members who cared more for socialism in other countries than in their own: Stalin's way of calling someone a Jew without sounding like a tsarist anti-Semite. At the same time, Jews were among Stalin's most loyal adherents; one among them, Lazar Kaganovich, headed the first Five-Year Plan's pitiless effort to forcibly collectivize the peasants of the Ukraine. Thus the urban Russian hated Jews because they were "rootless cosmopolitans"; the rural peasant hated them because they were ruthless oppressors. Speculators, petty traders, parasites, Bolshevik overlords, made up the image of the Jew in the eyes of most Russians.

In 1928 Stalin initiated an effort to settle Jews inside their own autonomous province in distant Birobidzhan, 23,321 square miles of territory near Manchuria, 8,000 miles from Moscow, and near the region of Solomon Slepak's forays into mainland Asia. It was a harsh, primitive land, ridden with disease, insects, rains. At its height, in the late 1930s, the Jewish autonomous region had 128 Jewish elementary schools with Yiddish as the language of instruction, a daily Yiddish newspaper, a medical school, a music school, and 27 Jewish state and collective farms. But little came of the effort. Crippled early on by the unwillingness of Jews to be concentrated in one area—particularly so distant from the centers of culture—it was further weakened by the purges of the 1930s, during which many of its leaders, accused of being Trotskyites, nation-

alists, and Zionists, were imprisoned, exiled, executed. By the end of the
1960s Jewish Birobidzhan was dead.

Stalin ended the New Economic Policy in 1928 with his first Five-Year
Plan to industrialize Russia on a massive scale and collectivize its agri-
culture. For that enormous effort a vast pool of highly trained workers
was necessary. Townlet Jews and village peasants poured into the cities
and entered the work force.

A photograph shows a group of young Jews in a workshop for the
training of metal laborers seated in front of a large portrait of Stalin, who
is wearing a white army-style jacket and holding a cigarette in his left
hand. By the end of that first Five-Year Plan, more than a million Jews
had become wage earners who worked with their hands, and salaried
bookkeepers, teachers, engineers. Gone were all the tsarist restrictions
that had barred Jews from entering higher education and the professions. In 1934–1935, the Slepak family's first year in Moscow after their
return from China because of Volodya's dysentery, fully 18 percent of the
graduate student population of Russia was Jewish.

Russian Jewry was dissolving into the larger body of the land and its
culture. Battered from without by the Communist Jews of the Evsektsia, weakened from within by Jews no longer willing to take on the bur-
dens of an ancient tradition and fearful of being branded Trotskyites or
Mensheviks, the Jewish religion and its institutions vanished or went
underground. So successful did Stalin think the anti-Jewish program to
have been that by the mid-1930s he was certain that the young generation of Jews knew nothing of Judaism. And he was in no small measure
correct.

About a decade and a half had passed from the time of the initial promulgation of those anti-Jewish decrees to that day when young Volodya
discovered his Jewishness. The family chronicles record his bewilderment on learning that he was a Jew, on being so defined by others, by
those who clearly hated him. They tell of his anger and shame. And his
sudden fear.

In school Volodya began to notice that some classmates would suddenly
become strangely sad and withdrawn. They stood alone in the play yard;
they were never called on in class; they sat silent and shriveled at their
desks. After some time they disappeared. Somehow everyone in the
school knew not to talk about them.

Volodya told his father about the vanishing students. Solomon Slepak explained that a new organization of secret political police had been established—the NKVD. It was made up of people who were cleverer and more talented than those in the previous political police forces, the Cheka and the GPU, and the NKVD was uncovering spies, enemies, and traitors who had not been discovered before. Those so uncovered were being arrested and sent away, together with their families.

One day Volodya saw his father remove some books from a shelf and toss them into the garbage; the authors had been arrested. Another time his father took down a history of the Russian Civil War and proceeded to ink out the photographs of Trotsky and others. In school Volodya's teachers told the students to tear out the pictures of this or that person who had just been discovered to be an imperialist spy. At home one day his father expunged with India ink faces of friends and relatives in their family album—all had been arrested. The features of Ambassador Bogomolov, with whom Solomon Slepak had served in China—erased. Volodya thought it a good thing that all those spies and traitors were being uncovered; now Russia would live safely without enemies.

His uncle Konstantin Shur, once Yosef Shur, was a tall, strong, jolly man whom the Slepaks often visited in his apartment. He was a member of the Communist Party and the director of the Soviet government's Department of Weights and Measures. Fanya Slepak's brother. He would toss Volodya up in the air, catch him, toss him up again. He had a wife and children, and the families were together often. Once some weeks went by and Volodya asked, "Where is Uncle Konstantin?" His father said, "Uncle Konstantin was arrested. He was a member of a hostile conspiracy. Don't ask about him; don't talk about him." Volodya, then about ten, obeyed and put his uncle out of mind and never saw him or his family again.

Fear hung in the air. People avoided looking into one another's eyes. Deep silences lay heavily upon food lines in stores, crowds in trams, workers in office buildings, dwellers in apartment houses.

The first time Volodya saw a photograph of Stalin was in the Russian Embassy building on the compound in Peking where he spent much of his early childhood. Almost all photographs of Stalin portrayed him in a khaki or white army-style jacket. Sometimes he was shown holding a smiling little girl. Volodya knew, of course, that Stalin was the leader of Russia, but he was five or six at the time and has no memory of how he reacted to his first look at the leader's face.

During his early school years in Moscow, Volodya read regularly the newspaper for youth, *Pionerskaya Pravda*, with its stories about Young Pioneers who helped catch spies, aided the old and sick, took part in harvesting. Many photographs of Stalin appeared in the pages of the paper, especially on occasions that marked Soviet or Communist Party anniversaries. The face in the photographs was never truly that of the leader, whose features were marked with smallpox scars always skillfully touched up by the photographers. And never actually shown was his withered left arm, the result of blood poisoning from a serious childhood injury. He had come from a life of terrible poverty in eastern Georgia. His father was a cobbler and a violent drunk, who often beat his wife and son; his mother was a peasant. In his youth he attended a seminary where he encountered, among the students, Georgian nationalism and a hatred of tsarist authority. An assiduous reader with a good memory, he was introduced by fellow students to the writings of Darwin and Lenin, as well as to the work of Plekhanov, who had insinuated the thought of Karl Marx into Russia. Stalin left the seminary in 1899 at the age of twenty and entered the ranks of professional revolutionaries. Into his blood and bones had penetrated a bitterness at the oppressions of the tsar, the capitalist, the landlord. He organized strikes and demonstrations, planned a number of bank robberies to help finance the Revolution, and wrote articles in which he agreed with Lenin's view that among the party's tasks was the need to "arm the people locally . . . to organize workshops for the manufacture of different kinds of explosives, to draw up plans for seizing state and private stores of arms and arsenals." The articles brought him to the attention of Lenin, who had urged the use of plundered funds in the waging of the Revolution. Eight times arrested and seven times exiled, Stalin managed to escape from each exile except the last—from which he was released soon after the abdication of Nicholas II. Together with Trotsky, he stood at Lenin's side during the early years of the Revolution, then outmaneuvered Trotsky in the struggle for leadership of the party after Lenin died in 1924. He was now ruler of a tumultuous and suffering Russia, which he was attempting to subdue to his own vision of communism and a centralized party.

Much of that vision involved crushing all opposition to his plans for collectivization, industrialization, and total control of the party. In this he followed closely the path set by Lenin—with a singular exception. No matter how bitter the quarrels within the inner circle, Lenin had never turned against those inside the party, especially his old comrades, the Bolsheviks who had created the Revolution. But Stalin saw in those very Bolsheviks—Ryutin, Radek, Kamenev, Zinoviev, Bukharin, and others—his most dangerous enemies, who had often aligned themselves against him in heated inner party debates. From 1930 to 1933 three attempts by high party officials to remove him failed. Most in the inner circle saw him as the only one who could lead the country and preferred the possibility of despotism under his rule to the probability of anarchy and the collapse of the Revolution were he to be ousted from power. Stalin failed in his effort to have Ryutin, who had instigated the second and third attempts to remove him, sentenced to death for political offenses. The Politburo hesitated, resisted, shied away from the arrests and executions of loyal party members. Sergei Kirov, a popular party leader, an excellent speaker, and the boss of the Leningrad party, argued strongly against the death penalty for Ryutin and persuaded others in the Politburo to oppose Stalin. Only Kaganovich sided with Stalin.

That reluctance dissolved with the December 1, 1934, murder of Kirov—a deed, it is now believed, Stalin himself arranged through the head of the NKVD, Genrikh Yagoda. The assassination of Kirov at the hands of a lone gunman in the offices of the Leningrad Soviet provided Stalin with all the weapons he needed against his actual and perceived enemies in the party. When news of the assassination reached the Kremlin, Stalin, together with Molotov and Yagoda, took the overnight train from Moscow to Leningrad. A blizzard of edicts and arrest orders issued forth from Stalin, with the swift and automatic approval of the Politburo—among them, an immediate death penalty for terrorists, with no possibility of pardon.

There took place in the wake of the Kirov assassination a paroxysm of shootings, as well as deportations to Siberia and the Arctic: from Leningrad alone, between thirty and forty thousand men and women in only a few months. The assassin, Nikolayev, a misfit who had been unable to find a job and bore a deep personal grudge against Kirov and the Leningrad party, was tried and executed. Also arrested were former leaders of the Leningrad party, among them Zinoviev and Kamenev, Stalin's opponents. The two Old Bolsheviks, makers of the Revolution and leaders of the party, were sent to prison.

In March 1935, death with no possibility of pardon became the penalty for espionage or for flight abroad. All the members of a family were now to be held responsible for the crime of any one of them; even those who had been entirely unaware of a crime could be sent into exile. And in April 1935 children from the age of twelve were made subject to the death penalty.

Kamenev and Zinoviev were brought back from prison in 1936 to stand trial, and were then shot. In 1938, it was the turn of Bukharin,

Rykov, Radek, and eighteen others—of the sixteen condemned to death, twelve were Jews. Among those shot in 1938 was the NKVD head, Yagoda, who had suddenly been arrested in 1936 and replaced by Nicholas Yezhov, one of the most repellent officials in all of Russian history, who was himself removed from his post in 1938 and replaced by Lavrenti Beria. From 1937 to 1940 there took place the trials and executions of eight commanders of the armed forces. One was Marshal Michael Tukhachevsky, who had denounced Stalin for a tactical blunder in 1920 that had cost the Bolsheviks the chance of victory in the war against Poland; Stalin seemed never to forget his detractors, bore his grudges against them forever. And on the very eve of the Second World War came the NKVD shootings of about forty thousand officers accused of plotting against Stalin.

Like a ponderous black glacier, the terror moved across the Soviet landscape, through cities and countryside, through every organization and branch of the party and government; the heads of industries, leaders in the republics, scientists and engineers, writers like Maxim Gorky and Isaac Babel among numerous others, poets like Osip Mandelstam, to the families of the accused, their distant relatives, friends, associates. Millions were arrested. Most of those who ended up in the labor camps were utterly confounded by the evil destiny that had shattered their lives; many believed that Stalin was unaware of what was going on, that it was all the doing of the sinister officials who ran the NKVD. For Stalin had cleverly distanced himself from the terror. He moved his offices from the building of the Central Committee on Staraya Square to new quarters behind the walls of the Kremlin; he ceased delivering major speeches; from 1937 to 1939 he did not appear in public save on rare occasions. Few were aware of his regular meetings with Yezhov, and that the terror was of his making.

And so the land lay atomized, all in fear of all, in a miasma of dread, with no possibility of organized resistance because the terror struck at individuals, each instance of it a separate and personal experience—the knock on the door, the abrupt arrest, the sense of shocked disbelief, the certainty that an error had been made and would soon be corrected— and everyone thinking, Don't look, don't listen, don't ask, how do I know, maybe he really was a spy, I'm not doing anything wrong, it won't touch me. People were terrified of intriguers, provocateurs, denouncers, even of their closest relatives and friends, who could be arrested, jailed, threatened, turned into informers.

It is believed that between 1929 and 1940 seventeen million Russians perished, seven million of them peasants who died in the 1932–1933 famine, and three million from forced collectivization. An additional nine million were in the Gulag, which is the Russian acronym for a department of the secret police called The Chief Administration of Corrective Labor Camps, the system of imprisonment of the "enemies of the people" begun by the Cheka under Lenin. Stalin probably killed more Russians during the 1930s than Hitler did during the Second World War.

Yet some survived: Maxim Litvinov, who slept with a revolver under his pillow so that he could shoot himself if arrested. Vyacheslav Molotov. Lazar Kaganovich. Nikita Khrushchev.

And Solomon Slepak.

One might gaze with a certain smugness upon the slaughter of Communist kingpins at the hands of their own leader were it not for the suffering the terror brought to so many innocent Russians—the blameless family members and nonparty people slain; the many tens of thousands of ordinary people who perished; the hell-on-earth of the Gulag; the unmarked mass burial sites recently uncovered near Minsk, Novosibirsk, Chelyabinsk, Kiev. Power was what Stalin wanted; vengeance for real and imagined opposition. And power over a terrified and anguished people was what he got—and held to the day he died.

Yet not everyone suffered. To enable Stalin to accomplish what he did required the cooperation of millions of Soviet citizens: from those in the Politburo to the NKVD to the legal system to the bureaucrats to the prison and labor camp guards. A photograph of a Leningrad café, taken in 1937, brings us into a sunny scene: Men in shirtsleeves and women in summer dresses sit about on wicker chairs along a riverbank, probably the Neva. Cloth-covered tables. Bottles of fruit juice, mineral water, beer, glasses of tea. A waiter in a white jacket and bow tie, a woman wearing a necklace, men bareheaded or with walking caps. Only three men out of the more than thirty people present are wearing soldier's uniforms. Trees and boats and riverfront homes along the opposite shore. A Russian idyll, a languorous moment in a Chekhovian landscape, a green calm surrounded by a bleeding land.

For many Russians the 1930s under Stalin was a time when life was actually improving. The two Five-Year Plans had wrenched the country out of its crippling illiteracy and agrarian backwardness and turned it into a largely literate, urban, industrial society. Millions of citizens worked very hard, received an education, sacrificed willingly for the Motherland—they were calling it that after 1934—and felt themselves economically well rewarded.

One day Solomon Slepak read in *Pravda* of the arrest and trial and sentencing of Karl Radek, one of the members of the original Politburo, and expressed astonishment to his family that the man he had known personally for years had all along been a spy. How fortunate the country was that he had been found out. He never talked of Radek again.

His major responsibility at Tass was to present daily to Stalin and the Politburo a digest of the foreign press. As well as to gather press information from all over the world, censor it, and disseminate it to the Russian people.

In 1938 Tass acquired a new director, a man named Khavinson, with whom Solomon Slepak soon found himself embroiled in endless quarrels. After some while he requested from the Central Committee a transfer out of Tass. A dangerous step: No one had the right then to quit a job; the punishment could be arrest and years in a labor camp. Mysteriously, permission was granted.

He left Tass and took a job as senior editor—that is, head censor—of a publishing house specializing in literary and nonfiction works designated for translation. He knew eleven languages well and was fluent in eight: Russian, Yiddish, English, French, German, Spanish, Italian, Polish. His was the decision which Russian books would be translated into foreign languages, and which books written by foreign writers would be published in the Soviet Union in the original languages. He supervised the publication in the USSR of the works of Theodore Dreiser.

Late one night in the winter of 1938, after Solomon had left Tass, he suddenly woke and, wearing his pajamas and robe, went to the door of the apartment, where he stood listening. (The apartment building was occupied entirely by those who worked for Tass; soon thereafter the Slepaks would leave it for their permanent home on Gorky Street.) That night, as Solomon stood at the door, Volodya woke and came out of his room and saw his father. When the boy asked what was wrong, Solomon silenced him, and Volodya, then ten years old, realized with astonishment that his father was frightened. After a while, Solomon told his son to go back to bed. Minutes later, Volodya heard his father return to his room.

Years later, his father explained that he had been afraid of being arrested. "But you were a member of the party!" Volodya said. "Sometimes," his father replied, "a disease requires that healthy tissue also be cut away." In order to be sure that all the enemies of the state were removed, Solomon Slepak quietly told his son, the NKVD would arrest all those close to the enemies. He himself, he said, had been very close to many who were later seen to be enemies; the NKVD might think he was involved with them. Even individuals who had once served with the secret police were arrested.

Solomon Slepak, loyal Old Bolshevik, waiting nights at his apartment door for the knock of the NKVD and the words "You are under arrest."

When Nicholas Yezhov, a dwarfish man who was living proof of the Russian proverb "Out of filth you can make a prince," replaced Genrikh Yagoda as head of the NKVD in 1936, he gave a talk to a number of his top officers and spoke of the many innocent victims who were bound to be caught up in their great effort to rid the country of spies and traitors. "Better that ten innocent people should suffer," he said, "than one spy get away. When you cut down the forest, woodchips fly."

Why wasn't Solomon Slepak one of the savaged trees?

Walking with his grandson one day in the late 1950s, he ran into the former secretary of the party organization at Tass, who seemed surprised to see him.

He asked Solomon, "When were you released?"

"I wasn't arrested," Solomon replied.

The man looked astonished. "I saw a list of Tass people who were to be arrested. You were on the list."

It turned out that the list had been drawn up soon after Solomon Slepak had left Tass. The man in Tass responsible for the addresses of those on the list had telephoned the NKVD and reported that Slepak no longer worked there. He was told to write "No longer works here" after Slepak's name. All the others on the list were arrested and shot.

Was he spared only through bureaucratic ineptness, sheer chance, repeated fortuitous slippings through the cracks? Did he have a sixth, saving, sense of danger that kept him always a step ahead of the secret police, staying one level below those in visible power, knowing when to leave a post? Was he perhaps in possession of ruinous information about those in power?

One of Solomon Slepak's closest friends was a man named Vassily Gorshkov, who had fought under him in the Lake Baikal region of Asia during the Civil War. He was a tall, strong man, with a deep scar across his head from a war wound. Life-loving, uneducated, always laughing. He often played with Volodya. Suddenly he disappeared, and was no longer talked of by the family.

One day in the mid-1950s there was a knock on the door to the apartment, and Volodya's mother went to open it. In the doorway stood a white-haired man, bent, leaning heavily on a cane. He peered intently at Fanya Slepak.

"Don't you recognize me?"

"No."

"I'm Vassily." He seemed a broken old man.

"Vassily? Come in."

He entered and stood a moment, gazing around. He asked quietly, "Are you receiving a pension for your husband? When was his reputation restored?"

"There is no pension. My husband is alive."

"Sam is alive?" He looked bewildered.

"Yes."

"Where is he?"

"He went out to buy bread."

"When was he released?"

"He wasn't arrested."

"But how is that possible? The main accusation against me was my link to the Japanese spy Slepak. I was sure Sam was in the next cell."

No one seemed to know why Solomon Slepak was not arrested in the purges of the thirties.

In August 1939 Soviet Russia's Foreign Minister Molotov and Nazi Germany's Foreign Minister Ribbentrop signed the German-Soviet non-aggression pact in Moscow, stunning the world. Each party to the treaty was to remain neutral should the other be attacked by a third party.

The two countries also secretly carved out spheres of influence in Central and Eastern Europe. The eastern half of Poland would go to the Russians, as would Lithuania, Estonia, Latvia, and Bessarabia. Now Germans could travel to Moscow as tourists, saunter about on Soviet streets, take in the sights.

How explain to twelve-year-old Volodya this sudden peace with the hated fascist enemy?

Solomon Slepak told his son that the Germans had begun to change in the direction of socialism and were now good enough to live with in peace. He spoke with wholehearted earnestness, and his son believed him.

On June 22, 1941, the Slepak family woke late, their custom on a Sunday morning. They sat around the table, eating breakfast, and did not

turn on the radio. The doorbell rang. It was Volodya's cousin Israel Dagman, his father's nephew, in Moscow on a business trip. He was invited
to have breakfast with the family, and Solomon asked him casually about
his life, his plans. Israel Dagman said that the family was fine, but what
kind of plans could he make after today's events? What events? Solomon
asked. Looking very surprised, Israel Dagman said that early in the
morning German planes had begun to bomb Russian towns and cities,
and German troops had crossed the frontier and were inside Russian territory. Solomon Slepak's face darkened. He switched on the radio, and
they sat listening to the news of the war between Soviet Russia and Nazi
Germany.

Believing the assurances that emanated day after day from the radio,
Volodya was convinced that the war would be over in two or three
weeks, with the Red Army victorious. But soon Leningrad was nearly
entirely encircled by one German army, while a second was advancing
on Moscow, and a third was swallowing up the Ukraine and the Crimea
and approaching the Caucasus. And then, a few weeks after the start of
the war, there came the startling announcement that the children of
Moscow were to be evacuated.

On a sunny day in August, Volodya went with his sister, Rosa, and his
parents to the railway station, which was crowded with children and parents. He and Rosa parted from their parents and boarded a special train
for the students of the Krasnogvardeysky district of Moscow. To the children aboard the train it all felt like an outing, a trip to a summer camp
for Young Pioneers; they would all be back in one, at most two, months.
All the parents waving to their children from the station platform
seemed oddly serious.

The train was soon out of Moscow. Many hours of travel went by
until it arrived in the town of Shilovo in Ryazanskaya Province, where
the children boarded trucks that distributed them among several nearby
villages.

The truck that carried Volodya and his sister and other children, together with some parents and teachers from the Moscow school, took
them to the small village of Iritzy, about fifty houses along the sides of a
dirt road that was a ribbon of dust in dry days and mud in the rain. Behind every house was a little vegetable garden. Some of the children were
placed in empty houses; others, with peasant families. A dining room
was organized, as well as a medical aid station staffed by a Dr. Abram Bogorad and a nurse. There was no shortage of food. The children worked
in the fields, gathering hay, harvesting.

In September they all moved to the larger village of Timoshkino, where there was a high school in which they attended classes. In October they began to hear artillery fire. The German Army was suddenly only a short distance away! Urgently the children were moved back to the town of Shilovo, which had a landing stage on the Oka River. They were quickly put on a boat.

More than three thousand people were on the boat, which normally carried no more than a few hundred. Younger children like Volodya were placed in the hold; older ones like Rosa slept on the open deck. Rosa had contracted malaria. There was little fresh water on board and no one could bathe, and soon there was an outbreak of lice. Twice a day the children were served hot tea; all the other food was cold. The boat took them down the Oka and then east along the Volga and northeast on the Kama. For most of the journey dense forests lined the riverbanks, broken at times by flat fields that extended to the distant horizons. Volodya kept wondering why the war wasn't over yet, how the Germans had advanced so deep into Russia; the radio had spoken with such confidence about the power of the Red Army! The adults, when questioned by the children, explained that the attack had been very sudden, that all of Europe was helping the Germans.

As they approached the city of Gorky, there came word that a boat on the Oka River carrying parents of children evacuated to the Ryazanskaya Province had been bombed by the Germans and had sunk with all its passengers. Volodya and Rosa feared that their parents might have been on board.

After about ten days, they arrived in the town of Okhansk in the Ural Mountains. They climbed onto horse-drawn carts and rode for hours on dirt roads to Bolshaya Sosnova, a town of some three thousand houses located on the Sosnovka River and surrounded by wide fields and dense forests.

That was October 1941.

The distant artillery fire the children had heard in the village of Timoshkino had come from the German Army moving through the Russian heartland. The Germans had advanced more than 1,000 miles in three months. In Moscow, factories were being disassembled for evacuation to the east. The Soviet government left for the city of Kuibyshev, 525 miles to the east. Stalin chose to remain behind.

By October 20 forward elements of the German Army were five miles from Moscow. There was panic in the streets and looting of shops. Solomon Slepak was given a shovel and, together with hundreds of others, told to dig trenches. Near the end of the month, mud and rain stalled the German advance on the city.

As Solomon Slepak dug trenches, German chiefs of staff of all the major units in Russia gathered for a conference in Orsha, the city to which Solomon had fled from the home of his mother at the age of thirteen. With temperatures around minus four degrees Fahrenheit, they decided to resume the offensive against Moscow.

By the end of November combat units of the SS were within seven miles of the Kremlin. Leningrad remained under tight land siege, and eleven thousand Russians died there of hunger that November. A number of German tanks came close to the heart of Moscow; their crews could see the spires of the Kremlin. That was the farthest point of the German advance on the city. The temperature suddenly dropped to minus 25.6 degrees Fahrenheit.

In the suburbs of Moscow some civilians who were digging trenches, Solomon Slepak among them, suddenly found themselves surrounded by German troops. They fought their way out, using their shovels as weapons.

On December 3, with the temperature at minus 36.4 degrees Fahrenheit, the Germans began to withdraw from the suburbs of Moscow. By then Solomon Slepak and the staff of the publishing house where he worked had been ordered to evacuate the city. A train brought him and Fanya southward to Engels, a city near the Volga River north of the Caspian Sea. About two hundred miles to the south lay Stalingrad, which remained under siege by the German Army until February 1943. Nearly nine hundred thousand Russians perished in that siege.

Solomon and Fanya Slepak knew nothing of the whereabouts of their children. And Volodya and Rosa, having written home repeatedly and received no reply, were certain by now that their parents were dead. It took Solomon several months of trying, through the office of the Supreme Soviet, before he learned where his children were. More months passed. Then, in April 1942, a letter from him arrived at the town of Bolshaya Sosnova, and Volodya and Rosa discovered that their parents were alive.

Rosa at the time was working in the munitions plant in the nearby city of Molotov (now Perm), making shells for guns. That winter the temperature in the village plummeted to minus fifty-eight degrees Fahrenheit. Volodya fell ill with rheumatic fever. He lay in bed for a month and survived only because of the care given him by Dr. Bogorad. Able to walk once again, he worked in the dining room, collecting and washing dirty dishes, then some weeks later in the kitchen, carrying water from the well, sawing and chopping firewood, and eating all he wanted. His health improved; he returned to school. During the summer he worked in the fields with the other children.

The months went by; the war raged on. Everyone knew by now about the sieges of Leningrad and Stalingrad. War news came to them from radio speakers that carried broadcasts twice a day from the Central Moscow Radio Station. There were no private transmitters; they had always been prohibited, even in peacetime. In the early days of the war the government had ordered that all radio receivers be turned in, to prevent the population from listening to enemy propaganda. You had to bring your receiver to a special store or you faced immediate arrest. Speakers were then distributed throughout the country; usually they were hung from a nail in a wall and connected to a special socket. Every town and village had a radio-receiving station that broadcast news from Moscow to speakers in houses and apartments and offices.

When the news arrived in the village of Bolshaya Sosnova that the German Army threatening Moscow had been defeated by the Red Army, one of Volodya's teachers, speaking to a group of children, expressed doubt about the victory. A day or two later he vanished and was not seen again.

Then rumors began to come—not over the speakers but by word of mouth—of the killing of Jews by the Germans. It was said that many thousands had been murdered near Kiev. But not until 1944, when Kiev was liberated, did the Russians learn of the slaughter of ninety thousand Jews in the ravine called Babi Yar.

In late January 1943, his health much improved, Volodya joined many others from his school who enlisted in a training course given in Moscow for munitions workers. That March they were informed that they would soon be going to Moscow, and some days later they climbed aboard horse-drawn carts and began a twenty-eight-mile journey to the town of Vereshchagino, which held the nearest railway station.

The air was glacial, the road frozen. They could not sit on the carts for any length of time but had to walk or run alongside to keep themselves warm. In the town of Ocher, they were given a brief respite and hot food. They waited two hours in the cold in Vereshchagino for the train that was to bring them to Moscow. It arrived at night and was crowded with children. All were traveling to Moscow from the region east of the Urals; all were enlisted in training courses for the munitions factories.

Volodya found a third-level upper bunk, normally used for trunks, and lay there trying to sleep. The train moved slowly and stopped often, taking on passengers. At some stations there were dining rooms for the children; at others, only bowls of soup or cereal. They were all hungry. At one stop Volodya exchanged his jacket for a loaf of bread and a bottle of milk. The train began to leave, and he raced after it and leaped from the platform to the step of the last car but could not push his way through the dense mass of passengers to get to his car. He rode outside in the arctic night until the next stop, when he made it to his friends, cold and blue as ice but with the food. They thought he had been left behind.

The trip from Bolshaya Sosnova to Moscow took four days. Volodya arrived in Moscow on the first day of April 1943. He had been unable to inform his parents of his time of arrival—not enough money for a telegram; a letter would not have arrived in time—so no one met him at the train station. He took the Metro home.

His father, who had been back in Moscow since the fall of the previous year, opened the apartment door and stood there a moment, dumbfounded. Then they embraced. Volodya's sister, Rosa, had returned home earlier that year and now came running out of a room and clung to her brother. Fanya had gone out to shop for food, and when she returned and saw her son, she began to weep. He was fifteen years old and had been away from home twenty months.

Their apartment on Gorky Street was the same as when he had left it. The wallpaper looked a little older. The city, too, was the same. Some additional broken-down houses; here and there an area fenced off because of bomb damage. At night there were no lights in the streets.

The apartment building had been completed in 1940, half a year before the Germans invaded the Soviet Union and at a time when the Stalin terror was coming to an end. The front of the building, which looked out on Gorky Street, was of light-gray stone; the rear, facing the yard, of plaster painted a grayish yellow. The Moscow Soviet—the city hall—down the street was of a reddish color. All the other buildings were white, gray, and yellow; nearly all had stores and restaurants on the first floors.

The building in which the Slepaks lived was clean save for the cockroaches that cascaded across floors and walls and against which one fought endless and futile battles. One entered from the rear, because the

Gorky Street side was entirely occupied by shops. The building had eleven entrances, with nine floors in its vast center section and seven in each of its two side sections. Each of the approximately two hundred apartments, in which there lived, all told, some twelve hundred people, opened onto an elevator and a stairwell; there were no hallways. The radiator on the wall near the stairwell always gave off ample heat, save during the years of the war. The inhabitants of the building were actors, musicians, journalists, architects, engineers, and a few workers. Rarely did friendships develop among the occupants.

The Slepaks lived on the eighth floor in two rooms of a three-room apartment that faced Gorky Street. The third room was always rented to another family, because Solomon Slepak thought it wrong for one family to occupy more rooms than it needed, especially during a housing shortage. The third room changed hands five times during the years Volodya lived there: a Tass clerk, a noted violinist, a retired colonel, a militia officer, a postal clerk.

In the next apartment lived the noted filmmaker Michael Slutsky, the producer of the remarkable documentary *Day of War*, and his wife, Mimi. The documentary had been shot on June 13, 1943, by hundreds of cameramen, and then edited by Slutsky. One night in the autumn of 1943—Volodya is uncertain of the time—the KGB came to the Slutsky apartment and arrested him. Some days later Mimi Slutsky knocked on the door to the Slepak apartment and showed the Slepaks the order she had received to appear at the office of the KGB. She returned some time afterward with the news that the KGB had informed her that because she had been born in Vienna, she would be interned as a German citizen. (All German nationals were imprisoned in special concentration camps during the war.) She produced the necessary documents to prove she was not German but Jewish, and was told she would not be interned but had twenty-four hours to leave Moscow. She gave the Slepaks her jewelry and some other possessions and asked that they all be handed over to her husband's brother, whose name Volodya does not recall. They never saw her again. Michael Slutsky's brother was ordered by the KGB to remove all the furniture from the apartment. Not long afterward a KGB colonel moved in.

About three years later Michael Slutsky returned from prison entirely exonerated. To this day no one seems to know why he was arrested. The KGB colonel and his family remained in the apartment.

Gorky Street had six lanes of traffic, a center lane, and wide sidewalks. Cars, trolleys, buses. No trucks save on days when military parades took place. On those days tanks, motorized artillery, and trucks carrying rocket launchers and soldiers assembled on the street on their way to Red Square. Most of the apartment buildings were seven to eight stories high. People crowded the balconies to watch the parades assemble and pass by below.

There were few parades during the war and few moments of celebration. The troops that paraded past the reviewing stand in Red Square on November 7, 1941, in commemoration of the Bolshevik Revolution, marched straight from the celebration to the front lines. And there were no speeches from Stalin save the one he delivered about ten days after the start of the war, when he was sufficiently recovered from the shock and depression that had all but paralyzed him in the early days of the German invasion: "Comrades! Citizens! Fighting men of our army and navy! Brothers and sisters, I turn to you, my friends. . . ."

In the Slepaks' apartment building on Gorky Street, there were never any public announcements of private grief. The notice that a soldier had been killed in action would come by mail from the local office of the military. Upon receiving the notice, the family might apply for a pension if the one killed was the breadwinner and request to be moved up on the list of those waiting for a new room or apartment. Inside the room or apartment there were tears for the dead. But very rarely were flowers or wreaths placed on doors or in windows. The Communist regime had done away with the old customs. Visible displays of grief were frowned upon by the authorities.

Volodya does not know how many families in his apartment building lost relatives in the war.

During the war years, universities and institutes found themselves hard pressed for students; most eligible young people were in the armed forces. Special courses were organized for those who had completed eighth or ninth grade to prepare them for their high school graduation exams.

The same month Volodya returned to Moscow, he underwent a medical examination and was informed, to his dismay, that the rheumatic fever he had contracted in Bolshaya Sosnova had damaged his heart. As a result, he was disqualified for the demanding toil required of munitions workers.

There was much discussion then between Volodya and his father about the future. Volodya began to study for his eighth-grade exams—the equivalent of tenth grade in America—which he took and passed in July. Passing meant acceptance into the institute of one's choice, where one could attend special courses toward a high school diploma. Volodya had selected the Aviation Institute, which was purported to offer highly specialized engineering courses in aviation engines, navigational equipment, radio electronics, aircraft armament. He chose radio electronics. It was, he thought, the most interesting area of aviation engineering. And the faculty was reputed to be excellent.

In September 1943 Volodya began the special course of study in the Aviation Institute, and the following August he passed his exams. He and his parents appeared in the large auditorium of the institute, together with hundreds of others. One after the other, the students were called to the podium, where the rector of the institute shook their hands and presented to each a certificate of graduation. A student then delivered a brief talk, thanking the party and the government on behalf of all the students.

One easily imagines Solomon Slepak in that auditorium, recalling the year 1913, when he was refused acceptance by the High Technological Institute of Moscow because he was a Jew. Now, one generation later, his pride in his son's achievement! And in that of his daughter, Rosa, a student in the faculty of philology at Moscow University. How vindicated, all the blood spilled in the cause of his Bolshevik dream of a new world for Jews and all humankind.

At that time Solomon Slepak still worked as chief editor of foreign books in a major publishing house and was also a member of the Jewish Anti-Fascist Committee, which had been created by Stalin in April 1942 as a means of influencing what he assumed to be the wealthy and influential Jewish community of the United States. The idea had originally been conceived by two Polish Jews, Victor Alter, an engineer, and Henryk Erlich, a lawyer, both of them leaders of the Jewish Labor Bund, who had fled from the advancing Germans in 1939, entered Soviet territory, and been arrested by the NKVD. Accused of being spies and counterrevolutionaries, they were sentenced to death, only to be set free about two years later. The Soviets had promised the Polish government-in-exile, which was in England, that all arrested Poles would be released.

In September 1941 the two Bundist leaders, who were then living in the Hotel Metropol in Moscow, received a request from Beria to submit a list of Jews who might serve on the committee. The list, which included the celebrated Russian Yiddish actor Solomon Mikhoels, was approved by Beria, who then asked that the two men write a memorandum to Stalin outlining the committee's tasks.

In the memorandum they urged that the Soviet government create a Jewish anti-Hitlerite committee to include members from Nazi-occupied countries, the Soviet Union, the United States (which had not yet entered the war), and Britain; that the committee mobilize the support of world Jewry in the war against the Nazis; that it undertake to care for Polish Jewish refugees inside the Soviet Union; that a Jewish Legion be established inside the United States to join the Red Army.

The memorandum, dated in the early days of October 1941, was duly delivered to Stalin.

With the German Army rapidly advancing on Moscow, the two Bundists then left for the city of Kuibyshev near the Urals, along with all the other Soviet leaders except Stalin. In the office of the Grand Hotel in Kuibyshev, on the night of December 3, 1941, a phone call summoned the two men to a meeting with Beria. They left the hotel and were never heard from again. Years later it was discovered that Stalin had penned on their memorandum the words *Rasstrieliat' oboikh* ("Shoot both of them").

A few days after the disappearance of the two Bundists, the Japanese attacked Pearl Harbor and Hitler declared war on the United States. The idea of a Jewish antifascist committee was not forgotten; a number of Soviet Jewish leaders began to discuss it openly. With America in the war, it seemed all the more imperative that the influence of Jews throughout the world, who had heretofore been cold to the idea of providing aid to Bolshevik Russia, now be mobilized to propagandize for the Soviet Union, raise funds for the war effort, and lobby for the speedy opening of a second front that would ease the appalling losses being suffered by the Red Army.

And so, in April 1942, the Jewish Anti-Fascist Committee came into existence, with Stalin's approval. It was the only Jewish institution in the entire Soviet Union officially recognized by the Soviet government, and it had in its ranks, among others, the writer Ilya Ehrenburg, the Yiddish poet Itzik Fefer, the Central Committee member Solomon Lozovsky, the actor Solomon Mikhoels, who was its chairman—and the Old Bolshevik Solomon Slepak.

At the request of Stalin, two members of the committee, Solomon Mikhoels and Itzik Fefer, traveled to the United States in May 1943. Stalin himself saw them off. Arriving in New York, they were greeted by

Evgeni Kisselev, the consul-general of the Soviet Union. There is a photograph of Mikhoels at the grave of Sholem Aleichem, the beloved Russian writer in Yiddish, who is buried in New York, and one of Mikhoels and Fefer with Albert Einstein in Princeton. All in this latter photograph are smiling; all seem relaxed. Einstein, in his sweater and flowing hair and shaggy mustache; Mikhoels and Fefer in jackets, shirts, ties; trees in the background; sunlight. Mikhoels and Fefer met with Senator Herbert Lehman, who had been governor of New York State; with President Roosevelt's noted friend Rabbi Stephen Wise; with Marc Chagall, who had painted sets for the Jewish State Theater in Moscow during the years following the Revolution, when Mikhoels had been the director.

That summer the two members of the Jewish Anti-Fascist Committee traveled throughout the United States, Canada, and Mexico and spoke to many Jews whose ties with Russia had been severed for more than two decades. They talked of future political and cultural links with their Soviet brothers and sisters, of the heroic role being played by Jews in the Red Army. At public and private meetings in Washington, Chicago, and Los Angeles, they recounted the valiant struggle of the Red Army against the Nazis and emphasized the need for Jewish support. The two men seemed to complement each other: Fefer was a colonel in the Red Army, an impassioned Communist; Mikhoels, astonishingly, was not even a member of the Communist Party. In the Polo Grounds in New York City, at a rally attended by nearly fifty thousand people, Fefer and Mikhoels spoke first; the writer Sholem Asch then lauded the Soviet Union for doing away with anti-Semitism; Ben Zion Goldberg, the Yiddish journalist and a son-in-law of Sholem Aleichem, spoke of Marshal Stalin as a great leader. And the actor-singer Paul Robeson sang Yiddish and Russian songs.

Mikhoels and Fefer returned home after two months, having raised more than two million dollars for the armed forces of the Soviet Union.

During the time they were away, about seven thousand tanks and self-propelled guns fought the largest land battle in history near the Russian city of Kursk, some 250 miles south of Moscow. In Moscow, where Solomon Slepak was working for the Jewish Anti-Fascist Committee and for a publishing house, and Volodya was studying for and then taking his eighth-grade exams, the Slepak family read the newspaper accounts of the nearly weeklong battle and heard it reported over the radio in their apartment. In the end the German Army lost more than ninety thousand soldiers and two thousand tanks; its attack along the central front was crushed. As with Stalingrad that previous February, where

Field Marshal Friedrich von Paulus had surrendered his armies, Kursk was a turning point in the war, the last major German offensive on the eastern front.

The family chronicles offer no details concerning Solomon Slepak's participation in the work of the Jewish Anti-Fascist Committee other than the bare fact that he worked in its press office. At the height of its activities, the committee had a membership of about one hundred individuals. It published its own Yiddish-language periodical, *Eynikayt* (Unity). The membership was not of one voice regarding the committee's goals. Some wanted to limit the committee's efforts to foreign propaganda, others hoped to make it a force for the revival of Jewish institutions and culture in the Soviet Union, and still others began to urge that the committee persuade Stalin to permit the creation of a Jewish republic in the Crimea in place of Birobidzhan. The Crimean Tatars had been permanently exiled in May 1943 for collaborating with the Germans—loaded onto cattle wagons by the NKVD and sent on a four-month journey across the barren steppes to Central Asia—thereby opening the Crimea to the possibility of colonization by others.

There seems to be no way of determining what Solomon Slepak's position was on any of those issues. No record of his views, if indeed he had any, can be found anywhere. His name does not appear in the only scholarly book known to me on the activities of the Jewish Anti-Fascist Committee. And at home he never talked about his work.

By March 1944 the Red Army had pushed the Germans back to nearly the western border of pre-1939 Russia. In White Russia the German lines extended to a few miles beyond Orsha on the eastern side of the Dnieper. In the fall of 1944, with the Red Army in the suburbs of Warsaw and the American Army assaulting the Siegfried Line in Germany, Volodya was attending the Aviation Institute as a first-year student in radio electronics. Daily he traveled by trolley bus to the Sverdlova Square Metro station and from there to the Sokol station. Classes were from eight-thirty in the morning to, at times, five in the evening. In addition to his classes in engineering, Volodya was required to attend three weekly lectures or seminars on Marxist ideology: the principles of Marxism-Leninism; Marxist philosophy; Marxist political economy. Absences from three or more such seminars without valid reason, or failure in the exams, meant expulsion from the institute.

The Aviation Institute was at the corner of Leningradskoye Shosse and Volokolamskoye Shosse, wide asphalt-paved streets with large office and apartment buildings and many shops. Like the compound of the Russian Embassy in Peking, where Volodya had spent the early years of his life, a wall surrounded the institute, with a guarded security entrance at one end and gates at the other. Behind the gates ran the railroad to Riga. Inside the compound were the buildings that contained the class-rooms, auditorium, and administrative offices, the hangar and wind tunnel, the machine shops and student club. At the entrance to the ad-ministration building stood a heroic-style bust of Stalin. As with almost all the buildings in Moscow, those of the institute were made of brick and covered in part with either plaster or stone or concrete blocks. There were also volleyball, basketball, and tennis courts and a soccer field.

In each of the five classes Volodya attended there were thirty to forty students, about 65 percent of them men. Fewer than 10 percent of the faculty were women. Around one-fourth of the students and faculty were Jewish. The student body of the institute numbered about seven thousand.

Volodya's only close friend was Valery Voitinsky, whom he had known for years, the son of his father's old friend from New York and China. They attended the Aviation Institute together, talked about the movies they saw, the books they read, their school problems. In summer they va-cationed together; in winter they went ice-skating and to the theater. But after about six months in the Aviation Institute, Valery decided to drop out, and enlisted in the Red Army. The friendship grew cool, slowly dis-solved, came to an end.

Volodya was five feet seven inches tall, and slim; his hair dark brown, almost black; his eyes were grayish green. He favored sports jackets and sweaters, but food and clothes were rationed, and he wore whatever he could. He had no overcoat and would have gone about cold were it not for a cousin who served in the Red Army and somehow procured for him a military greatcoat. His taste in music ran to the classics: Chopin, Tchaikovsky, Beethoven, Brahms. He attended concerts in the Moscow Philharmonic Hall, listened to music on the radio, owned a phonograph and Russian records. He liked Russian and Gypsy tunes and on occasion went to a jazz concert. He read in Russian the novels of Balzac, Hugo, and Dreiser, the poetry of Pushkin and Lermontov. He had little inter-est in sports.

One late afternoon in May 1945 came the announcement over the radio that the Germans had surrendered. The Great Patriotic War was over; the hated fascist enemy crushed! In the Slepak apartment—jubilation! Two of Volodya's friends were visiting at the time, and Volodya hurried out with them. His parents remained at home. In the streets strangers embraced. Volodya and his friends were swept up in the crowds surging through Gorky Street to Red Square. Music and dancing and fireworks. Red Square was packed with joyous people until morning.

Not long afterward Solomon Slepak learned of the fate of his brother, Aaron, whom he had left behind in Dubrovno and had last seen in 1936. Volodya's cousin Anatoly, one of Aaron's sons, who was in the Red Army, returned to Dubrovno soon after the war and discovered that his father, along with three of his seven siblings and his stepmother, had been killed by the Germans.

The Germans murdered one and a half million Russian Jews. Most were killed by the Einsatzgruppen, mobile killing units of the German security police that accompanied the army. The Slepaks read nothing of this in the newspapers, though it was known by March 1944, when a special government commission of inquiry into German crimes reported the killings and detailed the events at Babi Yar but made no mention of Jews. It was Soviet policy then not to single out the Jews as the primary victims in this Nazi drama of death but simply to state that those killed were noncombatants, slain with so many other innocents. A monument to the Jews slaughtered and buried in Babi Yar was put up only recently, after the demise of the Soviet Union.

Volodya did not attend the victory parade in Red Square on June 24 of that year. From the balcony of the apartment he and his family observed tanks and trucks and troops and rocket launchers rumbling along Gorky Street. For some while he kept seeing newsreels of the parade in movie theaters: Stalin, flanked by members of the Politburo, watching expressionlessly as units of the victorious Red Army marched by and placed on the ground before him flags of the destroyed German Army. The flags formed a tall mound. Stalin seemed a triumphant Caesar.

At the end of the war the borders of the Soviet empire extended from Vladivostok in the east to Berlin, Prague, and Budapest in the west. Never had Russia been stronger; never had the Communist specter it cast across the world appeared more menacing. All that despite the astonishing losses it had suffered in the war: more than twenty million dead and tremendous destruction of land and cities.

Inside the Kremlin, Stalin once again began to turn his attention to matters of internal Communist Party discipline and personal power.

Not that his iron hand had relaxed during the war: Millions among the national groups under Soviet rule had been expelled to Central Asia, Siberia, and the Arctic to forestall their possible collaboration with the Germans; after the Russian occupation of Eastern Europe in 1944–1945, half a million Germans, Poles, Hungarians, Bulgars, and Romanians were deported to Siberia; and even at the height of the war, anyone reported to have uttered or written a wrong word faced arrest and a labor camp. But the conflict had initiated an easing of cultural control inside the Soviet Union, as well as contacts with the West that now seemed especially menacing to Stalin and to Andrei Zhdanov, the man many thought would one day take the aging dictator's place.

Stalin had taken careful note of the work of the Jewish Anti-Fascist Committee and its inner discussions. The war over, he determined that he no longer needed the committee. It was an annoyance and a possible threat—all that talk about establishing cultural relations between Russian and Western Jews, about the renewal of Jewish national and cultural life in the Soviet Union, and the brazen proposal that the Crimea become a Jewish republic in place of the failed Birobidzhan.

Some claim that the actor Solomon Mikhoels often appeared before Stalin in the Kremlin as Shakespeare's King Lear, one of his most brilliant roles. Did he act the part in Russian or Yiddish? The sources do not tell us, but the image of Stalin listening to Mikhoels performing *King Lear* in Yiddish boggles the mind. Indeed, Volodya doubts that Stalin and Mikhoels ever met and regards as fanciful the various sources that claim otherwise. In any event, it is clear that Stalin had begun to detest the spirited activities of Mikhoels as head of the Jewish Anti-Fascist Committee and his self-assumed position as leader of the Jews, and finally came to regard the actor as a potential enemy.

On the night of January 13, 1948, Solomon Mikhoels was on the way back from Minsk, the capital of White Russia, where he had been reviewing plays for government prizes. He was hit by a truck and killed. That, at least, was the official account, briefly reported in the back pages of newspapers, where it was read and accepted as sorrowful truth by the Slepak family.

It soon became clear, however, that Mikhoels had been murdered, no doubt at Stalin's order. Some reported that he had been beaten. One eyewitness stated that a truck had repeatedly smashed him against a wall. There was even the grisly rumor that his head had been severed from his body. But at least two individuals who saw the body as it was being prepared for its coffin insisted that it bore no more injuries than one would expect from so severe an accident. Clearly, someone was not telling the truth, and it is likely that the details of the odd circumstances surrounding the death of Solomon Mikhoels will never be uncovered. But I have come across no one familiar with that event who today doubts that Mikhoels, like Kirov, was murdered at Stalin's behest.

Stalin accorded the revered Jewish actor a state funeral. The body was prepared for public viewing by Professor Zbarsky (aided, possibly, by his older son), the same man who had once attended to Lenin's corpse. For three days crowds moved silently past the dead actor in the building of the Moscow Jewish Theater to pay their final respects. Stalin, learning of the thousands of Jews filing past the casket, no doubt felt vindicated in his suspicion that Mikhoels had been a dangerous nerve center of Jewish national identity.

The subsequent brutal effort by Stalin once and for all to eradicate Jewish culture inside the Soviet Union was the absolute reverse of—and, ironically, was to a large extent fueled by—the foreign policy of the Soviet Union toward the new state of Israel.

Official Soviet policy after the war was heavily in favor of the nascent Jewish state and opposed to the presence of the British in the Middle East—even to the point of helping the new state acquire weapons it desperately needed in its war against invading Arab armies. In September 1948, Golda Meir, Israel's first ambassador to the Soviet Union, traveled to Russia and appeared in Moscow on the Jewish New Year. A vast crowd of Jews greeted her outside the synagogue, across the street from the school Volodya had once attended. She was surrounded and applauded. Militiamen ringed the crowd, and security police were everywhere, but they did not interfere. Astonishingly, from the crowd came a sudden cry in Hebrew: "The Jewish people lives!" Men and women wept with joy.

Stalin was confounded by that crowd, and raged at the Jewish nationalism he had thought long dead, perceiving it as an open threat to his power. Let one national group rear its head, others would soon follow, and anarchy ensue.

In November of that year, security police agents burst into the printing plant of the last Yiddish publishing house in the Soviet Union and disconnected the new linotype machines while they were running. Strongin, the director, and Belenky, the chief editor, were present, along with workers. A terrible silence suddenly filled the plant. "Your publishing house is closed down!" shouted one of the agents.

And at the end of 1948 the government ended the life of the Jewish Anti-Fascist Committee. Nearly all its leaders, including Itzik Fefer, ardent Communist and colonel in the Red Army, were arrested.

Arrested too were the poets Peretz Markish and Itzik Kipnis, the writers David Bergelson, Borukh Veisman, Moshe Notovich, Leib Kvitko. Articles began to appear in *Pravda* condemning "cosmopolitanism" in literature, the arts, music, scholarship. Of the writers, artists, and scholars singled out for criticism in the press, 70 percent were Jews.

Newspapers in all the Soviet republics trumpeted against "men with no background," "rootless cosmopolitans," "vagabonds without passports," "renegades foreign to Russia," individuals who had no grasp of the history and poetry of Russia, of the Russian soul—and everyone understood that these epithets were directed against the Jews, who were purported to lack deep feelings for the land of Russia and the Soviet way of life. Members of the erstwhile Jewish Anti-Fascist Committee were now declared to have been agents of American Zionism, plotting to create a Jewish state in the Crimea with the intent of using it to establish a bridgehead for American imperialism, a threat to the very heart of the Soviet Union. Jewish schools were closed. A tense incipient pogrom atmosphere pervaded much of the land. Jewish children were attacked in Russian schools. It became dangerous for Jews to walk the streets. Jews began to lose their jobs. To protect themselves, some Jews burned their Jewish books and broke off all contact with Jewish relatives and friends overseas.

In all, about four hundred Jewish writers and artists were arrested and exiled. One could never say with certainty that Stalin's fury was directed only against the Jews; always a few non-Jews, too, would be arrested, exiled, shot. With the termination of the Jewish Anti-Fascist Committee and the wholesale loss of Jewish writers and artists, there came to an end any open and effective Jewish culture in the Soviet Union.

Mysteriously, as in the purges of the thirties, Solomon Slepak escaped arrest. But this time he did not slip away entirely unscathed. Close friends in the Regional Party Committee and the Moscow Party Committee informed him that he would soon be dismissed from the publishing house. The reason? He was a Jew. And if that weren't grounds enough, his having lived so many years abroad was now of itself sufficiently strong cause for job termination. There was nothing they could do for him, his friends said, except request that he be given a party pension because of his service in the Bolshevik cause during the Civil War, even though he was not yet of pension age.

In October 1950, Solomon Slepak—dedicated Old Bolshevik, esteemed editor and translator, noted writer of articles for *Izvestia* and *Pravda* under the pseudonym M. Osipov, lecturer on international affairs of the Moscow Party Committee—was abruptly discharged from his position at the publishing house.

He received the pension and lived for nearly three more decades, writing, lecturing, translating. But his effective role as a player in the center of power had come to an end.

THE SON

The Enemy Within

At about the same time that Solomon's life as a career Communist was concluding, Volodya, having graduated from the Aviation Institute in June 1950 in the top half of his class with a master's degree in radio electronics, began to look for a job.

He applied to factories and institutes. The standard application form contained more than one hundred questions, among them: Have you any relatives abroad? Did you or any close member of your family ever live abroad? What was the nationality of your grandparents? Were you or your parents or grandparents members of any party other than the Bolshevik Party before the Revolution? Have you ever had any doubts concerning the policies of the Communist Party?

On his internal passport, his identity card, the line that revealed his nationality read, in Russian, *Evrei*. Jew.

For months Volodya went searching for a job. After handing in each completed application, he would wait two or three days and then call, only to be told that his services were not needed. He applied about a dozen times. Few who turned him away made any effort to hide the reasons for his being rejected. Volodya Slepak, son of Solomon Slepak, after six years in one of the leading scientific institutes in the Soviet Union and with a master's degree in radio engineering, was finding it impossible to get a job because during his childhood he had lived abroad, and because he was a Jew.

He told his parents often of his fruitless efforts. His mother commiserated and urged him to keep trying. His father said, "This is happening because there are many traitors and spies among Jews, especially with those who were abroad. Now our country is surrounded by enemies, we must build communism alone, and the party hasn't the time to check everybody. So they don't accept Jews into positions that are important to the state. Later, after careful investigation, everyone who is innocent will be given a job according to his education and knowledge."

Volodya unhesitatingly accepted his father's explanation. After failing for months to find work in the field of radio engineering, he took a job as a television repairman in a shop on Gorokhovsky Street in a Moscow neighborhood near the Kursky Railroad Station. The manager of the shop was a Jew.

In those days a television set cost approximately 500 rubles (five months' salary), the equivalent of about $250. The sets were the size of a microwave oven, with a rectangular fourteen-inch black-and-white screen. The box was of polished brown wood; the pictures were of poor quality. In the 1950s there was one television station in the Soviet Union and a wait of about five months for a set. If you lived in Moscow and your set suddenly no longer worked, you brought it to one of the five or six television repair shops in the city.

The shop in which Volodya worked consisted of a hallway and two rooms, each about two hundred square feet in size, with large windows, workbenches, and shelves along the walls. Into the shop one day walked one of Volodya's friends, who had been his classmate in the Aviation Institute, accompanied by a young woman. The friend had been visiting a woman named Rita and her cousin Masha. Rita had asked him to look at her television set, which wasn't working. It turned out that one of the tubes needed to be replaced, but a new tube could not be found in a regular shop, said the friend, because of the shortage of television parts. There was, however, this repair shop where he knew one of the workers, who might be able to get his hands on a new tube. He could go and be back in an hour. Did Masha want to accompany him?

She wore a knitted white and black wool hat and a beige sheepskin coat. Her skin was smooth, her face roundish, her eyes brown and alert behind glasses. She was in her fourth year in the medical institute in Ryazan, a town 125 miles to the southeast, and in Moscow for the weekend to visit her family.

As soon as his old classmate had left the television repair shop with Masha and a new tube, Volodya telephoned Rita and said that he wanted to come over and visit her next Saturday, and could she also invite her cousin Masha?

That Saturday Volodya met Masha again, in Rita's apartment. This time Masha's aunt was present, and they all had tea. Later he said he would walk Masha home. Her family lived not too far away in an apartment building in the center of the city, near the Moscow synagogue. It was February and very cold. They walked together for several hours.

Volodya has no clear memory of what they talked about; probably, he thinks, her studies in medical school, books they had read, concerts they had attended. Vaguely he recalls an attempt to explain why he was working as a repairman—a brief, guarded remark about anti-Semitism in the field of engineering—but he is not certain whether that happened then or later in their relationship. They did not discuss Israel or politics.

Her name was Maria Rashkovsky (in Russian, Rashkovskaya); her mother's name, Bertha. The chronicles record her fear of remembering too much. "I wish I knew more about my family than I do now," she tells us. "But there is nobody to ask. Before, it was dangerous for children to know, they could blurt it out. After the Revolution, people tried to conceal their past, bury it as deep as they could. I remember my mother filling out application forms, many pages, gray-colored paper. She would answer the question 'What class are you from?' with the words 'petty bourgeois' or 'lower middle class.' That terrifying question was on the first page of every application—for an apartment, a school, a job. Also: 'What parties did you belong to before 1917?' 'What views did you have?' The applications would stick to you all your life. So my mother tried to conceal as much as she could. Many things are gone with my mother."

Despite that, Masha's astonishingly retentive memory is rich in specificity and abundant with details. She remembers vividly her father, Sanya. A handsome stocky man, five feet seven inches in height, brown straight hair, his face smooth, close-shaven, glistening in the morning and bluish with beard by evening. He was born in Tiraspol into an assimilated family that had abandoned Jewish observance a generation earlier. He grew up in Odessa, served in the Red Cavalry during the Civil War, and rose to the rank of captain. After the war he settled in Moscow, where he met and married Bertha. Self-educated, well read, a devotee of opera, and the life of any party. His work in a secondhand bookstore and later in a government publishing house enabled him to indulge his passion for books. He owned a collection of about eight hundred rare leather-bound books printed before the Revolution: Boccaccio, Daudet, Flaubert, Balzac, Zola, Hugo, Shakespeare, Swift, Voltaire, Defoe, Maupassant, Pushkin, Gogol, Lermontov, Turgenev, Dostoevsky, Tolstoy,

Nekrasov. He loved the books, loved the smell and feel of them. He read them, knew the provenance of each. At his place of work he was able to remember the history of every book that came into his hands: the year of publication; where and by whom published; how many editions; the number of copies printed. He taught Masha to read and write and count long before she began to attend school; the first book she read on her own, in Russian, was *Little Red Riding Hood*. A short-tempered man, he once found Masha bending the corner of a page to mark her place in a book and shouted, "How *dare* you treat a book that way? It's so *low*, only uneducated people do such a thing. Do you know how many people labored to create *this one book*?"

Masha was born in Moscow on November 7, 1926, the ninth anniversary of the Bolshevik Revolution. Friends said to her parents, "You must name her Octyabrina in honor of the October Revolution." People were still euphoric about the Revolution, about the future; they gave their children names like Tractor and Industriya. Her father said she should really be named after her grandmother Miriam, but there were reasons not to choose a name like that. In tsarist times the Russians had been contemptuous of the Jews; now they feared and hated them, blamed the Revolution on them, saw them as conspiring to destroy the entire Christian world. And it was true that a few thousand Jews, sickened to blinding rage by tsarist oppression, had thrown away the very last marks of their Jewishness, joined the Bolshevik Party, and helped to make the Revolution. For them and all the other new leaders of Russia, the name Miriam was too Jewish. So Sanya and Bertha Rashkovsky named the child Maria, and at home called her Musya or Manya. It was Volodya who began to call her Masha.

Masha was the firstborn; then, five years later, came a boy, named Zinovy and called Zalya; and, afterward, a second daughter, named Henrietta and called Gera.

Sanya Rashkovsky left the care of the children and the house in the hands of his wife, whose cooking was a source of enormous pleasure to him. A supper of lamb stew and chicken soup with noodles: He would wrinkle his nose at the smells, rub his hands together with delight. He loved sweets, often told Masha tales of a mountain outside Odessa, a fantasy mountain of halvah, describing it so vividly she could taste its rich, honeyed sweetness. Cut flowers dismayed him. "Flowers die the instant you cut them," he said to Masha. "How can one gain pleasure from something that is dead?"

In the early 1930s he became ill with tuberculosis and spent the last months of his life in a sanitarium located in an evergreen forest outside Moscow. One month before he died, Masha and her mother visited him. Ten-year-old Masha could not recognize the wasted figure they said was her father. He was dying of starvation, slowly melting into death, unable to eat because of the searing pain in his intestines.

He died on January 17, 1937, and was buried three days later. Many attended the funeral. Masha watched the coffin being lowered into the ground and suddenly threw herself forward to halt its terrifying descent, screaming, "Daddy! Daddy!" Her uncle pulled her back. The chronicles record her comment: "My childhood was over."

Masha's mother was born in a small town on the Dnieper River in the Ukraine into a family of devout Jews. Her father, barely eking out a living as a maker of leather goods—belts, saddles, bridles—was at the same time a judge in the local Jewish religious court, a man so highly respected that the Ukrainians would often appear before him, requesting that he settle their differences. During the pogroms of 1903–1905 and the Civil War, Ukrainians tried to protect the family from Cossacks. Masha's grandmother bore across her face a long scar left by a mounted Cossack wielding a metal-tipped whip.

In the early 1930s Masha's parents took the children on visits to the grandparents, and Masha remembers Jewish folk prints on the walls and the warm smells of special foods for Sabbaths and festivals. Her grandmother lit candles on Friday evenings; her grandfather conducted the Passover Seder. The family gathered around the big dinner table for the Sabbath. At the head sat her grandfather; next to him his mother, Baba Malka; on the other side, his wife; then his children and grandchildren. Each knew exactly his or her place at the table. Then the blessing over the wine, the washing of the hands, the blessing over the bread, the scents, the food, the Sabbath songs, the Grace After Meals. She still remembers all those visits to the grandparents. And standing in the road alone one day in front of her grandparents' house, spinning her arms, and her grandfather calling out in Yiddish—he also spoke Ukrainian but could barely read Russian—"Hey, windmill, stop spinning your arms, you haven't gained a gram of fat, what am I going to tell your mother?"

Her mother had left her parents' home in the early 1920s, gone off to Moscow, lived under horrific conditions in a place called Hotel Chicago. She attended the School for Higher Education for Women, where she received a teacher's diploma, the equivalent of a university degree, with a specialty in preschool education. The winter of 1924 was especially severe in Moscow. On the day of Lenin's funeral she stood patiently in line with the tens of thousands who had come to view Lenin in his open coffin, to pay their respects to the leader of the Revolution. One of the guards near the coffin came over to her and said quietly that one side of her face looked severely frostbitten, she should tend to it immediately.

After her marriage to Sanya in January 1926, she ran one of the most successful kindergartens in Moscow, and Masha's very first memory is of sitting in her mother's classroom at the age of three, and watching her show flash cards about Lenin and Stalin and the Revolution. She remembers one evening her father sitting in his chair reading *Pravda* and suddenly saying in disgust, "What sort of newspaper is this, four pages of nothing, do you know what an English newspaper has?" and her mother looking around nervously and whispering, "Sanya, be still, the walls have ears." Masha was five. They lived in one room of a two-room apartment on Pokrovka Street near the Kremlin, directly under the slanting roof of a two-story pre-Revolution house. In the other, smaller room were two elderly men, factory workers. She remembers the fear on her mother's face when she said that: "The walls have ears."

The school authorities asked her mother to join the party, and she talked about it with her husband, who said that if she joined she would need to attend meetings and would have less time with the children, so she declined the invitation. Years later she told Masha that by not joining, she had probably saved herself, because had she joined she would have risen in the ranks, and all the high party members among her colleagues were arrested and shot.

The links to her family in the Ukraine wore thin through the thirties. Her father's leather shop was taken over by Communists, and in 1939 he died of a heart attack. The rest of the family disappeared into the storm of war.

In the early months of the war, with the German Army advancing upon Moscow, the city was at first chaotic, mobs of drunken and hysterical people roaming the streets looking for German spies, and then the streets were suddenly still, no traffic, no pedestrians, and nobody knowing what to do or where to run, and long lines at the bread stores. Masha waiting in a line one morning heard people say, "What are Jews doing here?" She was certain that if there were no bread or flour in the city the next day, all the Jews in Moscow would be killed. She waited in the cold for three hours, and someone pushed her out of the line and said, "Go to Palestine for bread." She ran home, weeping.

That October the family was evacuated from Moscow. A terrifying journey in a crowded freight car, one of more than ninety attached to two engines operated by men who seemed not to know their destination and took them at first south to the Caucasus and then east to the Urals, through vast fields and forests, the war sometimes nearby, the thump and crunch of artillery and German aircraft overhead.

After six weeks of travel the train deposited them in the exotic world of Tashkent, the capital city of Uzbekistan in Central Asia, where they lived for a while in a shack. It was winter, the rainy season, and very cold. In a bazaar one morning they watched as soldiers loaded onto a truck the corpses of starved children recently arrived from the Ukraine, and some minutes later a hungry boy was beaten to death before their eyes by a raging crowd for stealing an apple from a stall. Masha's mother decided they would not remain in Tashkent, and they traveled south and lived in a village not far from the border of Afghanistan. There they survived the winter through the grit and wits of Masha's mother, who seemed to understand how to deal with the local people, bartered clothes for food, worked at odd jobs with Masha, who was fifteen years old, on a collective farm for a daily payment of a loaf of bread each, and nursed Masha's sister through the measles that took the lives of all the other refugee children stricken with it.

In the summer of 1942 they returned to Moscow—after months of a nightmarish journey on slow trains teeming with refugees, after bouts of serious illness along the way, after Masha and her little brother had been separated from their mother and sister as their train pulled out and left them behind, and they spent a week hopping rides on freight trains and army trucks, making their way to Moscow without papers or money, and found their mother in the apartment, beside herself with grief over her two lost children and overwhelmed with joy at the sight of them.

Masha discovered to her dismay that much of her father's precious library of leather-bound books had been stolen, some of it sold for food, some of it burned for warmth. The two elderly men who were their neighbors in the communal apartment stared at them icily when Masha's mother asked about the books. What did she think was more important in wartime, her husband's books or Russian lives?

They had been away from the city a long time and needed a new residence permit in order to obtain ration cards for food. There was no certainty the permit would be given them. Masha's mother said to her, "You have to come with me to the militia station; you will bring me luck. You have that luck; it's within you." Masha did not understand. They went to the local precinct and were given their residence permit and papers to fill out. Her mother took her everywhere she needed to go to get the papers approved. She began to call Masha "my little amulet." Whenever she had to go somewhere on a serious errand, she would say to Masha, "Come with me; you'll bring me luck."

In 1943 they moved to another building because the walls of the old apartment, weakened by German bombing, began to crumble. The new apartment was enormous, with one sink, one toilet, nine rooms, nine families, about thirty people in all, among them ten children; nine tables in the kitchen, each with a kerosene burner; cooking, laundry, gossip, arguments in the kitchen, children running about; buckets, pails, clothes, a bicycle hanging from a wall, boxes filled with books. Quiet only when everyone slept.

In Uzbekistan, Masha had not attended school and missed her seventh and eighth grades. When they returned to Moscow, she studied on her own, took the examination for ninth grade, and passed. Along with other young people, she became a member of Komsomol. In their first apartment her parents had spoken to each other in Yiddish and with the children in Russian; her mother sang songs and told stories in Yiddish and Russian. Now, in this apartment and on the street, the Rashkovsky family spoke only Russian. In school and around the neighborhood Masha had Jewish and Gentile friends. She distanced herself from anyone known to be even remotely anti-Semitic; she avoided trouble; she never spoke to anyone about politics.

After high school she began to attend the Institute of Historical Archives because it was nearest her home, and at the end of her first semester she told her mother that she wanted to leave school, she was bored. Her mother said, "If that's the case, then either you will study to become a doctor or you will go to work in a factory." Her mother thought that the practice of medicine would be good for a woman.

That was in 1947, before the kindling of Stalinist-style anti-Semitism. To attend medical school then, you needed to have graduated from high school and passed examinations in chemistry, physics, and Russian language. During the summer of 1947 Masha did whatever preparatory study was necessary and had no difficulty gaining acceptance into medical school.

There followed two years of lectures and class work and memorization. And sessions in Marxism, Leninism, Stalinism, political economy, history of the Communist Party, dialectical materialism, historical materialism, little of which, according to the family chronicles, the medical students took seriously. They brought their notes to the examinations and immediately afterward forgot what they had memorized.

Masha's parents had observed no religious traditions; her mother did not light Sabbath candles. When Masha met Volodya, she was as indifferent to religion as he was. They considered themselves citizens of the Soviet Union, with the word "Jew" appearing routinely as a mark of identity after the word "nationality" on their internal passports.

Masha was able to leave the medical institute in Ryazan for Moscow only on weekends. The fifth time she and Volodya met, he brought her to the apartment on Gorky Street and introduced her to his parents. Volodya's sister, Rosa, no longer lived there; she had received her master's degree in philology from Moscow University in 1948 and was married that same year. To Volodya's parents, Masha seemed bright, engaging, thoroughly Russian, and suitable for their son. That was in the early spring of 1951.

They went out together nine times in all before Volodya proposed marriage. Masha accepted. The marriage took place on the seventh of that June, a civil ceremony in the municipal registration office. Afterward there was a small party for them in the apartment of Masha's family and another later in the Slepak apartment on Gorky Street.

The next day Masha left Moscow to begin her summer internship in a hospital in the small town of Lebedyan in Ryazanskaya Province, about 220 miles southeast of Moscow. She returned in late August, moved into Volodya's room in the Slepak apartment, then went back to the medical institute in Ryazan to continue her studies and soon discovered that she was pregnant.

She did not want to have the baby in Ryazan and decided to apply to the Ministry of Health for a transfer to a medical institute in Moscow. She and Volodya proceeded, with much effort, to tread their way through the bureaucracy and the paperwork: numerous applications; documents that confirmed their marriage; papers from Masha's physician verifying her pregnancy; an affidavit concerning Volodya's workplace and position.

On weekends she traveled to Moscow to be with Volodya in his little room with a balcony facing Gorky Street.

Weeks passed while Masha's request for transfer slowly wound its way through the bureaucracy. Finally, to her joy, the request was approved. At the end of the semester, after passing her exams, she was transferred to the Second Moscow Medical Institute. That May she entered the local maternity hospital on Stanislavsky Street to deliver her baby. Hours of difficult labor, during which she remained largely unattended, reduced her to utter exhaustion and an ominous silence. The medical staff then labored long and hard to save her and the baby. She gave birth to a son, who was given the name Alexander and the nickname Sanya, after her father. Some weeks later Masha Slepak returned to the medical institute.

All was tranquil in the Slepak household on Gorky Street during the summer and fall of 1952: Masha, in her final year of medical school; Volodya, working as a senior engineer in the Electro-Vacuum Factory in Moscow, a job he had obtained when the manager had chosen to ignore the fact that he was a Jew, because skilled specialists were now needed if the Soviet Union was to overtake the West in radar technology; and Solomon, the Old Bolshevik, approaching his sixtieth year and at peace with himself despite a recently diagnosed heart condition, his grandson embodying for him a sense of continuity and accomplishment, his life-long dream of a new order to a great extent fulfilled. Adding to his feeling of personal achievement must have been the enormous satisfaction of having witnessed, in 1949, the termination of the Civil War in China and the creation of the Communist Chinese People's Republic, under the leadership of Mao Tse-tung.

Then, suddenly, in November 1952, Stalin ordered the arrest of his personal physician, A. N. Vinogradov. Arrested, too, were others on the medical staff in the Kremlin hospital-clinic that serviced the ruling class of the Soviet Union. The stunning accusation: involvement in a plot to poison the entire leadership of the country.

Masha Slepak, attending her final year at the Second Moscow Medical Institute and, as part of her studies, working in Moscow City Hospital Number 4 as an intern, knew many of the arrested doctors. On an evening in November, after a day at the hospital, she returned to the apartment in a state of great agitation. She took Volodya aside and spoke to him. Then they went into the room of his parents.

Fanya Slepak was out. Solomon Slepak sat alone, reading.

"I just came from a meeting in my hospital," Masha said.

Solomon looked up from his newspaper.

"It was terrible," Masha said.

Solomon asked what had happened.

Masha said, "It was a meeting of the staff. Almost every day the authorities of the hospital organize such a meeting. All the students and doctors and professors must attend. Each time a party activist comes to the stage, and right after his speech they put on a Jewish doctor, who talks against Jewish traitors and the Jewish conspiracy and Jewish professors who are poisoners."

Solomon said calmly, "It's true that among Jews, and especially Jewish doctors, there are traitors."

Masha said, "But many of the professors who were arrested are my teachers. I know them. They're honest people."

"Perhaps they are," said Solomon.

"They can't be traitors or spies."

"Perhaps they are entirely innocent."

"Then how can they be arrested?" asked Masha.

Solomon explained patiently. "The class struggle is now in its fiercest and most dangerous stage. Look at us, we are surrounded by capitalist enemies. Isn't it better to arrest and prosecute a hundred innocent people and catch among them one spy than to let the spy go free?"

"I can't accept that," Volodya suddenly said.

" 'Whenever you cut down trees, chips will fly in all directions.' " Solomon Slepak quoted the old Russian proverb.

"I will never accept such a philosophy," said Volodya.

"You understand very little," said Solomon, his voice rising.

"I understand enough."

"What do you understand?"

"I understand enough to know that I will never join your party!"

For Solomon Slepak, the Communist Party possessed the power of a church, the authority of an order, the force of a communion of faith. It had given him self-respect, a dream to strive for, a strong and revered leader. One imagines his raging thoughts: *your* party! Such disrespect and ingratitude! And what dangerous talk. *Your* party! His face flushed, Solomon shouted at his son, "You understand nothing!"

"I understand plenty," said Volodya.

"I risked my life fighting for your future, and you are talking to me this way!"

"I understand there is too much blood on your hands," replied Volodya. "*That* I understand!"

Volodya and Masha left the room. Minutes later Volodya saw his father enter the kitchen and pour some of his cardiac medicine into a glass and with trembling hands raise it to his lips and drink it down.

In July of that year, 1952, twenty-five distinguished Jewish writers and public figures had been put on trial, and in August many were summarily executed, among them David Bergelson, Binyamin Zuskin, Peretz Markish. Also shot was the poet Itzik Fefer, Stalin's passionate admirer. All charged with being spies, Zionists, traitors.

Then, according to many sources, a young radiologist named Lidia Timashuk, who was an informer for the secret police, wrote to Stalin accusing certain doctors of plotting to assassinate him and others through poison and improper medical treatment. No one seems to know why she wrote that letter, if indeed there ever was a letter; it may have been concocted by the secret police from an earlier report she had sent concerning her suspicions about the doctors who treated party leader Andrei Zhdanov when he suffered a serious and subsequently fatal heart attack in August 1948. In any event, that November a number of leading Kremlin doctors were abruptly arrested, directed to confess, beaten when they refused, ordered to name other conspirators in the plot.

On January 13, 1953, a portentous article appeared in *Pravda*, announcing the arrest of nine doctors—six of them with obviously Jewish names, and purportedly connected with the Joint Distribution Committee, the philanthropic organization founded during the First World War to aid Russian Jews and, according to *Pravda*, a known arm of American intelligence. The three remaining doctors were said to be British agents. All the Soviet people, proclaimed *Pravda*, now condemned those nine doctors, who had confessed to having poisoned Andrei Zhdanov in 1948 and before him Alexander Shcherbakov, a secretary of the Central Committee; condemned, too, were their foreign masters and "the well-known Jewish bourgeois nationalist, Mikhoels." Western agents were everywhere, the paper warned, even inside the heart of the Soviet Union. It was necessary to be vigilant against sabotage and to be wary of Jews, whose links with Western powers enabled them to take on the work of imperialist spies and collaborators; it was necessary to crush such "loathsome vermin," destroy the "enemies of the people."

For bravely exposing the insidious doctors and helping alert the country to the Jewish "enemy within," Lidia Timashuk was awarded the coveted Order of Lenin.

Rumors proliferated: Jews were putting poison into medicines, infiltrating vacation areas and homes of the aged to carry out nefarious schemes, establishing nests of Zionist spies in the government and in universities. On buses and in classrooms people shouted at Jews, "You poisoners! You poisoned all our great leaders!" Russians stopped going to their Jewish doctors. In many regions of the country, demonstrations took place against Jews. Mid-twentieth-century industrial Russia had resurrected the medieval image of the Jew as demonic poisoner.

As in the past, it was not only the Jews who were the targets of Stalin's denunciatory campaign. Old Mensheviks, Trotskyites, various Soviet minorities, writers, and artists influenced by the West, Russian intellectuals from economists to physicians, anyone suspected of even marginal contact with foreigners—the people were urged to denounce them all.

By and large, workers remained untouched; they were the audience for the denunciations, not the target. For all others there was in the air the terrifying probability of yet another mass purge of the party. The final act of an old and ailing despot, who saw enemies everywhere, found delight in the subservience and humiliation of others, preferred loyalty out of fear rather than conviction, and raged at the advancing years that were slowly sapping his strength, reducing his powers of concentration, inexorably forcing him to loosen his hold on the vast apparatus of government. One more cleansing of the party, decisive and shattering. But first, he had to solve once and for all time his problem with the overbearing, cerebral, stubborn Soviet Jews.

Masha read with deep apprehension the newspaper reports of the arrested doctors—surgeons, internists, neurologists, pediatricians—all accused of having murdered patients during surgery or prescribing poison as medication. Because she knew many of the doctors personally or by reputation, she was able to persuade Volodya that those named were innocent. They began to sense the start of a vast organized campaign against Soviet Jewry. What better way to direct the anger of all the Soviet people against the Jews than to reveal them as agents of an international conspiracy to murder the country's leaders? But to what end? What lay behind the anti-Semitic campaign? What did Stalin have planned for the Jews?

On a number of occasions they tried to discuss the matter with Solomon Slepak, but the talk would inevitably degenerate into loud arguments. At times, in the midst of a heated flurry of words, Solomon would abruptly glance at his wristwatch, announce that he had to meet someone, and rush from the apartment. Masha and Volodya ceased talking to him about the doctors.

Day after day, in the pages of *Izvestia, Trud, Pravda,* and the popular satirical magazine *Krokodil,* appeared savage lampoons of Jews and a torrent of furious articles attacking the "despicable gang of killer doctors." Anti-Semitic hysteria increased, distended to proportions never before known in the Soviet Union. The entire nation was being readied for pogroms, a bloodbath.

Then new rumors swept through the bitter-cold winter air of

Moscow. Secret meetings were taking place in the Kremlin. A carefully prepared scenario was being arranged by Stalin for the Jews. Versions of his plans floated about like insidious poisons. One version—later confirmed by MGB Major Alexei Rybin, who was present at two meetings where the details were worked out—had it that there was soon to be a public trial of the doctors, who would all be found guilty and sentenced to be hanged from scaffolds on Red Square. Then, as the sentences were about to be carried out, the prisoners would be torn away by a raging crowd and lynched, despite the heroic efforts of the guards. Nationwide pogroms would then follow, the Soviet people venting uncontrollable rage against the Jews. Added to these rumors were accounts about barracks being constructed in Siberia on a stupendous scale that made sense only in the face of an impending mass deportation of Jews; about the appearance of freight trains in marshaling yards near Moscow; about lists of Jews being prepared in police precincts. Jews in the major cities of Soviet Russia would be given two hours to pack, allowed one bag per person. All who perished on the tortuous journey were to be thrown from the trains into the frozen fields and forests in the thirty-below-zero air of the Siberian winter.

Chilling confirmation of these rumors came by chance to Masha Slepak. At six o'clock one morning a Russian woman named Nadezhda Naumovna, an old and close friend of Masha's mother, showed up suddenly in the mother's apartment. She had been orphaned in her early years and taken in by a Jewish family in the city of Gomel in White Russia. Her Yiddish was fluent. She lived in Davidkovo, a village very near Moscow that has since been swallowed by the western part of the city and no longer exists. Agitatedly she told Masha's mother what she had witnessed that night, a clear, moonlit night: Trucks suddenly appearing and rumbling up to the houses where Jews lived, and people emerging from the houses with children and small bundles and climbing into the trucks. And the trucks rumbling away. And silence. In the morning all the Jews of Davidkovo were gone.

The frightened woman finished her tale and quickly left. Masha's mother immediately called Masha and asked her to come to the apartment, where she told her daughter what she had just heard. Masha related it to Volodya. Both saw the events of the night as a rehearsal for things yet to come. They said nothing to Solomon, who, they felt certain, would have called it a wild and baseless story, a slander against the party.

The truth was, however, that the deportation of the Jews, when it was finally to take place, would not be concealed from public view. On the contrary, it would be accomplished in the open—as a magnanimous act by Stalin, as the only possible way of saving the Jews from the wrath of the people, and in the wake of an urgent, importuning letter to the editor of *Pravda* signed by leading Soviet Jews. We Jews who live in the Soviet Union, the letter would say, are privileged to enjoy fully all the rights guaranteed by our constitution. We participate willingly as workers in the factories and institutions and scientific institutes of our land. But a militant bourgeois nationalism has infected the entire Soviet Jewish people. And in order for that people to atone properly for its murderous doctors and corrupt nationalist sentiments, in order for it to be protected from the righteous wrath of the Soviet people, the Jews whose signatures appear on this letter ask Comrade Stalin to send the Jews of the Soviet Union to the farthest corner of the land for reeducation.

The letter was composed by historian Isaak Mintz and philosopher Mark Mitin, along with the *Pravda* journalist Yakov Khavinson. Perhaps they believed their act might save them from being added to the lists of deportees. In the offices of *Pravda*, Khavinson and another staff member, David Zaslavsky, Jews slavishly obedient to Stalin, worked the switchboard, contacting Jews all over the country and requesting that they come to Moscow to sign the letter that was to save Soviet Jewry.

Many yielded and signed; many, despite the clear personal danger, refused. Outlines of the letter were later traced from memory by some who were asked to sign it; the letter itself has yet to be found in the Kremlin archives. It would have had to be approved by Stalin, but most likely did not go through the normal bureaucratic chain that required its being registered and numbered at each level, hence is not in its proper file. No doubt it will surface one day.

During the time signatures to the letter were being collected, Solomon Slepak, loyal Bolshevik and chairman of the house committee of the apartment building in which he lived, walked one day into the building office. In the Soviet Union all apartment houses belonged to the state; in each there was an office responsible for the building's plumbing, electrical network, gas, heating, rent collection. Salaried government clerks ran those offices, aided by house committees of volunteers, who were usually pensioners. The clerks were in close contact with the local militia, who in turn reported to the security police. Inside the office that day, Solomon Slepak found himself looking at a list of the Jewish residents in the building. His name was on the list.

All through the night of February 28–March 1, 1953, Stalin caroused in the Kremlin with his closest comrades: Georgi Malenkov, Lavrenti Beria, Nikita Khrushchev, and Nicholas Bulganin. He was in a good mood and became quite drunk. The party ended at six o'clock in the morning. He summoned no one all that day, and thus his apartment door remained closed. In the early hours of the second of March his maid entered and found him collapsed on the floor. Guards immediately summoned Beria. Soon Malenkov arrived, followed by the others of the inner group. They remained a long time, gathered around the sofa on which Stalin had been placed. Then they left—without calling a doctor.

The next day they returned with a doctor, who diagnosed a stroke. Stalin lay bereft of speech and partially paralyzed. They stood around, watching him die.

He lay there for three and a half days, in agony, slowly strangling to death, his face turning black.

He died on March 5, 1953. Three days later his death was announced over the radio.

Solomon Slepak was stunned and wept openly. Even in the labor camps, many cried. What would now be the future of the Motherland? Masha and Volodya admit that they were frightened. Who would rule the country, hold it together?

Volodya made his way to the Hall of Columns near Red Square, where the coffin with Stalin's body had been placed for public viewing. People poured from side streets onto Petrovsky Boulevard. A solid jam on Pushkin Square. Gorky Street closed off. A tumultuous crush of humanity moving slowly toward the Hall of Columns at the House of the Trade Unions. The despot lay dead in his coffin, walrus mustache looking stiffly waxed, heavy-lidded eyes forever closed. An armed soldier stood guard nearby. Stalin dead! How astonishingly small and helpless he appeared now, slightly ludicrous even, unseemly, with his dyed red hair and pocked face. The uniformed corpse lay wreathed in flowers; lavish bouquets encased the coffin.

On March 9 the body was borne to the mausoleum on Red Square by his son, Vassily, a chronic alcoholic, and by Malenkov, Beria, Khrushchev, Molotov, and Voroshilov. The mummified corpse was placed alongside the figure of Lenin. On the streets men and women wept, even though he may have sent their loved ones to a labor camp. Many privately celebrated his death, but most feared that someone worse might soon rule—the dreaded Beria, perhaps. In Moscow from time to time the vast crowds grew suddenly frenzied, and distant screams could be heard as many among the mourners were crushed to death. Even when dead, Stalin took life. Some murmured that had he been able to, he would have taken all of Russia with him to the grave.

The despot had died around the holiday of Purim, when Jews celebrate the deliverance of an ancient Persian Jewish community from annihilation at the hands of a minister of state named Haman. No one in the Slepak family, however, knew enough about anything Jewish to make such a connection.

On April 4, one month after the death of Stalin, came an announcement over the radio concerning the "Doctors' Plot": "The people guilty of perverting the inquiry have been arrested and summoned to trial to bear the responsibility for their criminal guilt." And, added the announcer, the Order of Lenin was being taken away from the chief prosecution witness, Dr. Lidia Timashuk.

April 4 was the third day of Passover, the festival that marks the Israelites' deliverance from slavery in Egypt, an occasion no doubt overlooked by Solomon Slepak, who by that time must have read in *Pravda* that those accused in the "Doctors' Plot" had been imprisoned "without any lawful basis" and were being released. A *Pravda* editorial declared Solomon Mikhoels innocent and referred to him as "an upright communal worker."

Some years later Volodya wondered aloud in the presence of his father if there had ever been a deportation list of the Jews in their apartment building during the time of the "Doctors' Plot." His father would not respond. Masha said that she had heard of the lists and that each apartment house had one. Volodya said to his father, "How was it possible you didn't know, you were the chairman of the house committee?" Masha said to Solomon, "You must have known." Solomon then admitted to having seen the list in the apartment building's office. Volodya said, "You saw the list and you said nothing to us?" Solomon glanced at his wristwatch. Volodya said, "Were you on the list?" Solomon said, "Yes, I was on the list." Volodya said, "You had to be crazy to help them do this against yourself." Solomon got to his feet and walked out of the room without another word.

Behind the thick walls of the Kremlin, a raging war of succession was being fought among the contentious heirs of Stalin: Malenkov, Beria,

Molotov, Khrushchev. In Asia the Korean War was still dragging on. Along the western border Soviet satellite states were growing restive with the end of Stalinist rule.

At first Malenkov and Beria and Khrushchev appeared to be ruling together, an ungainly troika: Malenkov as chief of state, Beria as head of security, and Khrushchev as apparent leader of the party. Then, at the end of June 1953, after strikes and demonstrations in Czechoslovakia and a surprise workers' uprising in East Berlin, Beria, whose job it was to anticipate such events, seemed to vanish, his name stricken from the *Pravda* list of the party hierarchy present one night at the Bolshoi Theater. In July the Korean War came to a negotiated end. In September, Khrushchev gained the position of general secretary of the party. And on Christmas Day 1953 there appeared in *Pravda* the announcement that Beria and seven of his closest collaborators had been brought to trial and shot earlier that month. Sometime afterward the *Great Soviet Encyclopedia* asked its subscribers to remove with a razor the article on Beria and his photograph and to replace it with an entry on the Bering Sea.

By then Solomon Slepak and his son rarely talked about politics. But the family chronicles add, in Volodya's voice, that had his father been asked to explain the demise of Beria, he would have responded with an exultant "You see how honest the party is, how it cleans its own house. Beria, not Stalin, must have caused the doctors to be arrested. Beria, that imperialist agent, was all the time deceiving Stalin."

In 1954 the MGB, Ministry of State Security, which had replaced the NKVD in 1946, was reorganized and renamed the KGB, Committee for State Security. One year later Malenkov, whose economic policies had proved disastrous, was abruptly removed from his position and replaced by Nicholas Bulganin. He and Khrushchev now ruled the Soviet Union.

In the labor camps lived close to ten million prisoners. Slowly they began to be released, and their reputations and pensions were restored. The "crimes" of many who had perished were erased from the record, and their families sent back from exile.

The danger to the physical existence of Soviet Jewry appeared to have ended. In 1959, following eleven years of silence for Yiddish books, three works in Yiddish suddenly appeared, the selected writings of the greatest of the Yiddish writers in the tsarist period: Mendele Mocher Seforim, I. L. Peretz, and Sholem Aleichem. Books in Yiddish by surviving writers were published sporadically during the years that followed, but no Jewish institution or school was reestablished, no professional theater returned to life.

On Gorky Street the Slepak family seemed to be enjoying a comfortable and serene Soviet life.

Little Sanya Slepak attended Special English School Number 31 on Stanislavsky Street, one block from where he lived. The school, which was designated as an English school in 1963 (there were other schools that specialized in French and Spanish), serviced many of the children and grandchildren of the Soviet ruling class. It was named after the Scottish poet Robert Burns and had a brother school in Glasgow, named after the Russian poet Alexander Pushkin. It had an excellent faculty and began the teaching of English in the second grade rather than in the fifth, as was typical of regular schools. It gave more hours to English than did other schools and possessed the most up-to-date language-teaching equipment. English was studied in small groups, five or six students to a teacher; some subjects, such as geography and history, were taught entirely in English.

Why, one might ask, was English so eagerly sought and openly taught among the Soviet elite at a time when public policy at the highest levels was so belligerently opposed to foreign cultural influences? In fact, the school was a training ground for children of the elite, their beginning preparation for contact with the world outside the Motherland, where the international language was English. About one-third of the students were from families in the diplomatic corps and would end up in English-language institutes or the Institute of International Relations. Others would one day work as interpreters and translators in Soviet radio and television. There were only two or three English schools of that caliber in Moscow, all of them near the Kremlin.

Among those in Special English School Number 31 around that time were the grandson of Khrushchev, the grandchildren of Politburo member Anastas Mikoyan, the daughter of Minister of Culture Demichev, the daughter of Beria, and the children and grandchildren of many high-level bureaucrats. It was nearly impossible for an average Russian family to have a child admitted into that school. When Sanya Slepak reached school age, Solomon Slepak went to the school and had a talk with the headmaster, Gregory Suvorov, reputed to be a decent and honest man, a man of high principle. The details of Solomon's conversation with Suvorov are unknown, but afterward Sanya Slepak was permitted to take the entrance examination, which he passed.

Masha, after five years of additional medical training, was a radiologist in City Hospital Number 30 on Krestyanskaya Zastava and later worked in a polyclinic named after Felix Dzerzhinsky, the founder of Lenin's secret police; the clinic was in Kitaysky Proezd ("Chinese Way"), in the center of Moscow.

A sudden change in fortune occurred to Volodya in 1957: The Moscow TV Research and Development Institute invited him to work as a senior engineer in a laboratory where experiments were being conducted with measuring and control equipment for television transmitters.

Then his mother died of cancer, in 1959. A year later his father married a Russian woman and moved to her house on Mashkova Street, about three miles from the Gorky Street apartment, which he relinquished to Volodya and Masha, who now had two children; another son had been born to them in May 1959 and named Leonid, after no one in particular. Masha liked the name.

Astonishingly, in 1962, the institute where Volodya worked asked him to lead a laboratory; he was to be the chief designer of a special project. His new position needed to be confirmed by the Ministry of Radio Industry; the project was part of a contract between the Ministry of Radio Industry and the Ministry of Defense. Apparently the former ministry was less interested in his Jewishness than in his ability to fulfill the latter ministry's contract.

Volodya Slepak was now involved in the development of the Soviet air-defense system.

The Soviet Union was girded by a dense network of radar stations that relayed their sightings to a central computer that in turn sent signals to antirocket and antiaircraft systems, as well as to airfields and to the air defense general staffs. General officers and their staffs needed to have the signals translated onto huge screens in situation rooms, where defense and attack positions could be read on maps that showed moving rockets and aircraft. Each aircraft and rocket on the screen had to be accompanied by its appropriate characteristics: type, speed, altitude.

It was the responsibility of Volodya and his laboratory to design the most up-to-date display screens. To obtain that position, it had been necessary for him to receive First Form security clearance, second only to the top security clearance known as State Secrets.

Volodya Slepak, son of Solomon Slepak, had risen to the very summit of nonpolitical life in the Soviet Union and now stood on the frontier of the Motherland's national defense.

A year or so before he obtained that sensitive new job, Volodya had purchased for about eighty rubles in a Moscow shop a radio called a Spidola,
a black-and-yellow plastic box, about twelve by eight by four inches.
A radio powerful enough, after certain modifications, to receive the
Russian-language broadcasts of the BBC, the German Wave, the Voice
of America, the Voice of Israel. The voices of the enemies outside.

The Radio in the Forest

A t first Masha had wanted to be a surgeon. But she quickly realized that surgery was not for her; she had a child and couldn't put in a surgeon's hours. And it would not be easy for a female surgeon to find employment in a good hospital.

She began to work as a general physician, traveling half of each day about the city to treat the sick and the injured in their homes and spending the remainder of the day tending to patients in the hospital. The regimen soon exhausted her.

She considered leaving medicine. Then she learned that the hospital sorely needed a qualified radiologist and was prepared to support any staff member willing to undertake that course of study. Masha applied and was accepted. Colleagues warned her against the dangers of radiation and talked about how radiologists were always retired early because of the X rays. But she found herself fascinated with radiology, became expert at it, and soon when there were doubts in the hospital about the reading of an X ray, it would be brought to her for review.

During her years in medical school, she had watched with growing bewilderment and dread as her country began to change before her eyes, had read in its heart the deepening fury against Jews. She knew there had always been many who hated Jews; but in the past, the Soviet authorities had reined in that hostility, especially during the war. Suddenly, in the late 1940s, came the torrent of abuse at "imperialists," "bourgeois nationalists," "cosmopolitans," "Zionists," "foreign influences," "enemies of the people"—so blatant, so venomous, and so clearly organized from above—all openly aimed at the Jews.

She remembered hearing on a number of occasions during the years immediately after the war that Russian soldiers who had been captured by the Germans were, upon their release, transported directly to Siberia. That had seemed cruel to her, sending your own soldiers away to the labor camps, repaying them like that. But one said nothing about such matters in those days, not even to the members of one's own family. And then there were rumors that those who had been released from the camps after serving ten-year sentences were being arrested again. And in 1948, there was that business about the three thousand biologists fired from their jobs for disagreeing with the genetic theories of Trofim Lysenko, who claimed that he had disproved the laws of heredity and that man could easily overthrow the laws of nature and control the environment. All of that, together with the articles in journals and newspapers endlessly attacking "cosmopolitans." Somewhat fearfully Masha had begun to wonder what was happening in her country: Why the imprisonment of its captured soldiers, the persecution of its intellectuals, the attacks against its Jews?

Then came the strange order to efface all foreign names from medical school textbooks. In one of Masha's classes the professor lectured one day about the Blumberg Symptom in cases of painless appendicitis and said that it had really been discovered by a Professor Shchyotkin and was from now on to be known as the Shchyotkin Symptom. When, two years later, someone stumbled upon the fact that Blumberg, a professor of medicine in Odessa, was actually a Russian and not a Jew, they took to calling it the Blumberg-Shchyotkin Symptom.

The reaction of the students to the various rewritings of medical history ranged from docility to concealed contempt to anger they suppressed because it was believed there were MGB agents attending classes.

One day in April 1951, while interning in Ryazan, Masha was arrested by the secret police. The charge against her: possession of a concealed weapon. Two agents interrogated her for eight hours. "With whom are you friendly?" they wanted to know. Dismayed by the arrest and frightened by the interrogation, she still had the wits to answer, "With everyone." "We mean among the students," they said. "With all the students," she said, and mentioned no names. Apparently, two students in her class had been arrested for anti-Soviet activity, and the agents wanted from Masha names they might use as witnesses against them. She was released after signing a paper that she would not leave Ryazan without MGB permission, and she spoke to no one about her arrest.

She kept away from groups, felt there was danger in being part of any coalition. Indeed, Soviet law made membership in a clandestine group a worse crime than acting alone. She had at the time only one close friend and said nothing of her arrest even to him.

The arrest had followed an MGB search of her mother's apartment in Moscow. The agents, looking for concealed weapons, had found nothing. When Masha returned to Moscow for her June marriage to Volodya, her frightened mother told her of the search, and Masha informed her mother of the arrest and interrogation. They said nothing to Volodya.

The two students who had been arrested were tried, found guilty, and sent to a labor camp.

The summer of 1952, when Masha returned to medical school some months after giving birth, she was startled by a sudden message from her very close friend, who asked urgently to meet her alone. This friend was a fellow student, a non-Jew, who lived in Siberia. His father was an interrogator in a procurator's office. They met on August 20 of that year, months before the arrest of the doctors, and he told her he had information that there was to be an action against the Jews in the near future, all the Jews would be transferred to Siberia from central Russia, and the conditions of transport would be such that half would not survive the journey. He said, "I can save you and the child. Your son is blond, and I will give him my name and take the two of you to Siberia far away from all cities," and Masha said, "No, I will go with my own people, with my brothers and sisters." She trusted him completely and told no one, not even Volodya. In February 1953 he came to her again and said that the final decision had been made and very soon the action against the Jews would take place, and Masha said, "I haven't changed my mind, I can't save myself this way," and he said, "At least you can save your child," and she said, "No." She had known him for years, he was a completely honest person, and she believed him. He had come from Siberia to study medicine, was a very good student, determined to do well. He said to her angrily, "You are a weak people, spoiled by civilization, and in forty years I will be a professor." Today he is a member of the Academy of Sciences and holds the august rank of Academician. The family chronicles do not reveal his name.

Masha Slepak had witnessed the staged meetings at the medical institute and the hospital, the cruel fulminations against Jewish doctors, · the crude admissions of Jewish guilt, and asked Volodya to talk to his father, solicit from him an explanation for what was happening; after all, he was a party member, he seemed to know high party people. Why were innocent Jewish doctors the target of official rage and persecution? And then the fierce quarrel took place in the Slepak apartment. And weeks later the nine doctors were arrested and trains stood waiting and lists were being readied. The predictions of Masha's friend from Siberia were proving true. The Soviet Union was about to rid itself of the Jews.

Using the figures in official Soviet censuses and taking into consideration the enormous difficulties in defining who precisely was a Jew in the Soviet system, we can estimate that there were a little more than two million Jews in the Soviet Union at the time of the "Doctors' Plot."

In 1939 the Jews had numbered about three million. One out of every three Jews perished in the war, thereby reducing them from 2½ to around 1 percent of the total population. Jewish losses in the war were proportionately four times higher than those of the population as a whole.

Stalin's intention was to rid the major population centers of Jews and bring to an end his perceived troubles with that arrogant people. Instead he died.

In February 1956 Khrushchev stood for about three hours before the Twentieth Party Congress and delivered a twenty-thousand-word speech, carefully prepared in advance, that exposed many of the horrors of Stalin's rule and stunned the Communist world. There is a photograph of Khrushchev speaking behind the podium, a phalanx of microphones like blackbirds before him, and the rows of deputies, some staring, some with eyes averted, some whispering to one another. Delivered in closed session, the speech was to have remained secret—notes could not be taken; questions could not be asked; no one was permitted to leave during the reading—but it made its way to Communist parties in the West and to the CIA and the American State Department and into the offices of party officials throughout the Soviet Union. Accounts of the speech tell of dense, shocked silence in the vast meeting hall of the congress, an icy silence punctured from time to time by cries of outrage, buzzes of anger, waves of disquiet, and applause. Stalin, said Khrushchev, had moved far away from Leninist principles, had been guilty of despotism, mass terror, brutal violence, and the cult of personality. Upon his head lay the guilt of the country's lack of military preparedness and its costly defeats in the Great Patriotic War. Kirov's murder in Leningrad in 1934 should be looked into again, for Stalin may well have had a hand in it. A full 70 percent of the members of the Central Committee elected at the Seventeenth Congress in 1934, as well as over half the deputies, had been executed on Stalin's order. He was a cruel, bloodthirsty, and sickly-suspicious tyrant, who had slaughtered the innocent along with the guilty in his purges of the party and the army. He had deported the Volga Germans and other loyal nationalities. The "Doctors' Plot" had been a fabrication initiated by Dr. Lidia Timashuk, and Stalin had personally advised concerning the conduct of the investigation and the method of interrogation, himself calling the investigating judge and telling him he was to "Beat, beat, and, once again, beat," until confessions were obtained. It was not the party that had been at fault, said Khrushchev, but one man, its leader, Stalin, whose aberrations the party now needed to correct so that the country could once again be ruled with the same vision and effectiveness it had known in the time of Lenin. He said nothing about the party before 1934; about the innumerable peasants and nonparty people starved and slain; about the Ukrainian intelligentsia he himself had ordered killed; about his own participation in Stalin's brutal endeavors; about the millions of prisoners still in labor camps; about the plan to climax the "Doctors' Plot" with mass deportations of Soviet Jews.

To this day there is no generally accepted explanation of why Khrushchev gave that speech. To consolidate his position in the party by openly opposing the Stalinist faction: Malenkov, Kaganovich, Molotov, Shepilov? To put an end to the terror and the secret police that were stifling Soviet art and culture? To make some sort of restitution to the innocent victims of Stalin's paranoia?

About one month after the Twentieth Congress, Volodya's superior at the Electro-Vacuum Factory asked him if he wanted to read Khrushchev's secret speech. Volodya said, "Yes, of course." The man said, "Go to my office. It's on the desk. I took it from the office of the party committee." At about that same time, the speech was read aloud to the medical staff during a meeting in Masha's hospital. She and Volodya had known in outline much of the history related in the speech but were astonished by the details and by the fact that party leaders were now talking openly of the horrors perpetrated by Stalin.

The family chronicles relate the calm reaction of Solomon Slepak when he learned of the speech: "Stalin was certainly a great person. He did many positive things for our socialist state. Yes, he made mistakes. The party will correct them." But one wonders about that response.

The speech and the furious reaction of the Communist Chinese to Khrushchev's de-Stalinization and liberalization of Soviet life, a reaction that by 1963 was to become an irreparable rift between the two centers of world communism, could hardly have brought much joy to the Old Bolshevik's ailing heart.

By the early summer of 1957, some months after the autumn 1956 Hungarian rebellion had been crushed by Soviet troops, Khrushchev further tightened his hold on the Soviet Union when he persuaded the Presidium to oust his opponents—Malenkov, Molotov, Kaganovich, Bulganin, Voroshilov, Mikoyan, Shepilov. Then, in March 1958, Bulganin resigned as head of the government and Khrushchev took over the premiership. He was now head of both the party and the state. A self-made man, whose father had been a Ukrainian peasant, now ruled the Soviet Union: brash, hearty, overbearing, as well as cunning and devious, and schooled since the twenties in the Byzantine politics of the party.

The Twenty-second Party Congress, which met in October 1961, confirmed Khrushchev's leadership and documented more of Stalin's atrocities. Newspapers carried articles detailing facets of the great purge. And to the added astonishment of Masha and Volodya and countless others, the body of Stalin was removed before the end of the year from the mausoleum in Red Square, an event widely reported in the Soviet media and by the BBC and the Voice of America. And the city of Stalingrad was renamed Volgograd.

How did Solomon Slepak, then sixty-eight years old, react to the unceremonious removal of Stalin from his resting place beside Lenin? The chronicles, silent on the Old Bolshevik's response, record Volodya's conjecture about his father's possible reply: "You see how the party cleans its own ranks? Even the great Stalin cannot evade the watchful eyes of the party."

According to Volodya, as far as his father was concerned, events were moving inexorably along the correct course. The original cult of the party was now appropriately replacing the unseemly Stalinist cult of personality.

The body of Stalin was reinterred in a grave between the mausoleum and the Kremlin wall, beneath a stone and a bust of the tyrant.

Volodya and Masha began to wonder if the country had turned a corner, if life had moved onto a new plane for the people of the Soviet Union, especially for the Jews. Or was it all merely a period of political infighting, a nervous pause rather than a permanent redirection of purpose? By then Volodya and Masha, together with some very close friends, were listening regularly to the overseas broadcasts of the BBC and the Voice of America.

Warm weekends and summers Volodya and Masha traveled to the forests outside Moscow, where they camped with their friends amid the pines and alders and maples and junipers. Parents brought children. Each family slept in its own tent, purchased in a Moscow sports shop. Hiking, fishing, swimming, boating; gathering mushrooms and berries—much as Volodya had once done in his childhood with his father, during the thirties.

It was a circle of about six to ten friends: engineers, doctors, scientists. Their talk centered on new movies, books, music, concerts; on recent achievements in science, medicine, engineering, biology; on world events. They expressed to one another their astonishment that the Soviet authorities had approved the publication, in 1962, of Alexander Solzhenitsyn's *One Day in the Life of Ivan Denisovich*. It was not so much the contents of the book that were of interest to them—they were familiar with many of the details—as the very fact of the book itself, what its appearance signaled and its worth as literature. They wondered what comparable works might soon follow.

Very much on their minds was the atmosphere of relaxation in Soviet culture that had succeeded the death of Stalin: Ilya Ehrenburg's 1954 novel *The Thaw*; the rehabilitation in 1955 of the writer Isaac Babel, who had been arrested during the purges of the thirties and was thought to have perished in a labor camp; the journal and newspaper articles lamenting the stagnation of Russian literature. There was a sudden freeze on the arts following the Hungarian revolt in October 1956, but then a thaw once again, with the appearance of the poetry of Joseph Brodsky and Yevgeny Yevtushenko, and the public readings attended by thousands in Moscow's Mayakovsky Square and Luzhniki Sports Palace, where a new generation of young poets read works that openly declared rebellion against their fathers and mothers. Volodya and Masha did not attend the readings but knew of them. They were aware, too, that the authorities had finally put a stop to the readings; organizers and poets were arrested, some sent into exile and others to psychiatric hospitals.

Arrested in the late fifties for reading poetry to his friends, exiled to Siberia, and released in February 1961 was the mathematician and poet Alexander Yesenin-Volpin, whose mother was Jewish. Some of Volpin's friends were arrested in February 1962. When they were brought to trial for "anti-Soviet agitation"—they had read their poetry to a crowd in Mayakovsky Square—Volpin tried to enter the courtroom, but was stopped by guards. The trial was closed to friends and relatives. On a sudden impulse Volpin showed the guards a copy of the new criminal code, which contained the promise made by the new Soviet leaders that henceforth trials would be open to the public and conducted with "Soviet legality." The guards, after some hesitation, permitted him to enter.

There are those who, in retrospect, regard that seemingly insignificant event as the instant of conception for the civil rights and human rights struggle in the Soviet Union.

That same year, 1962, there appeared Anatoly Kuznetsov's novel *Babi Yar*. Like the great poem of that name by Yevgeny Yevtushenko, it deals with the 1941 German slaughter of ninety thousand Jews in the ravine outside Kiev. One might have thought that the Soviets were finally acknowledging the unique dark destiny of the Jews in their midst. But then, in 1963, the Ukrainian Academy of Sciences published twelve thousand copies of a book called *Judaism Without Embellishment* by Trofim Kichko, a reworking of the turn-of-the-century tsarist police hoax known as *Protocols of the Elders of Zion*, Jewish bankers and Zionists allied with Western capitalists in a conspiracy to take over the world. The book was studded with ugly racial cartoons reminiscent of the Nazi era.

Volodya and Masha and their friends talked at length about those events during their weekend and summer excursions in the forests outside Moscow. In the evenings they sat around a campfire, listening to the broadcasts in Russian that came from the world beyond the borders of the Soviet Union. Those who planned the programs knew Russian work patterns and broadcast only in the early morning and from late afternoon into the night. Words from the world outside emerged from portable radios and drifted through the woods: news from Britain, Germany, America, Israel. Turbulent times, the fifties and early sixties: Presidents Eisenhower and Kennedy in the American White House, Joseph McCarthy in the Senate, civil rights demonstrations in the streets; everywhere the Cold War and the armaments race; the Sinai War in the Middle East, the launching of *Sputnik*, the space race, the Cuban missile crisis, the growing American involvement in Vietnam. And the news from the United States seemed to be coming over the airwaves raw and uncensored, the good and the bad alike. Volodya repeatedly asked himself, What sort of country broadcasts to the world in such sordid detail its domestic turbulence, its ugly riots, the assassination of its leader? A strong and free country, he thought, and said so often to his friends.

Among his friends were David and Noemi Drapkin, Leonid

Lipkovsky, Victor and Elena Polsky, Alexander Gilman, Alla Futer, Vladimir Prestin, Pavel Abramovich.

In the winters they went to the forests to ski. Again they brought their radios, listened to voices talking of distant worlds.

None of the Soviet shortwave radios available in shops had the frequencies needed for foreign broadcasts; to net the outside voices, one had to retune the frequency bands. With his knowledge of radio electronics, Volodya found the retuning a simple matter: Rewind some coils and change some capacitors. He did it for himself and for his friends. As more and more people began to listen to foreign stations, it became possible to find technicians who, for not a great deal of money, would unofficially retune one's shortwave radio.

Soviet law did not explicitly prohibit citizens from tuning in to foreign radio stations; such a law would have been tantamount to forbidding the movement of air. The authorities tried to prevent reception by jamming broadcasts, thereby producing a screen of noise the voices of the enemy could not penetrate. Jamming was costly, however, and centered mainly on the large cities and even there was not entirely successful. In forests and fields, retuned shortwave radios were able to pull in the signals that relayed to Volodya and Masha and their friends events in America and Europe and Israel, the hum of new possibilities.

Though there was no specific law against listening to the outside world, a hint of habitual tuning to those voices might easily have resulted in suspicion being cast upon one's loyalties and the beginning of mistrust on the part of one's superior. And one doubt leading to another and still another. And perhaps one day the loss of one's job, and the KGB at the door.

Why, then, did they do it? Why all that clandestine listening by those very successful, very assimilated Russian Jews, that circle of accomplished men and women, many with families and in splendid jobs, virtually all, despite some doubts, committed to Marxist ideology and conditioned to the Soviet way of life? Why that beginning effort by Volodya and Masha and the others to dismantle the Soviet core of their beings, to bore tunnels to their individualities, to discover their separate selves?

Volodya had repeatedly felt his father's brutal single-mindedness of purpose. Alone among his circle of friends, he had a father who was an Old Bolshevik, one who had mysteriously survived all the Stalinist purges, and whose sudden rages and evasive answers in defense of party policies had caused his son to view him as an uncompromising Soviet ideologue, a man of relentless cunning and cruelty on political issues, including those pertaining to Jews, in the matter of which he seemed to acquiesce entirely to party instructions, at times to the point of groveling servility. Indeed, though the notion never occurred to Volodya, it is not too far-fetched to wonder if in ideology and temperament his father was only a few steps removed from the ruthless Lazar Kaganovich, the sole Jew left in the Politburo, who had long ruled with Stalin.

As Volodya continued working on the air-defense system of the Soviet Union, his sense of his personal future began to be increasingly somber. He was aware that Jews could no longer enter the ministries of Foreign Trade and Foreign Affairs; that the upper echelons of the party and the secret police, where Jews had been so heavily represented from the time of the Revolution until the mid-thirties, were now closed to them; that there were proportionately increasingly fewer Jews in local soviets, in republic-level legislatures, in the Supreme Soviet. He knew too that from 1958 to 1961, for the first time in the history of the Soviet Union, not a single Jew was to be found among the numerous government ministers. Until mid-1957 many Soviet Jews had thought that some kind of cultural and religious rebirth might be at hand: A few Yiddish books had appeared; the authorities had even permitted amateur theatricals in some cities; synagogues were undisturbed; a theological seminary had been added to the synagogue in Moscow; and three thousand prayer books were published in Moscow. Indeed, during the first half of 1957 about thirty thousand Soviet Jews were repatriated to Poland as part of a Soviet-Polish agreement to allow the return to their homeland of pre-1939 Polish citizens and their families; many soon left Poland for Israel and elsewhere. There were the visits by Israeli athletes, and the Israeli participants in the 1957 international youth festival in Moscow, and the tourists from Israel and other countries, and the concerts given by Israeli performers. But abruptly, as if awakening to the fear that it might have opened its doors dangerously wide and that things might soon go spinning out of control, the Kremlin again reversed itself. An antireligion campaign began to sweep through much of the country in mid-1957, intensified in 1959, and continued in ferocity until 1964. It was directed against not only Judaism but all faiths. About fifty synagogues—"nests of speculators," rose the cry from the local press—and thousands of churches were shut down. The last synagogue in the city of Minsk had its roof removed during a service and was turned into a club. Baking the traditional unleavened Passover flatbread, matzah, was forbidden. And a campaign against economic crimes netted an astonishing number of Jews, whose names were prominently announced in the press. More than 500 trials took place in the early 1960s for the crimes of embezzlement, speculation in foreign currency, bribery, and connections to foreigners; 117 individuals, of whom 91 were Jews, received the death penalty. That so many Jews were among those arrested is no surprise, as Jews were prominent in certain areas of the economy. But it is not unreasonable to wonder why the number of Jews executed was disproportionately so much higher and to regard with dismay the atmosphere of hatred generated by the anti-Semitism in the Soviet press, so starkly reminiscent of the late forties and early fifties under Stalin.

Back and forth went the Soviet Union in its relationship with the Jews, now warming to them, now freezing them out. As in tsarist times, a dizzying policy of peace and war, progress and retreat, acceptance and rejection, yawing this way and that: the classic, paralyzing Russian ambivalence. No pogroms anymore, nothing quite so crude as that, especially with the world always watching. Khrushchev was not a boorish anti-Semite; the butchery of pogroms, which he had witnessed during his early years in the Ukraine, was unseemly to him, unfit for a superpower attempting to influence the third world. Still, the Jews had to be dealt with. They were too easily attracted to Zionism and bourgeois nationalism, far too intellectual, too quick to avoid collective labor and group discipline, too exploitive of Gentiles, too eager to attend universities, too entangled with ancient superstitions, too individualistic. Deviants. Best to just barely tolerate them, to treat them as marginal, and as forever incapable of entering the Soviet mainstream.

That attitude toward the Jews was at times brought home to Volodya on the job. In 1963 the laboratory he headed had a staff of about twenty-five people, all working on improving the air-defense system of the Soviet Union. On occasion he informed the deputy director of the institute that some additional engineers were needed, and each time the response was: "Please find good engineers, and they will be accepted. But they must not be Tatars or Jews. I can do nothing for them."

Masha never encountered anti-Semitism on the job, because most of the doctors in her hospital were Jews. But she knew of Volodya's experiences, was intensely aware of the poisoned air of the country. She and Volodya asked themselves often how they could raise a family in that atmosphere. Even those who wished to assimilate could never be certain that they would not be told one day, "You come from Jewish grandparents and parents, and therefore you cannot be fully Russian." And those with excellent jobs today might be fired at any time in the future simply because they were Jews, and then arrested, exiled, shot. On the one hand, Jews were being deprived of their culture, their religion, their history; on the other hand, the authorities bluntly refused to acknowledge that they could ever become an integral element of the Soviet people. For all the foreseeable future, "Jew" would be the word on the fifth line under "nationality" on the passports of Soviet Jews, save in those instances when one parent was not Jewish and one chose to adopt that parent's nationality upon turning sixteen. The identity of Jews was being defined for them by their enemies. Even Volodya's father—who had helped to make the Revolution, who had metamorphosed the core of his being from village Jew to Bolshevik fighter—was regarded as a potentially menacing outsider by the very party to which he had always shown nothing but blind loyalty! What kind of a land was this in which to bring up children? What security could Volodya and Masha hope to have in a country where their lives might be destroyed one day by some cruel and violent upheaval? Were Jews so helpless everywhere in the world? Was there someplace where they were differently treated?

So Volodya and his friends turned to overseas voices in the forests. And in 1963 he and Masha began to listen to their shortwave radio inside their apartment, in which he had located certain areas where the metal construction within the walls screened more of the jamming signal than it did the signal from the radio station. Depending upon the earth's atmosphere and the sun's activity, it was often possible to hear the words through the jamming. When he was alone, Volodya used earphones. When he and Masha were together, they kept the volume low. The walls in their building were of good quality and thick; thus no one outside their apartment could hear the radio's foreign voices. The children never listened with them.

Most of the time they listened in the evenings. They followed closely over the Voice of America the reporting of the assassination of President Kennedy and over the Voice of Israel, events in the Middle East. That was the period when the Kremlin had begun to court the Arab world, and Soviet relations with Israel were cooling. But connections between the two countries were still being maintained—the Soviets worried about the many millions of dollars' worth of Russian property in Jerusalem, and the Israelis had awakened to the realization that vast numbers of Russian Jews might yet be saved for Zionism—and there were fully functioning embassies in both countries and diplomatic personnel traveling back and forth.

Volodya and Masha had no way of knowing about the covert operation then being run in the Soviet Union by the Israeli intelligence agency Mossad. In the judgment of those who conducted it, and others, that operation had a startling ripple effect on the destiny of Soviet Jewry—and on the future of the Soviet Union itself.

Israel made a slow entry into Soviet Jewry's dissident movement and, once inside, seemed to walk an overly cautious path. Geopolitical interests forced upon it a proceed-with-care policy: It needed Soviet support and could not become involved in overt criticism of the Soviet Union or in its disputes with contentious nationalities.

A few in Israel thought that what could not be achieved openly might be done secretly. To that end, in 1952 a small group of people in Israeli intelligence, with the approval of Prime Minister David Ben-Gurion, set up an operation whose main task was the classical Zionist one: Contact Jews in the Baltic regions and Soviet heartland, especially those who had once been members of Zionist youth parties, and establish escape routes to Israel in case of Stalinist pogroms. At the same time, begin to bring certain reading material from Israel into the Soviet Union through diplomatic channels.

It was not, by any ordinary standards, a spy operation: no clandestine meetings that might be interpreted as a threat to Soviet authority; no sub rosa photography; no thefts of classified documents. Inordinate care was taken to avoid the inevitable agents provocateurs: the beautiful woman who offered to slip into your bed; the young man who promised you a fortune in icons; the anxious writer who pleaded with you to smuggle out his manuscript. During the period of Khrushchev, who was abruptly removed from power by the Politburo in October 1964, and all through the suffocating years of Leonid Brezhnev and the leaders who followed, there were no precarious spy games. Just a small number of Mossad agents, at times with their wives, entering as tourists or as embassy personnel, carrying into the Soviet Union books forbidden by Soviet law—Hebrew Bibles, grammars, Jewish calendars, Israeli newspapers, periodicals, Zionist tracts—and leaving behind with seeming carelessness a Bible here, a periodical there, in a synagogue, an apartment, on a park bench, at a summer beach, as one might discard a newspaper after a train ride. Everywhere in the Soviet Union meeting anxious and forlorn Jews—in an old bazaar in Samarkand, a resort on the Black Sea, a synagogue in Lithuania, a village in the Caucasus, a town in Georgia—often by chance and at times by design, enabling them to experience the presence of an Israeli, and witnessing in those Jews a sudden spark of astonishment, a rushing buoyancy of spirit. The Mossad operation is one of the reasons why, when the Soviet Jewish dissident movement finally began to take form after—in a few places even before—the 1967 Six-Day War in the Middle East, there were at least some books in place, some Hebrew grammars available, for study and duplication.

In addition, a number of invaluable old books were within reach—classics by Leon Pinsker, one of the pioneers of Zionism in nineteenth-century tsarist Russia; by Simon Dubnow, the Jewish historian; by Theodor Herzl, the founder of political Zionism; and others—because of the work of a few Russian Jews who had chanced upon them in forgotten private libraries, recognized their cultural value, and dusted them off for possible use by a new generation of young people.

Volodya and Masha Slepak could not know that during the sixties, before the Six-Day War, they were part of a still-shapeless tide of dissidents slowly rising in the Soviet Union.

How did the movement begin?

Singling out its elements is like trying to take hold of waves in a swelling sea. The death of Stalin in 1953, the corrosive infighting of the Politburo, the astonishing secret Khrushchev speech at the Twentieth Congress in 1956—all gave early impetus to the unraveling, especially among some of the young intellectual urban elite, of the Communist web of belief, and also led to the rise of small friendship circles known as *kompanii*, like-minded young men and women who would come together, talk about literature, music, journalism, sing to a guitar, read forbidden poetry, tell somewhat perilous jokes (*Question:* What will happen after Cuba builds communism? *Answer:* It will start importing sugar. *Question:* What's the difference between capitalism and communism? *Answer:* Under capitalism, man exploits man; under communism, it's the other way around)—and feel themselves fully alive outside the suffocating framework of Soviet life. Those *kompanii*—bearded men in homemade sweaters bearing Russian pagan symbols; smart, chain-smoking, keen-witted women—were the germinating seeds during the late fifties of the dissident movement, which rose in various forms throughout the land during the 1960s: long-suppressed nationalism sparking among Ukrainians, Lithuanians, Latvians, Georgians, Armenians, Crimean Tatars, Soviet Germans; Leninists who wanted a return to the pristine communism they believed had graced the dawn of the Revolution; democrats and humanists seeking a form of government free of political ideologues; Russians dreaming of a pre-Revolutionary Russian culture and a restored Orthodox Church; Baptists, Seventh-Day Adventists, and Pentecostalists awaiting the opportunity to garner new souls; and Jews fighting for the right to emigrate to Israel.

For many of the Russian intelligentsia—those among the early *kom-*

panii who remained troubled and alienated after the phenomenon of the *kompanii* began to burn itself out in the early 1960s—the turning point came with the arrest, in September 1965, of Yuli Daniel, a Jew, and his friend Andrei Sinyavsky, Soviet writers whose works had been banned in the Soviet Union.

Using the writer Boris Pasternak as a kind of model—his novel *Dr. Zhivago* had been published in Italy during the late 1950s; "tamizdat" publishing, the Russians called it: "published over there"—Daniel and Sinyavsky had some of their manuscripts smuggled out and published pseudonymously abroad under the names Nikolai Arzhak, for Daniel, and Abram Tertz, for Sinyavsky.

Their arrests, coming less than a year after the sudden ouster of Khrushchev, were read by many as a signal of the new regime's hostility to "samizdat" ("self-publishing"), which was then accelerating among intellectual circles. It was a painstaking, time-consuming process: covert duplication of uncensored literature, poetry, and political material by means of typewriter and carbon paper and then its illicit distribution, sometimes of foreign writers whose works were no longer available in translation, like Koestler's *Darkness at Noon* and Orwell's *1984*; often of writers like Sinyavsky and Daniel and others whose works had been rejected by official Soviet publishing channels.

The arrest of the two writers, at first unannounced by the Soviet authorities, caught the attention of the world. For the first time foreign stations began to broadcast news of a KGB action. Shortly after the beginning of the foreign broadcasts, the Soviet press reported the arrests and proceeded to condemn the writers for their slanders of Soviet society. Frightened friends and relatives envisioned with dread a return to the horrors of the thirties: torture and confessions and further arrests; execution by a pistol shot to the head, by a firing squad.

Volodya and Masha cannot recall how they first learned of the arrests. The radio, the newspapers. Very soon everyone knew.

Early in December 1965 the mathematician Alexander Yesenin-Volpin—the man who had gained entry into a 1962 trial by showing a copy of the new criminal code to the guards, with its promise that trials would henceforth be open to the public—composed a statement and arranged for it to be typed in numerous copies and distributed as leaflets around various institutes and Moscow University.

The leaflets told of the arrests of the writers and the concern that their trial would violate the laws regarding public court proceedings, and proclaimed: "Citizens have the means to struggle against judicial arbitrariness: public meetings, during which one well-known slogan is chanted—'We demand an open trial'—or is displayed on placards. You are invited to a public meeting. . . ."

For a number of Soviet citizens, the line of submissive endurance had been breached.

On the evening of December 5, 1965, about two hundred people, among them many students, assembled in Alexander Pushkin Square in Moscow, near the statue of the poet. At a prearranged signal they raised placards on which appeared the words "Respect the Soviet Constitution" and "We demand an open trial for Sinyavsky and Daniel."

The demonstration ended almost as soon as it had begun. Hardly had the placards been displayed by Volpin and others than they were torn away by KGB agents and militiamen in the crowd. Flashbulbs popped on the cameras held by foreign correspondents who had assembled to witness and report the event. About twenty of the demonstrators were taken away in waiting cars—and released after a few hours. Some days later around forty people who had participated in the demonstration found themselves abruptly expelled from their institutes.

Thus ended the first human rights action with placards and slogans in the history of the Soviet Union.

In the years that followed, demonstrators assembled in Pushkin Square on the night of December 5 to commemorate that first peaceful public protest. One of those present in 1966 was Andrei Sakharov, the physicist who had helped the Soviet Union develop its hydrogen bomb. He came each year for the next decade.

Volodya and Masha heard of the demonstration immediately after it took place. One day in Volodya's institute, during a lunch break in the cafeteria, two engineers from the design bureau sat talking about the demonstration and books written by Sinyavsky and Daniel that had been published illegally in the Soviet Union or overseas: *This Is Moscow Speaking, Hands, Ice-Covered Earth, The Town of Lyubimov*. Someone must have overheard the conversation and informed on them. Their desks were searched; the books found. Two days later the engineers were fired.

The trial of Sinyavsky and Daniel—the first of many show trials that were soon to extend across the country—took place during four days of arctic cold in February 1966. Sinyavsky received seven years, Daniel five, both at hard labor—for "anti-Soviet propaganda," a charge taken from the criminal code and used for the first time against intellectuals. The sentences suddenly made real the vision of a return to Stalinist repression. True, neither writer had been subjected to beatings, and there had been no allegations of terrorism against the state, but the price imposed for their dissent was inordinately cruel.

The arrests and trial of Sinyavsky and Daniel are regarded as a watershed moment. With that event was born, in the eyes of most historians, the human rights movement in the Soviet Union. Letters began to be written, petitions signed and sent: to deputies of the Supreme Council, to the procurator general, to Brezhnev. Letters and petitions had been sent often to Stalin, who at times responded with arrest, years in a labor camp, a bullet in the brain. But in the post-Stalin Soviet Union of 1966, the Kremlin seemed uncertain at first about how to respond.

Then many of the letters were published in a samizdat edition of a work titled *The White Book*, which also carried newspaper accounts and an abbreviated, unofficial transcript of the trial. That brought the patience of the authorities to an abrupt end, and in 1968 four young samizdat activists, all part-time students—Yuri Galanskov, Alexander Ginzburg, Vera Laskova, and Alexei Dobrovolsky—were arrested and accused of having smuggled the book out to the West. Their trial, which came to be known as the Trial of the Four, and the lengthy prison terms they received evoked still more letters and petitions. Protest, arrest, trial, further protest and arrest: A self-perpetuating escalation toward the doom of one side or the other, or both, had begun.

A few who signed petitions in the years 1966–1968 soon found themselves in labor camps; many signers who were party members were dismissed from the party and their jobs; nonparty people lost their positions or were transferred to minor posts; students were expelled from their institutes, artists and writers from their unions; scientists could not complete their dissertations. Those with their names on letters and petitions, once full and thriving participants in official Soviet society, were suddenly shunned, excommunicated. Still, the letters went on being written, signed, sent.

And in 1968, Larisa Bogoraz, the wife of Yuli Daniel, and Pavel Litvinov, the grandson of Maxim Litvinov, former foreign minister of the Soviet Union, wrote a letter protesting the Trial of the Four, addressing it not only to the world inside the Soviet Union but, in a sudden departure from past practice, to the West as well. A typed draft was handed to the Reuters correspondent in Moscow and soon appeared in the foreign press. Overseas radio stations repeatedly broadcast the entire text of the letter into Soviet homes.

A cycle of communication had been established: wronged Soviet citizen to foreign press and back to ever-wider circles of Soviet citizens.

At about that same time, the mid-1960s, the civil rights movement had begun to grow in the United States. Strangely, simultaneously, in both countries, from radically opposite poles of the political spectrum, people of limited power had begun to protest against their pariah status: Crimean Tatars, Kalmyks, Chechens, among others, in the Soviet Union; African Americans, Native Americans, women, homosexuals, among others, in the United States. Restless, disillusioned youth in both cultures embarked upon the creation of angry countercultures. Volodya and Masha listened to the Voice of America describe riots and demonstrations; news of the escalating war in Vietnam penetrated the forest and the apartment. There were times when Volodya and Masha felt better informed about the tides of protest in the United States than about those in their own country.

Thus it was that, in September 1964, they knew nothing of a man named Iosif Chornobilsky, a locksmith from Kiev, who handed a woman visitor from Detroit a statement claiming that the Soviet Union hated Jews "with a wild anti-Semitic hatred" and was crushing "the rights of Jews in their education and work." The statement, translated, was published in the *Detroit Jewish News*. After obtaining a number of signatures, in 1966, on a petition requesting a Jewish national theater in Kiev—rejected by the Ukrainian Communist Party—Chornobilsky was arrested. In the file the KGB had on him were copies of his statement in the *Detroit Jewish News*, letters to his sister in Israel, accounts of his meetings with tourists, and a list of books he had received about Israel.

Nor were Volodya and Masha Slepak aware of the few Jews in the Soviet Union who were attempting to revive the study of Hebrew: Rachel Margolina-Ratner, Felix Shapiro, Michael Zand, Hillel Butman, Zev Mogilever, and others. Nor did they know that American Jewish organizations, at the urging of the activist theologian Abraham Joshua Heschel and a few others, had begun to waken to the reality of Soviet Jewry's suffering. Moshe Decter, an advocate for Soviet Jewry since the 1950s, organized a Conference on the Status of Soviet Jewry, which was held in October 1963. In the years that followed, the issue of Soviet Jewry began to appear with increasing frequency on the agendas of Jewish and non-Jewish American organizations, institutions, newspapers, the halls of Congress. Rallies were held at which U.S. senators spoke: Robert Kennedy and Jacob Javits urged the Soviet government to abide by its own constitution and grant the Jews their lawful rights. Catholic clergymen, labor leaders, and others joined in the protest. The Soviet government, mindful of world opinion, reacted in 1965 by ending its economic persecution of the Jews, rescinding its prohibition against the baking of unleavened bread for the Passover festival, and permitting some Jews to emigrate.

In the meantime a bridge of tourists was slowly being built between Western Jewry and the Soviet Union. American rabbis journeyed to Moscow. In 1965 Rabbi Israel Miller of New York City headed a delegation of Orthodox Rabbis and addressed the aged congregants of the Moscow synagogue in Yiddish, an event without precedent. In the summer of 1966 a group of American Reform rabbis visited that same synagogue, and the young son of one of the rabbis was called to the Torah to recite the blessing. Astonishment and tears filled the eyes of the old worshippers; it was the first time in forty years a youth had taken part in a service.

A vague, confused reawakening of identity seemed to be taking place among Jews in the Soviet Union; so some tourists reported when they returned home. They reported, too, on vague and distant stirrings: the unusually frequent borrowing of certain books, like *Hebrew-Russian Conversation*, often found in the reading rooms of institutes for Oriental literature; the constant perusal, with the help of a Hebrew-Russian dictionary (ferreted out of an old pre-Revolution private library? or left behind by a Mossad agent?), of the official Communist Party Hebrew newspaper *Kol Ha-Am* ("Voice of the People"), published daily in Israel and available in Moscow's Lenin Library; the use of those books and newspapers by pensioners to learn Hebrew so they could then teach the language to the young. But in truth, only a few old and young Soviet Jews were part of that reawakening in the early and mid-sixties. A very few.

Volodya and Masha Slepak knew nothing of those embryonic cultural stirrings. Though listening frequently to foreign radio broadcasts and made uneasy by anti-Semitism and the apparent re-Stalinizing policies of the Brezhnev government, they were still to all appearances exemplary Soviet citizens—Masha a highly respected radiologist in an urban hospital; Volodya a skilled, prominent engineer in highly secret defense work that at times took him to strategic air bases and radar installations; their two sons in a superior special English school.

Less than a year later the shortwave radio was to bring into the apartment and the forest news of distant events that ultimately caused Masha and Volodya Slepak to transform their lives.

Journeys

The change in Masha and Volodya began slowly. That it began at all was in part a consequence of experiences private and personal: Masha's terrifying arrest by the KGB; Volodya's distressing encounters with anti-Semitism on the job; their gnawing awareness of the ruthless deeds of Solomon Slepak in China. And in part on account of events public and political: the demythologizing of Stalin; the candor of the Khrushchev years and the sudden poisoning of the air with the arrest and trial of Sinyavsky and Daniel; the possibilities, borne by radio voices, of alternative lives for themselves and their children. The change came reluctantly at first, with considerable anxiety and hesitation. Until the final visceral change, caused by the overwhelming terror and triumph of a distant war.

The family chronicles tell of summer boat trips that Masha and Volodya often took during those Khrushchev-Brezhnev years. They went on one such trip in the summer of 1966—the year Sinyavsky and Daniel were tried and sent to labor camps for "anti-Soviet propaganda"; the year the locksmith Iosif Chornobilsky unsuccessfully petitioned the Ukrainian Communist Party for a Jewish theater in Kiev and was arrested; the same summer American Reform rabbis visited the Moscow synagogue and a youngster accompanying them became the first youth called to the Torah in forty years.

The boat they sailed on that summer was named *Dolphin*. Built in East Germany, it was 16.5 feet long and 5.5 feet wide and had two sails and an engine. Its wooden frame was covered with rubberized textile, and it could be easily disassembled and packed into several bags.

They sailed for two weeks along the Neringa Spit, a 75-mile length of sandbar—its width from half a mile to 2.5 miles—that separates the Kursh Gulf from the Baltic Sea. Also aboard were their friends Victor and Elena Polsky and Leonid Lipkovsky, all engineers whom Volodya had met while working in the Electro-Vacuum Factory in Moscow.

The boat took them from Klaipeda, a Lithuanian city on the Baltic, to the city of Königsberg, which the Soviets had renamed Kaliningrad, in the former state of East Prussia. They would sail for a day on the gulf side of the spit and then go ashore and make camp and put up tents and remain for one or two days, swimming, lying in the sun, fishing, picking berries. At night they built a campfire and Leonid Lipkovsky played the guitar and they sat around singing comical ditties and old Russian songs about love, the sea, nature, and long journeys, and listening to the various voices over the radio, and then quietly talking. They were a close, intimate circle of friends. In those Brezhnev days, the smaller the friendship group, the safer you were: fewer chances of running afoul of informants. No conspirators in this band of intimate friends sailing along the Neringa Spit that summer of 1966 and camping on its white dunes away from civilization, save for the three times they went into the towns on the spit for supplies, where they bought bread, sugar, pasta, and other staples.

On the gulf side nearly the entire shoreline was of white clean sand, some of it rising to a height of one hundred feet. It was exciting to slide down a high dune into the shallow water of the gulf, which was fed by the freshwaters of the Neman River. There were many fish, and they caught and fried bream and bought eels from the fishermen and cured them in smoke.

In the places where the spit widened there were forests beyond the beaches. Exploring one of the forests, they came upon the hunting lodge once used by Nazi Field Marshal Hermann Göring. Its walls had long been removed and used as firewood by people who lived nearby. Only the inlaid floor remained. All around the ruined lodge ran a wild garden with deserted stables and henhouses. Berries grew from bushes in the garden, and the Slepaks and their friends picked many and enjoyed them.

For two weeks they were connected to civilization only by radio. The men let their beards grow. On their last day of sailing the skies darkened and the wind rose, and there was a storm with waves six feet high. Arriving in the town of Zelenogradsk, they disassembled the boat and packed it away. Then they rented a small truck and drove to Kaliningrad, where they visited a barbershop. After his haircut Volodya gazed at himself in the barber's mirror. Thirty-nine years old. Rugged, handsome, unshaven features. Grayish-green eyes; full lips; prominent, slightly curving nose. A Muscovite, urbane, intellectual, a bit too masculine, too attractive, the way Masha's father had been. He turned to Masha and said in his throaty voice, "Maybe I will leave the beard?" Masha said, "You can try."

The abrupt decision to let one's beard grow. An assertion of identity, of self, to counteract growing inner uncertainty? Or an attempt to hide behind a dawning hurtful truth?

They spent the rest of the day touring the city and out of a sense of homage visited the grave of the great German philosopher Immanuel Kant, one of the legendary figures of the eighteenth-century Enlightenment. That night Volodya and his friends boarded a train back to Moscow, and Masha, who had one more week of vacation, took a train to Klaipeda and rode from there by bus to Palanga, the Baltic Sea resort town where her mother was staying with the children.

That was the last summer of the Soviet paradise for the Slepaks, the last year of servile imprisonment for many Jews in the Soviet Union.

In 1926 there were more than one thousand synagogues in the Soviet Union; in 1966, sixty-two. Each synagogue now functioned separately, fighting its own battle for survival; there was no central religious Jewish organization. Thirty of the synagogues were located in non-European regions of the Soviet Union, in which lived less than 10 percent of the country's total Jewish population. The Oriental Jews of those regions would have fought to the death against any attempt to close their synagogues, and the authorities mostly left them alone. More important, Oriental Jews did not have the sense of Jewish nationalist consciousness that existed among Western Jews, for whom religious ideas invariably ignited the fires of nationalism. Thus the Soviet authorities fought hard against overt manifestations of religion in the ranks of Western Jews. And those Jews, largely assimilated and yielding to government harassment, had witnessed over the years the regime's anti-Semitic propaganda campaigns, the closing of synagogues, the uprooting of institutions that might afford opportunities for assembly and separateness; had witnessed, silently until now, the gradual collapse of Judaism all around them: the absence of academies of higher Jewish learning; the suppression of the religious education of children; the gradual rise in the average age—now above seventy—of rabbis, ritual slaughterers, and circumcisers; and the expunging of all public references to explicitly Jewish contributions to Soviet life past and present. Synagogue life, controlled; a Yiddish press, dead, save for showpiece publications. Clearly, it was the intention of the government to throttle the living organism of Judaism until such time as it would indeed cease to exist, thereby demonstrating the truth of the announcement of its demise.

Astonishingly, the brutal crushing of Jewish nationalism led some young secular Jews on journeys for other forms of expression, on quests into heretofore unexplored regions of religious worship, and they discovered the noisy, blatantly public territory of Simchat Torah, the exuberant festival when Jews mark the end and the new beginning of the annual Torah-reading cycle, its fervid enthusiasms only loosely codified by Jewish law. The passion, the openness, the frenzied exhilaration. They danced; they sang; they played their guitars.

And so in the fall of 1966, only a few weeks after the sailing trip of the Slepaks and their friends, hundreds of young people gathered inside and outside the Moscow synagogue, milling about, singing, dancing, marching with the Torah scrolls, brazenly celebrating the holiday in the presence of the KGB and the militia, which had set up two huge floodlights and were photographing everyone who entered the synagogue. Also present were Elie Wiesel and a number of tourists, who then journeyed home and reported what they had seen.

The style of the KGB was first to watch and follow and then to pounce and arrest. Much of the time they did the watching openly; part of their style of terror was to let you know that you were being stalked. The Slepaks felt certain that there were no informers in their small circle of friends because no one was watching them.

Among the members of that circle were Victor and Noya Drapkin. He was an engineer; she, a biologist. They had a daughter, Vika. Victor Drapkin, who later changed his first name to David, was a tall, gray-eyed, balding man in his mid-forties, with a slightly hoarse voice and a limp from a childhood fall beneath a tram that had shorn off part of one foot, leaving him only his heel. He was a noisy, argumentative, excitable man, who despised Jewish assimilationists; from his lips the term *assimiliant* issued forth as an epithet. Noya, or Noemi, Drapkin—in many ways the opposite of her husband: dark-haired, dark-eyed, short, restrained—had been born in Riga, where she received a good Jewish education, the Baltic states having been acquired by the Soviet Union as recently as the Hitler-Stalin nonaggression pact of 1939 and not subjected to radical religious cleansing because they lay along the rim of the empire. She knew Hebrew, had experienced traditional Jewish life, and each year visited her relatives and friends in Riga, where there was a vigorous Jewish community. She had convinced her husband of the virtues of Zionism, and the two of them lost no opportunity to talk about Israel as they sat with their close friends around campfires.

Those friends, skilled engineers and scientists trained in the finest institutes in the Soviet Union, had talked during the early years of their friendship about what they thought were the real reasons Khrushchev had delivered his secret speech; about their samizdat reading; and, in later years, about the arrests and trial of Daniel and Sinyavsky; about rumors of Jews leaving from border cities of the Soviet Union to be reunited with their families in Israel. At first it was only a few Russians talking about a few other Russians, all the discourse plainly illegal. The sole reason for their interest in those outside events: curiosity. They had no wish to join any movements, not the least inclination to enter the perilous arena of party politics. In the beginning there were no activists among those friends; they were merely a few young inquisitive people who only wanted to talk.

Then, gradually over the years, inside the ambience of intimacy and safety they created for themselves, they began to widen the landscape of their curiosity, tentatively extending it at times to take in Israel, where, they understood, there were collective farms known as kibbutzim. How did the kibbutz compare with the Soviet Union's kolkhoz? the friends wondered. And they listened to the Voice of Israel, drawn from the air by the radios they carried into the forests and on summer journeys.

In the early years they had no feeling that they were anything other than Russians, no connectedness to Israelis. Only David and Noya Drapkin kept insisting that they were all part of one people. The others maintained that if they were Jews at all, they were Russian Jews and had nothing to do with Israel; but yes, wasn't it interesting what the Israelis were trying to build, their clearly thriving collective farms, their strong citizen army, their socialist government, their open society?

As the years went by, with no abatement of anti-Semitism, some among the friends ventured to wonder aloud from time to time if they were really part of the world of Russia. And soon others began to murmur to one another about the twilight land they inhabited. No real sense anymore of who they truly were: Russians, Jews, what?

It was clear by now that the chauvinistic Slavic groups would never accept them as part of the Russian people.

They said to one another, "Even if we tell them we're Russian, they tell us we're Jews." "Are we ever invited to any of their parties? And even if we were invited, would we go?" "Maybe during and right after the war, yes, we would have gone. Then there was the feeling we were all one country, one people. That was the only time I ever felt like a whole person and not one part of me Russian, another part of me Jewish. But then, after the arrest of the Jewish Anti-Fascist Committee, the shooting of the Yiddish writers, the 'Doctors' Plot,' the endless articles condemning Jews—no, we wouldn't go. The long history of anti-Semitism in this country has really turned us into a separate people."

A friend once wondered aloud, "What if there had been no anti-Semitism at all?"

Volodya said, "Then we would have joined the country as another nationality and vanished, and my father's dream would have come true."

Masha agreed. There had been many intermarriages during and right after the war, when it seemed the dream was becoming real. Now, fewer and fewer.

"Why haven't the Russians seen that?" someone murmured.

"Because they hate us too much," said Masha.

And one day, in 1965, she suddenly and clearly saw herself and her family emigrating to Israel, an idea she had only vaguely conjured up before. She mentioned it to Volodya, who thought her impulsive, a woman, a dreamer.

And sometime during the final weeks of the summers of 1965 and 1966, one of the friends said he was going to the Simchat Torah celebration in the Moscow synagogue and did Volodya want to come along, and Volodya said it was not a good idea, the KGB and militia would be there, too, and he didn't want to jeopardize his security clearance.

Only decades later did Volodya and Masha come to realize that their circle of friends was one of thousands like it in the Soviet Union, a society shriveled by terror and reduced to forming, by way of instinctive response, the smallest and safest communal units. Among those friendship circles were a minuscule number of the intelligentsia, which included a few of Russia's finest writers. It was the initial battles fought by the friendship circles that prepared the ground for the later Jewish struggle, which in turn, when it gained force, helped shore up the democratic human rights movement of the dissident Russians. Those early circles were microcosms of small turbulences that would one day link up and play a major role in bringing about the sudden, reverberating implosion of one of the mightiest empires in human history.

Each of those circles, from Siberia in the east to the Baltics in the west, was detonated into action by diverse events: the horrific tales told by prisoners released from labor camps; the secret speech of Khrushchev in 1956; the show trial of Daniel and Sinyavsky in 1966; the Trial of the Four and the Soviet tanks that crushed the Prague Spring in Czechoslovakia in 1968; the constant arrests, trials, physical violence, internal exile to provincial towns, sudden loss of jobs or expulsion from institutes, long sentences in the labor camps—indeed, the near-crushing of the dissident movement in the 1970s and early 1980s—that marked the re-Stalinization policies of Brezhnev and his successors, Yuri Andropov and Konstantin Chernenko, ailing men dedicated to the entrenched old order. But each repressive effort by the regime ignited additional fires among the dissidents. No one seemed aware of it then, but inexorable events had been set in motion, eerily reminiscent of those that, starting around the turn of the century, had climaxed in 1917 with the overthrow of the tsar.

For Jewish circles like those of the Slepaks and their friends, the quickening moment was the 1967 Six-Day War in the Middle East.

As the summer of 1967 approached, conflict in the Middle East appeared inevitable. Egypt had blockaded the Strait of Tiran; the United Nations, yielding to the demands of the Egyptians, had withdrawn its buffer troops from the Sinai Peninsula; Arab nations were calling for a holy war against Israel. It set the air shivering, the likelihood of another Holocaust befalling a large segment of the Jewish people as the world stood by, watching. But Israel was not the Warsaw Ghetto, and the Israelis, taking a page from Clausewitz's classic work on war, struck first. Soviet foreign policy now favored the Arab cause, and the Soviet media condemned the preemptive strikes of the Israeli armed forces, told repeatedly of Arab victories, and then fell abruptly silent. Volodya and Masha and their friends tried to pick up the overseas voices on their radios and were able to catch the speech of Soviet Ambassador Fedorenko in the United Nations, a spewing forth of venomous hate against Israel and Moshe Dayan. Suddenly all the Soviet media erupted with invective toward Israel and Jews as, after the few days of fighting, the full dimensions of the Israeli victory began to become apparent. On June 15 *Izvestia* announced that the Israelis were killing prisoners of war and executing women and children. Magazines and newspapers compared the Israelis to the Nazis. At factory meetings, workers passed unanimous resolutions condemning the "aggression" of Israel. The very air throbbed with official hysteria directed against Jews, who were accused of being Nazi collaborators, a genocidal people. Public celebration of the Israeli victory was, of course, out of the question; a number of private celebrations by Jewish students resulted in police harassment, searches, arrests.

There now occurred inside the circle of seven families of which the Slepaks were a part a sudden electrifying collective and exhilarating awareness of power over their enemies, of life-enhancing alternatives to the degradations of Soviet life, of a triumphant goal to be fought for: emigration. For some members of the group, those thoughts still lay far below consciousness; for others, they were full-blown but remained for the time being unspoken. For all, the possibility of emigration became a permanent condition of their lives. Unlike the Russian democratic dissidents, who sought to remain and reform the system, these Jewish dissidents, and the movement they were soon to be part of, abandoned all hope for themselves within the system, cut the cord of destiny that had until then bound them to Russia, and now, with a slowly growing sense of belonging to the Jewish people, began to cast about for ways to leave the Soviet Union.

Diplomatic relations between Israel and the Soviet Union came to an end that June. The Israeli Embassy in Moscow was directed to close down. A few days later, on June 13, a twenty-one-year-old man named Yasha Kazakov—he had been raised in an assimilated home, subjected to some anti-Semitism, and had begun on his own to read books on Jewish history—suddenly decided that if the Soviet Union was breaking off relations with the state of Israel, he would break off relations with the Soviet Union. He sent a letter from his parents' apartment in Moscow to the Supreme Soviet renouncing his citizenship and demanding what he claimed was his right to emigrate to Israel. The letter went unanswered. He then wrote to U Thant, secretary-general of the United Nations, hand-delivered the letter to the American Embassy, and was then arrested by the KGB, and interrogated at length. "You will never receive an exit visa," he was told upon his release. "You were born in Russia, and you will die in Russia." He continued to write letters demanding that he be allowed to leave the country, and in early 1969 he received permission to emigrate to Israel. Yasha Kazakov was the first Jew in the post-Stalin era to challenge personally and openly the Soviet regime and succeed.

Around the same time another Jew, Boris Kochubievsky from Kiev, who had applied to leave the Soviet Union in 1967, was refused. He applied again, was arrested, placed on trial in May 1969, and given three years in a labor camp. The Soviet pattern of arbitrary and capricious handling of visa applicants had been set, a roulette wheel of justice. It was to characterize the twenty-year period of the visa war.

In July 1967, following the Six-Day War, the Slepaks and their older son, Sanya, spent two weeks on the shore of Lake Tzesarka near the

Lithuanian city of Vilna. Together with them were David and Noya Drapkin and their daughter, Vika; Victor and Lena Polsky and their daughter, Marina; Volodya and Lyalya Prestin and their son, Minya. They had one motorcycle, one car, the boat *Dolphin*, and a kayak. Each couple shared a tent. There was one tent for the two girls, and one for the two boys. They sat around campfires every night listening to overseas radio broadcasts and talking about the Six-Day War. The sons and daughters understood that what was said around those campfires and inside their apartments was never to be repeated to anyone anywhere.

After the two weeks of sailing and camping, the Drapkins and Prestins returned to Moscow, and the Slepaks and Polskys drove to Vilna and Kovno, where they visited the ghetto areas of the Nazi occupation and the site where several thousand Jews from Kovno had been murdered. They motored through Latvia, Estonia, and northwest Russia, talking often of the recent war in the Middle East and listening to the radio.

Over the shortwave radio in the course of the next year came the shocking news from the United States of the assassination of Martin Luther King, Jr., in April 1968; of riots in the streets of Washington, Chicago, Detroit, Boston; of troops guarding the American capital. First, President Kennedy; now, Dr. King. And in June, exactly one year after the onset of the Six-Day War, came the news of the assassination, in Los Angeles, of Senator Robert Kennedy by a twenty-four-year-old Christian Arab who had been born in Jordanian Jerusalem. Volodya and Masha and their friends wondered about the nature of American society, its stability, its violence, its future.

That summer the Slepaks and their friends vacationed on a large island in the Dnieper River about one hundred miles southeast of Kiev. The island was unpopulated; the nearest habitation was the village of Prokhorivka across the river. Once again they talked among themselves, without inhibitions. Around the campfire they listened to news over the shortwave radio: Volodya, Masha, and Sanya Slepak; Leonid and Fanya Lipkovsky; Mara Abramovich; Volodya and Lyalya Prestin and their son, Minya; David, Noya, and Vika Drapkin; Victor and Lena Polsky and their daughter, Marina. They had with them the sailboat *Dolphin*. In a camp about three hundred feet away was another circle of friends, dissidents who had no wish to leave the Soviet Union; the excitable David Drapkin referred to them scornfully as *assimiliants*. The two camps sat together around the campfire, listening to unfriendly voices over the radio, talking quietly, singing to the strains of Leonid Lipkovsky's guitar.

From those unfriendly voices they learned, in the third week of August, that the Soviet Union and four of its Warsaw Pact allies had invaded Czechoslovakia. Communist tanks and troops had quickly and with little bloodshed shut off the hum of democratic possibilities emanating from that sovereign socialist country: an end to censorship; a candid critique of Soviet-style communism; a liberal socialism.

The small circle of friends was enraged, sobered, frightened by that news, and confirmed in their conviction that they should leave their country. Surely the death of liberal Czechoslovakia meant the end of liberal hopes in the heart of the Soviet Union as well.

Volodya and Masha and their friends returned to Moscow some days after the invasion.

On August 25 seven men and women staged a demonstration in Red Square, raising banners that read LONG LIVE FREE AND INDEPENDENT CZECHOSLOVAKIA and TO YOUR FREEDOM AND OURS. They were arrested by the KGB.

Volodya did not attend the Simchat Torah celebration in the Moscow synagogue that fall of 1968. Again, the reason he gave was concern over his security clearance.

In the course of a press conference in Paris on December 3, 1966, Premier Alexei Kosygin had remarked that "as far as the reunification of families is concerned, if some families wish to meet or if they wish to leave the Soviet Union, the road is open to them. . . ."

There is a spring 1967 photograph of Jews on a crowded platform in the rail station in Riga, men and women in their thirties and forties, with some children, starting out on the first leg of their journey to Israel. Jews were being let out, about one thousand people every year, from the southern and western Ukraine, the Baltic states, Hungary.

One day in the fall of 1968—around the time when Richard Nixon was elected president of the United States—the Drapkins informed the Slepaks and their circle of friends that a group of Jews from Riga had been granted exit visas and would soon be leaving for Israel from Moscow. Did the Moscow circle want to meet some of the people from the Riga circle when they arrived in Moscow to pick up their visas? That was how it was done: You went to Moscow from Riga, visited the Dutch Embassy for your Israel visa and the Austrian Embassy for your transit visa, had all the required documents photographed, returned to your city to collect your family, traveled back by train to Moscow with the family, then boarded a flight to Vienna. Yes, the Moscow circle did indeed want to meet with some of the people from the Riga circle.

The meeting occurred on December 25, 1968, in the Moscow apartment of the Drapkins. Over the past months the Drapkins had introduced the group to a number of former prisoners who had been in labor camps for Zionist activities. One had served a sentence of six years. The circle had listened to accounts of the camps and to plans for the reorganization of Zionist groups. Other visitors had told of meetings that were dealing with the possible beginnings of a nationwide movement of Soviet Jews and the start of a Jewish samizdat press. David Drapkin and his wife had already decided that they and their daughter would one day emigrate from the Soviet Union. In the meantime, to sever himself entirely from assimilation, he had stopped eating Russian food and reading Russian authors.

Now, in the Drapkins' apartment, the circle talked with six people from Riga, among them a man named Mark Blum, in his late twenties, who was not returning to Riga because he was unmarried and had no family there. Instead he was to leave for Israel shortly via Vienna. Did anyone in the group wish to give him the personal data needed by the Israelis in order for them to send the official invitations that were necessary for Soviet visa applications? Names, addresses, children, dates of birth, names of parents, relatives in Israel. He would give the information to the Israelis, who would then search for the relatives. In cases of the total absence of relatives, the Israeli authorities would look into the possibility of other arrangements.

Members of the group began to write down the information.

Volodya and Masha sat looking at each other. It was late evening. The curtains were drawn against the winter gloom outside. Masha got to her feet and took Volodya's hand, and they moved to a dark corner near a window and a desk and stood with their backs to the others.

Masha said quietly, "This is a special opportunity. Who knows when it might happen again? Are you ready to do it?"

Volodya, lost in fearful hesitation, did not respond.

Fighting back her apprehension about the consequences of their act upon their children, Masha said, "We must use this opportunity."

And Volodya, after a brief silence, said, "Let's do it," and felt they had suddenly fallen into deep and icy waters.

The family chronicles record Masha's uncertainty about what she might have done had Volodya refused. Made a further effort to persuade him, she maintains. There is a vague hint of divorce, but sober reality put that out of mind: Under Soviet law, she might have gained her visa to Israel and lost her young children to Volodya.

That evening Volodya and Masha transmitted to Mark Blum the necessary data on their family. That was the day, December 25, 1968, when three American astronauts flew around the moon, seventy miles above its forbidding surface, and one of them recited, for all the world to hear, the opening verses in the Book of Genesis: "In the beginning God created the heaven and the earth. . . ."

The Slepaks had informed their older son, Sanya, then sixteen, that they intended to emigrate; but the younger son, Leonya, nine years old, knew nothing, and they would have to talk with him. Masha's mother knew; she had given them her blessing, said she wanted to leave with them; indeed there was a remote possibility that she had cousins in Israel. Volodya's father was unaware of his son's and daughter-in-law's intentions; he, too, would have to be told. But not immediately. First, they wanted to see what would come of the information they had given Mark Blum—who, in Israel, changed his name to Mordechai Lapid, became very devout, and in 1993 was killed by an Arab terrorist.

Now they waited. And lived their lives on the surface as if that evening meeting had never taken place. No one shadowed them; all appeared normal in the apartment building and in the workplace. But they had moved out of the ranks of the people and were now disloyal citizens, indeed would have been regarded as near criminals in the eyes of their Russian colleagues and coworkers had their plans become known.

During the time of their waiting, the dissident movement began to grow. Individuals of extraordinary stature, honored by the Soviet government and central to Soviet life, citizens of high privilege and national pride, such as the celebrated physicist Andrei Sakharov and the noted scholar Roy Medvedev, moved into the ranks of the human rights movement. Their works entered the illicit world of samizdat publications: Sakharov's *Progress, Coexistence, and Intellectual Freedom*, a critique of the Soviet Union's social structure; Medvedev's *Let History Judge*, an exhaustive and chilling study of the Stalinist era.

The samizdat journal *Khronika* was established in April 1968 by the poet and editor Natalya Gorbanevskaya: a bulletin containing only basic information, without commentary; one copy typed with several carbons, the copies handed to others for retyping, the tissue-thin sheets stapled together and passed from hand to hand. No one seems to know how many that journal reached. Volodya and Masha were among those who read it. Reports of secret trials and the persecution of Lithuanian and Ukrainian Catholics, Seventh-Day Adventists, Buddhists, Jehovah's

Witnesses; stories of prisoners in psychiatric hospitals, of hunger strikes, protest letters, sudden loss of jobs, searches of apartments, arrests, visa requests, prison camps. One knew nothing of the fetid corners of the Soviet house from the official media; those stories were to be found only in publications like *Khronika* and, later, in others, including the clandestine Jewish publications that began to appear in the 1970s.

Early in 1969, soon after Mark Blum had left for Israel with the information the Slepaks and their friends had given him, Volodya asked his father to come to the apartment for a visit. Solomon Slepak was then seventy-six years old, silver-haired, stocky, a rugged, robust-looking man, with smooth pink features and clear brown eyes that effectively concealed the difficulties he was having with his heart.

The three of them, Masha, Volodya, and Solomon, sat in the large room of the apartment. Solomon looked uncomfortable and kept glancing at his wristwatch.

Volodya told him in a quiet voice that they had decided to apply for an exit visa to Israel.

Solomon Slepak stared at his son.

Volodya said they had asked for an official invitation from Israel, and as soon as it arrived, they would send in their visa application.

Solomon jumped to his feet. "You are crazy!"

"We've made our decision," said Volodya.

"You are enemies of the people!"

Masha sat silent, observing the tempest of father and son.

"Israel!" Solomon Slepak said with contempt. "I could understand if you had decided to go to America or Canada for a better life. I was in both countries, I know how people live there. But to go to Israel, to a fascist state!"

Volodya said, "We've made our decision."

"I lived among Jews. I know what it is like."

"We won't change our minds."

"I warn you," Solomon raged, "we'll be on opposite sides of the barricades!"

"We are going," said Volodya.

"I am telling you now, I will do everything in my power to stop you!" shouted Solomon, and stormed out of the apartment, slamming the door.

Volodya remembers the reverberating air in the suddenly silent room and the fury and dread he felt as he wondered how much influence his father still had in the post-Stalin Communist Party.

The official invitation from Israel arrived in the mail in March 1969. It consisted of two sheets of paper fastened together. The first, directed to the Soviet authorities, was from the woman who claimed to be a Slepak "relative"; the Slepaks, official inquiry had revealed, were without true relatives in Israel. It stated the names, addresses, and dates of birth of the Soviet citizens who were her "relatives," the precise nature of the "family relationship," and an assurance of providing for them. The second sheet of paper was a statement from the Foreign Ministry of Israel, certifying the signature of the inviting "relative," joining in her request, and guaranteeing that those invited would be given citizenship after their arrival.

The invitation was the core element in the tortuous visa application process they were about to undertake: the key to the exit door of the Soviet Union and the entrance door to Israel. Looking at it closely, Volodya saw that his and Masha's names were replete with egregious spelling errors that could not be corrected. He was dismayed. They would now have to wait for a second invitation.

Volodya knew that all letters from abroad, before being delivered, were opened and read by the authorities. It was only a matter of days until the KGB informed the head of the institute that engineer Slepak was planning to emigrate. He would be fired immediately. He now needed to find someone else who was emigrating to Israel. More months would pass before the second invitation arrived. To apply for the visa, he needed *kharakteristika*, references from his place of work. He would have to tell people with whom he had worked for years that the references were to be directed to OVIR, the Department of Visas and Permissions, for an emigration visa. How mortifying it would be to have to ask for *kharakteristika* from his current place of work after being fired because of the KGB report. The institute chiefs would subject him to a barrage of meetings filled with derisive talk, humiliating questions, degrading accusations.

He decided to leave his work at the institute, find a simpler job, and ask for *kharakteristika* from there.

A day or so after he had received the invitation from Israel, he handed the deputy director of the institute a statement to the effect that he wished to leave his job and, according to the rights granted him by law, would no longer come to work after two weeks.

The astonished deputy director asked, "Why?"

Volodya said he had found a new job.

The deputy director asked, "What job? Where?"

Volodya said he preferred to keep that information to himself.

The deputy director asked, "Would you stay if you were made head of the department and given a higher salary?" The head of a department was normally in charge of three to five laboratories.

Volodya said, "No."

Two weeks later he gave up his job.

He asked his friends to find him a new job, and after a short while obtained work in one of the offices of the Trust Geophysica, which was involved in oil prospecting and was mapping the strata of the earth's crust in certain regions of the Soviet Union. Small explosive charges would be set off at a depth of five to eight feet. Located around the charges at distances of two or three miles were devices that would record onto magnetic tapes the oscillating waves that rolled through the earth. By comparing the frequencies of those waves, one could obtain a picture of the earth's crust in the area of the charges. Such comparisons could be made only by a computer, but the signals on the tapes were in analog form, which a computer could not read. Volodya's job was to design an electronic instrument that could transform analog signals into digital ones, which computers could read and analyze.

The office of the Trust Geophysica was near the Povarovka Railway Station on the Moscow–Leningrad railway, a half hour train ride from the Leningradsky Railway Station. The work paid considerably less than what he had been earning at the institute.

About six months later, while walking along a street in Moscow, Volodya met one of his former colleagues from the institute and was told that one month after he had left the job, there had been a meeting in the institute of all the party members and heads of departments and laboratories. The sole topic of the meeting was Volodya Slepak and his plans to emigrate to Israel. In the course of a furious speech against Volodya, the party secretary had said, "How blind we were not to see that among us was a traitor, an enemy of the people!"

Masha retained her job as a radiologist because her chief received no instructions to dismiss her. He was an upright man and would not fire her on his own even though he knew that she intended to emigrate. Besides, there was a dire need in Moscow for radiologists.

David and Noya Drapkin submitted the necessary documents to OVIR, requesting permission to emigrate. In April 1969, about the time that Volodya gave up his job at the institute, David Drapkin received a call from OVIR and was told that his request had been refused.

"There are too many of you Jews," the OVIR official said over the telephone. "We will not let you leave; we will finish you off here."

Volodya's new job at the Trust Geophysica began in June. Because he had no vacation coming to him, he and Masha and Sanya remained in Moscow that summer. The weather was hot; the air dusty, brown. Some weekends the Slepaks went with friends into the forests. And listened to the news over the radio. That was the summer two American astronauts walked on the moon. In Moscow the political atmosphere was portentous with neo-Stalinist resonances after a year of increasing repression and the surprise overpowering of Czechoslovakia the previous summer. Leonid Slepak, then ten years old, spent his vacation in a Young Pioneers camp.

A man from Leningrad, Sasha Blank, an old friend of the Slepaks', emigrated to Israel that August, carrying with him the data for a second invitation. Many were being refused visas at that time because according to the OVIR officials, those sending the invitations were not "close" relatives; hence Masha's mother had asked Sasha Blank to find an Israeli woman about fifty years of age, who was to claim in the invitation that she was her daughter. Masha's mother had contrived a lengthy story to tell the emigration officials about how during the Civil War she had suddenly fallen ill with typhus and fainted on a train; after having been removed from the car, she woke in a station to find her daughter gone. The amulet the daughter had worn around her neck all through the years had finally led to her mother.

The same August that Sasha Blank left for Israel carrying with him Volodya and Masha's data and the story of Masha's mother's "daughter," eighteen Jewish families from the Soviet region of Georgia took the astonishing step of sending a petition directly to Prime Minister of Israel Golda Meir, with the request that it be forwarded to U Thant. The petition solicited his backing for their constantly thwarted attempts to emigrate to Israel. "It is incomprehensible that in the twentieth century people can be prohibited from living where they wish to live," read the petition. "We will wait months and years, we will wait all our lives, if necessary, but we will not renounce our faith or our hopes."

The petition, which seemed to signal the start of a mass movement, was read to the Israeli Knesset and presented by the government of Israel to the United Nations as an official document. News of the petition filtered into the major cities of the Soviet Union: Moscow, Leningrad, Minsk, Riga, Vilna, Odessa, Kiev. More petitions and letters followed, from individuals and groups, addressed to the United Nations, to Soviet Premier Kosygin, to the Soviet Ministry of Foreign Affairs, to President Zalman Shazar of Israel. For years we have suffered humiliation, the letters and petitions said; we have the right to request a new home in a land of our choice.

Volodya and Masha, barely aware of those letters, had no notion that they were becoming part of an expanding horizon of opposition to tyranny. But with his job at the institute now lost, Volodya knew that he no longer needed to be concerned about his security clearance. And so that fall, for the first time in their lives, he and Masha and their sons walked from the apartment on Gorky Street to the Moscow synagogue on Arkhipova Street, where they became part of a multitude of Jews celebrating Simchat Torah.

They would not enter the synagogue, avoided contact with the rabbi and state-hired officials of the Jewish community, all of whom, they had been told, were under the control of the KGB. One of their friends, David Chavkin, had brought along a self-made amplifier with two powerful speakers, a tape recorder, and cassettes. Jewish music resounded through the street. Volodya and Masha were caught up in the tumult and enthusiasm of the huge crowd, thousands of people. Militia stood along the rim of the crowd, and everyone there knew that KGB agents in civilian garb were among the crowd—some may even have been participating in the singing and dancing—but no one seemed to care. The celebration lasted until midnight.

The Slepaks went often to that synagogue from then on, on Sabbaths and festivals. They never entered but stood on the street with friends and other dissidents, watching the crowds grow from year to year.

In late 1969 dissidents from Moscow, Leningrad, and Riga met and decided it was now time to initiate collective letters of protest to the authorities and make them public. That was the first clear move toward organized open confrontation with the regime. In early 1970 Jewish dissidents in Riga issued the Jewish samizdat bulletins *Iton Aleph* ("Newspaper A"), and *Iton Bet* ("Newspaper B"), a few copies on poor paper in Russian, the first independent public voice of the embryonic movement: an interview with Golda Meir; an article about the Israeli Army; a passage from a book about the 1943 uprising of the Jews in the Warsaw Ghetto against the Nazis; the texts of letters to government officials by Soviet Jews voicing their right to emigrate; the words of Israel's Declaration of Independence.

The second invitation to Israel arrived in the Slepak mailbox on a day in January 1970—from a different "relative." This time the names were correctly spelled. Volodya and Masha went to the OVIR office for the necessary application forms and to learn from instructions posted on the walls how to complete the forms and what accompanying documents they were required to submit.

It took them nearly three months to assemble all the necessary documents. The application form alone was six pages in length. It asked for your name, address, date and place of birth, place or places of work for the past five years, were you a member of the Communist Party or Komsomol, had you ever lost your membership and why, your nationality, names of your closest relatives, had you ever been abroad, where when why, who among your relatives had been abroad with you, had you ever before applied to leave the USSR, when, were you refused, why, who in your family was now applying with you, what country did you intend to enter, who in that country was your relative, why and from where did the relative leave the USSR, list all your communications with that relative, when did you receive the most recent communication, how did you discover where that relative was living, explain why you wanted to emigrate from the Soviet Union.

Together with the application, you needed to submit to OVIR: your autobiography; the invitation from the relative in Israel, certified by the Foreign Ministry of Israel; the *kharakteristika* from your job, stating that it was addressed to OVIR specifically for a visa application and signed by the director of your place of employment, the party secretary, and the chairman of the trade union committee; a certificate, also specifically directed to OVIR, from the office running your apartment building regarding your status as a resident of Moscow and the condition of your domicile; a signed statement from your parents, if alive, about how they looked upon your desire to leave the country and whether they had any financial or other claims upon you, with their signatures certified either at their places of work or by the office of their apartment building; certificates of birth and, wherever applicable, of marriage, divorce, parents' death; copies of diplomas; four photographs; two blank postcards with your home address; receipt from the bank certifying your payment of the special tax for the exit visa application; internal passport, military record, trade union card, work book, pension card.

Sometime in March 1970 Volodya telephoned his father and asked if he would write and sign a statement about how he felt concerning his son's wish to leave the country. He explained that he needed the statement to complete his visa application documents.

"I will never write or sign such a statement!" shouted his father. "Do not call me again! I will have nothing to do with an enemy of the people!" And he hung up the telephone.

After repeated failed attempts to obtain the statement, Volodya decided to include with the documents an affidavit written and signed by him and certified by a notary to the effect that his father had refused to take part in the visa application process.

That same month Volodya requested from his chiefs at the Trust Geophysica the *kharakteristika* he needed for OVIR. They agreed, on condition that he resign from his position. It was three months before he found another job.

By the time Masha and Volodya completed gathering all the documents, everyone at Masha's place of work and in their apartment house knew that they were applying to emigrate from the country.

On April 13, 1970, Volodya and Masha boarded a dark blue city minibus on Alexander Pushkin Square, one block from their apartment, rode to Pokrovskiye Vorota, and then walked a block and a half to the OVIR office on Kolpachny Pereulok, where they submitted their visa application for emigration to Israel.

An official from the Ministry of the Interior checked the documents attached to the application form for proper stamps, signatures, and answers. Pausing over Volodya's statement regarding his father's refusal, the official insisted on the need for a statement from his father.

Volodya said it was impossible. His father was an Old Bolshevik; he would never write and sign such a statement. Why wasn't Volodya's own statement to that effect sufficient?

After a moment the official yielded. Gathering up the application form and the documents, he said tersely, "You will be informed about the decision."

Volodya and Masha went out of the OVIR office and rode the minibus back to the apartment. Volodya was forty-three years old, Masha forty-four.

Their sons, Sanya and Leonid, seventeen and ten, knew that their family was applying to emigrate to Israel. They continued to attend school without incident. No one seemed aware of their family's plans.

One day two KGB officers appeared at the school and told the principal, Gregory Suvorov, that the family of one of his students, Leonid Slepak, was applying for a visa to Israel. The KGB was requesting, said the agents, that the principal and all the teachers in the school organize themselves into a pressure group to persuade the student, Leonid Slepak, to change his mind about going to Israel and to incite him against his parents.

Gregory Suvorov was a Russian, a teacher of history, and a member of the party. All in the school held him in high esteem; many loved him. Politely he informed the KGB agents that they had their business and he had his; he was responsible for everything that took place in the school and would not allow any interference with his work. He then asked them to leave the premises. Soon afterward he met with the teachers and told them that they were not to say anything about the status of Leonid Slepak; they were to make him feel warm and welcome.

No further incidents occurred in the school over the Slepak family's emigration plans.

Weeks went by. The Slepaks heard nothing from OVIR. On a day in June, after having waited about two months, Volodya telephoned the OVIR office.

The official who answered said, "Your name is Slepak?"

"Yes."

"We have just received the decision of the commission." He said nothing about the nature of the commission or who had served on it. "Your request for a visa has been refused."

"What is the reason?" asked Volodya.

"Secrecy," the official said. "According to regulations, you have the right to reapply after five years; then your case will be reviewed." And he hung up.

In the single word "secrecy" Volodya read the true and complete response of the Soviet authorities. His years of scientific work on the air-defense system of the Soviet Union had given him access to vital state secrets. He was a major security risk, and quite probably would never be permitted to leave the country.

The Visa War

On the afternoon of June 15, 1970, some days after the telephone conversation with OVIR in which Volodya was informed that his exit visa application had been refused, he and Masha were alone in the apartment when they heard the doorbell ring. Masha went to the door, while Volodya remained in the smaller of their two rooms. He heard the door being opened and called out, "Who is there?"

Masha returned to the room. "They came to make a search."

From somewhere outside, a man said, "Please come here!"

Volodya followed Masha out of the room. In the hall near the entrance door stood five men in civilian clothes and one in a militia uniform. One of the men in civilian clothes said in a soft voice, "I am Major Nosov of the KGB." He had on a dark gray suit, a white shirt, and a tie. Under his jacket he wore a pistol. "I have a warrant to search your apartment," he said.

"In connection with what case?" asked Volodya.

"The case of Yuri Fedorov," said Major Nosov. He was very polite.

"What is he accused of?"

"Anti-Soviet activity," said Major Nosov. He pointed to the man in uniform. "This is a representative of the militia. These two are witnesses, and these two are my aides. So, if you please, give us voluntarily all the anti-Soviet material that you have in your possession. Otherwise we will begin to search."

Volodya said, "I don't know Fedorov. I know nothing about his anti-Soviet activity, and I have no anti-Soviet material."

The men proceeded to search the apartment. They went about the search slowly and with great care. Major Nosov read English fluently. He began to look through the English-language books, listing their titles in English, which he then translated into Russian. He came upon shelves that held lawbooks, hundreds of lawbooks.

"You're an engineer, why these books?" he asked.

"I'm interested in Soviet law," said Volodya.

Sanya Slepak, eighteen years old, watched the search in fascination, imagining himself inside a movie, remembering films he had seen about tsarist police ransacking the living quarters of courageous Bolsheviks. At one point he said he needed to go to the bathroom, and one of the men in civilian clothes accompanied him to the small water closet. Sanya remained awake throughout the eighteen-hour search, witnessing the gradual confiscation of much of his father's library. His younger brother, Leonid, eleven, went to sleep.

The men riffled the pages of every book, turned over every sheet of paper. Books and journals printed in a foreign language were impounded, together with personal letters and notebooks. Also seized were tape recorders, tape cassettes, the shortwave radio, even a broken typewriter once owned by Solomon Slepak. Those devices might be used to spread anti-Soviet propaganda, explained Major Nosov politely.

In the course of the search, two friends of the Slepaks, Norman Sirkin and Mark Elbaum, appeared in the doorway of the apartment on a visit and were ordered by Major Nosov to remain until the search was completed. The KGB did not want them informing anyone that a search was in progress because that would attract people to the apartment house. Especially to be avoided was the annoying presence of the foreign press. At about two in the morning Volodya fell asleep in an armchair. His noisy snores brought from an astounded Major Nosov the comment "I have never had anyone fall asleep during a search. Sometimes they jump out the window or hang themselves in the toilet by their tie." Norman Sirkin later told Volodya that he said to Major Nosov, "Only a person with a clear conscience can sleep in a situation like this."

The search came to an end at six o'clock in the morning. Major Nosov presented Volodya with a list of the items the KGB was about to remove from the apartment and requested that he sign it. Volodya refused. He said the search was against Soviet law and the confiscated objects had no connection to anything illegal. Without further ado, Major Nosov folded the list and slid it into an inside pocket of his jacket. The men left, carrying with them four large sacks of the Slepaks' possessions. Nothing they took was ever returned.

The chronicles record Volodya's odd comment that books confiscated by the KGB often ended up in prison camps. Some of the most politically unreliable books in the hands of some of the most intractable political prisoners! And books that might help one learn a foreign language. And take one on a journey into forbidden lands. Asked what kind of logic there was to that, Volodya responded, "If you want logic, you have to go someplace else."

Ten days earlier, on June 5, Volodya and seventy-four others had signed a letter to Secretary-General of the United Nations U Thant, who was soon to visit Moscow. The letter, which has come to be known as the Letter of the 75, was read on overseas radio stations and appeared in newspapers around the world. It was an appeal to U Thant that he intercede with the Soviet government for the right of the signers to emigrate to Israel.

Volodya did not know Yuri Fedorov, the man named by Major Nosov as the reason for the apartment search, and was unaware that he had been arrested in Leningrad in the morning of that same day on the charge of having hijacked an aircraft for the purpose of fleeing from the Soviet Union. Also searched that day were the apartments of others who had signed the letter to U Thant.

In Leningrad, as Volodya later discovered, nine Jews and three non-Jews had been arrested at eight-thirty that morning while walking to an aircraft about to depart on a scheduled flight. They were a group of men and women who had been repeatedly refused exit visas. Made desperate by loss of hope, they were caught up in the possibility set before them by one of their number, Major Mark Dymshitz, who had been a pilot in the Soviet Air Force: They would hijack an aircraft, and he would fly them to Sweden. There is the clear possibility that someone in the group was a KGB agent, for the hijacking never occurred; they were arrested before they got to the aircraft. Nevertheless, the charge brought against them was hijacking, and hijacking—as well as betrayal of the Motherland, which is an act of treason, and anti-Soviet agitation and complicity in an anti-Soviet group and preparation of a crime—was what most of those involved were tried for that December in Leningrad's City Court, found guilty, and sentenced.

The prosecution had demanded the death penalty for two members of the group, Mark Dymshitz and Eduard Kuznetsov, and five to fifteen years for the others. And on December 24 those were the verdicts handed down by the court. A worldwide wave of protests and demonstrations followed: appeals from religious and political leaders; from Communist parties in the West; from the Soviet Human Rights Committee, established by Andrei Sakharov and others without official sanction in November 1970. The Kremlin found itself in the uneasy position of having to explain its actions to a court of world opinion that was constantly being fed information on events heretofore kept sealed inside Soviet borders. True, the authorities had control of the press and radio, but the dissenters circulated samizdat publications, slipped vital information to Western journalists, sent crucial documents abroad in the luggage of sympathetic tourists. Another regular source of inside news for Western journalists was Andrei Sakharov. Adding to the embarrassment of the government was the coincidence of the trial of Basque nationalists taking place in Spain at that same time, a trial repeatedly denounced by the Soviets; the Basques received death sentences, which Franco then commuted. And so, finding it necessary to respond to the protests, the Kremlin appealed the verdict to the Soviet Supreme Court, which, on December 29, commuted the death sentences to fifteen years and ordered that a number of the other sentences be reduced.

Clearly, the regime was using the hijacking as a pretext for a major effort to crush the entire Jewish dissident movement. From the time of the arrest of the so-called hijackers in June to their trial in December, dozens of activists were arrested and jailed—in Leningrad, Moscow, Kishinev, Riga. More trials took place: May 1971 in Leningrad; May 1971 in Riga; June 1971 in Kishinev. The government linked all those tried to the Leningrad hijacking. Alarm, disarray, and depletion in numbers occurred among the ranks of Jewish activist leaders. It was a while before new people joined the dissident movement, most especially in Leningrad.

To this day it is not entirely clear whether the hijack attempt was instigated by KGB provocateurs. It is conjectured that at the highest levels of Soviet policy-making, a decision was reached, in the spring of 1970, that Jewish dissidence had become too widespread and worrisome and needed to be put down. The hijack scheme was either a KGB operation or a convenient moment seized by the Kremlin for its own purposes. Much as Stalin used the murder of Kirov as a springboard to eliminate his opposition, so the Kremlin now used the hijack attempt to bear down relentlessly upon Jewish dissidents.

Volodya and Masha Slepak were aware of the trials—through word of mouth and samizdat publications. They were aware, too, that in the wake of the trials there had been a sudden upsurge in immigration requests, the reverse of what the Kremlin had expected. Some of their friends soon received exit visas. There is a photograph of Volodya standing amid a group gathered in the airport in Moscow to bid good-bye to a departing dissident. About twenty people, all posing, many smiling. In the front row is Anatoly Shcharansky, the Jewish dissident who would one day be accused of spying for the CIA. Volodya and Masha attended many such farewell gatherings.

Volodya had lost his job at the Trust Geophysica, whose management had agreed to give him his *kharakteristika* on condition that he leave. For three months he looked for work. Friends found him a job in the Institute of Organic Chemistry of the Academy of Sciences. The head of the department, a decent man, knew that Volodya had applied for an exit visa but said nothing about it to his superiors.

Volodya worked with electronic equipment for measuring nuclear magnetic resonance; the institute was researching the structure of organic molecules. As head of a laboratory in the Moscow TV Research and Development Institute, he had earned 250 rubles a month; at the Geophysica, 140 rubles; now at the Institute of Organic Chemistry, 160 rubles. One day KGB agents showed up at the institute and inquired into Volodya's behavior. His situation became known throughout the institute. The head of the department asked Volodya to leave; his own job was at risk, he said. The institute heads did not want a person of Volodya's dubious political status on their staff.

That was in September 1971. Volodya then found a job sharpening pens for a little workshop. During the mornings he would visit design offices in the area of the workshop, places where technical drawings of one kind or another were made. He collected draftsmen's pens that had been blunted by use and brought them to his apartment, where he sharpened them. The next day he returned the sharpened pens and again picked up blunted ones. He would show up at the office of the workshop, on Prospekt Mira, to drop off his receipts and collect his salary, about 130 rubles a month. Then KGB agents began to appear at the workshop almost every other day, inquiring of the manager about Volodya's behavior, how many hours a day he worked, where he was at any given moment. Finally, in September 1972, harassed beyond endurance, the manager asked Volodya to leave. That was Volodya's last official employment in the Soviet Union, the final job recorded in his government work book until his arrest and trial in 1978.

Masha retired from her work as a hospital radiologist in December 1971. Her pension was seventy-six rubles a month. From the end of 1972 on, she and Volodya lived largely on the kindness of others: money from a special fund organized by refuseniks, the name soon given to the Jewish dissidents whose visa applications were being repeatedly refused; visitors from abroad who left behind clothes and things that she and Volodya could sell through secondhand shops.

Volodya experienced a slow sinking into an abyss of ever more shabby jobs—elevator operator, hospital orderly; he had to work at something in order to avoid the serious charge of parasitism—and a growing sense of worthlessness. For the Soviet Union's highly educated dissident scientists, self-worth was measured by achievement. Now Volodya faced psychological torment as a result of the barriers that blocked his work, accomplishment, progress, recognition—all the things that made his life meaningful.

The suffering was caused not only by the status of pariah in which he and Masha were living but also by a bitter awareness that what was happening to them was touched with an outrageous illogic over which they had no control. In the matter of visas to Israel there were no clear and consistent guidelines from above; hence local officials felt themselves able to mete out capricious decisions from below. It was all so arbitrary, so pitiless. "You'll never get out until you grow old," one visa applicant would be told, and to another an official might say, "You'll rot here." Families with sons in their mid-teens were refused because they had not yet served in the army. Those whose sons had served were refused because as former soldiers they knew state secrets. People in their fifties and sixties were refused because their parents or former wives or husbands would not give them the necessary written permission to leave for Israel. Yet in seemingly haphazard fashion, others would be granted approval and were soon on their way out of the country.

In the early 1970s a number of Jewish scientists, denied visas and plunged into professional limbo after losing their jobs, organized seminars to help themselves stay informed of developments in their various fields. The seminars met on Sundays. In a photograph of one such seminar, Andrei Sakharov sits, chin in hand, listening attentively.

Volodya attended the Sunday seminars and remembers that among the many subjects dealt with were mathematical logic, radio physics, the architectonics of computers, the chemistry of polymers, quantum mechanics, computer programming, genetics, cybernetics. He could do little, however, to keep up with the field of engineering, for which special equipment was needed. Every Soviet citizen who attended those seminars stood the risk of sudden arrest, imprisonment, exile. But the knowledge gained, the fraternity experienced, the heartache assuaged, made the risk worthwhile.

At the same time, clandestine study groups where Jewish history and Hebrew could be learned were formed throughout the Soviet Union. In 1969 there were about ten groups in Moscow, a hundred or so individuals, studying Hebrew. By the 1980s many thousands in major cities of the Soviet Union attended secret Hebrew classes, with the result that a significant number of Soviet Jews arrived in Israel already knowing the language. I remember teaching one of the Moscow groups in the mid-1980s: the silent climb up the dim staircase of the apartment building; the warm, crowded room; the hushed voices; the quiet lecture; the subdued discussion; the silent climb down the staircase; the sudden snowy street; and the icy wind like a stinging slap across my face.

Volodya and Masha often helped duplicate textbooks for the groups, but, save for a class in Hebrew held on occasion in their apartment, neither participated seriously in Jewish study. That was not their weapon of choice in the visa war.

Volodya had been told by the OVIR authorities that he would have to wait five years before he could apply again for an exit visa. It was OVIR policy not to return documents; thus in order to reapply, one had to repeat from the start the entire documentation procedure. Volodya refused to wait and would not reprise the nightmarish grind and embarrassment of document acquisition; the first effort had taken about three months. Repeatedly he addressed applications to OVIR requesting that his case be reopened. Regularly he called the OVIR office, only to be told that his application had been refused. And when he asked for the reason, the response always was "Secrecy."

Refusals from OVIR were communicated orally. If, however, one's application for a visa had been approved, one received a postcard in the mail. On March 11, 1971, an OVIR postcard arrived for Masha's mother, who had recently suffered a heart attack and was in the hospital. "You are permitted to leave for Israel. To obtain your exit visa, you must appear at the office of OVIR with these documents." A list followed.

Masha went to see her the following day and showed her the postcard. After a long moment of silence, her mother said she would go alone.

"The trip is difficult," said Masha. "Will you be able to make it?"

"It's up to God. Begin the process."

Masha spoke with her mother's doctor, who said the trip would kill her. Masha said it was her mother's decision; she would go.

Volodya and Masha went about collecting the necessary documents. The only place where her mother, weak and shaky, had to appear in person was the Austrian Embassy, for her transit visa.

Four days later, Masha and her mother were in the apartment on Gorky Street; Volodya had been arrested for participating in a sit-in. They drank tea and talked about the family, about Israel. Mother and daughter were up most of the night. "I'll heal," said her mother. "I'll go to Europe and America. I'll speak everywhere about you. I'll be a bridge for you and get you out of here." She seemed tortured by her decision to leave. "I am not abandoning you. We will see each other soon."

She left the country on a stretcher and flew to Israel. She settled in Jerusalem and lived on a government old-age pension until her death in the desert city of Beersheba in 1980. Masha never saw her again.

By the early 1970s non-Jewish Russian dissidents of what had come to be called the democratic movement had established clear channels of communication to the West, along which flowed a steady stream of information about their activities in the Soviet Union and the efforts by the authorities to silence them. The refuseniks began to use the channels of the Russian dissidents to communicate with the West. Lists of Jews in refusal were slipped to foreign correspondents, along with carefully documented information concerning human rights violations. The lists also appeared in the Russian dissident samizdat publication *Khronika*.

The Slepak family chronicles are particularly clear on the help the refuseniks received during the early 1970s from those in the Russian dissident movement. Volodya recalls the day, March 13, 1971, when Vladimir Bukovsky, one of the leading Russian dissidents, suddenly appeared at the apartment on Gorky Street, accompanied by two men. Volodya had met Bukovsky some months before and had since that time been regularly giving him information to relay to foreign correspondents. A tall man in his early thirties, with broad shoulders, brown hair, brown eyes, and a wide face with a prominent nose and cheekbones, Bukovsky had been arrested for dissident activity while still on the faculty of biology at the University of Moscow. Assuming that the Slepak apartment was bugged by the KGB, he proceeded to write on a magic slate, from which the script could be easily and repeatedly erased: "I know that I will be arrested in two or three days. The KGB agents are following me day and night, making no effort to hide. It took me about two hours to lose them so we could come to you without the KGB tail. When I'm arrested, you can be in direct contact with these gentlemen, and through them with other foreign correspondents." One of the two men was Bob Catlin of Reuters. The other was the UPI correspondent, whose name Volodya does not now recall.

The next day Volodya met one of the correspondents—he does not remember which one, but the agreement was that all information related to one would be communicated by him to the other—and informed him that on the following day he and a group of others were going to the Supreme Soviet with a list of grievances against the Soviet Union. Volodya was arrested March 15 and given fifteen days in jail. While he was serving his fifteen days, the KGB arrested Bukovsky, who was sentenced to seven years in a labor camp and an additional five years of exile.

That was the start of Volodya's direct contact with the foreign press, the public word in the outside world, one of his weapons in the visa war.

There were other weapons.

On March 15—a cold, cloudy day, with melting dirty snow on the ground—a group of about fifteen Jewish dissidents whose visa applications had been refused, arrived at the building on Pushkinskaya Street that housed the Office of the General Procurator. The entrance to the building was from the rear, which faced Sovietskaya Square. Earlier that morning, they had gone to the office of the Presidium of the Supreme Soviet on Mokhovaya Street near the Kremlin only to be told that their grievances had first to be presented at the office of the general procurator of the USSR. Now they waited in the receiving room of General Procurator Roman Rudenko's office, after having informed the clerk that they wished to present their applications for exit visas, together with a number of demands: (1) that those arrested in Leningrad, Riga, Kishinev, and other cities for requesting visas to Israel be released and (2) that OVIR comply with Soviet law and send refusals in written form, stating the reasons for the refusal, the date of the refusal, and when the refusal would be terminated and the applicant free to leave the USSR.

After two hours they were told by the clerk that no one would speak with them. Spontaneously they determined not to leave and informed the clerk of their decision: They would wait until the general procurator or one of his aides responded to their demands. They sat in the receiving room until the office had to be closed. An officer of the militia arrived with several militiamen and said that if they did not leave immediately, they would all be arrested. The group refused to move.

Eventually about thirty militiamen came into the room. They removed the dissidents by force and pushed them into a bus, which transported them to the prison in the Moscow City Department of Militia on Petrovka Street. Each member of the group was separately interrogated in a small room furnished only with a table and two chairs: Your name? Your date of birth? Who is the organizer of this action? Do you personally know the people in the other cities who were arrested for their anti-Soviet activity and whose release you demanded? Do you know that their activity was inspired by foreign intelligence? Do you know any foreigners? Do you know that if you do not stop your anti-Soviet activity, you will never leave the Soviet Union? Do you know anyone in the so-called democratic movement?

Each interrogation took about twenty minutes. The members of the group gave their names and dates of birth and refused to answer the other questions or sign any statements. Instead they insisted upon their release and repeated their demands. Most stated that if they weren't released immediately, they would go on a hunger strike. Volodya told his interrogator that he would answer none of his questions, not even about the weather, unless he was shown an official protocol accusing him of a crime.

All were put into cells, two to a cell, where they spent the night. Each cell contained two iron beds, a table with iron legs, and two benches, all screwed into the concrete floor. In the corner there was a tank instead of a lavatory. An iron door with a tiny sliding iron window sealed the cell from the outside. A high iron-barred window permitted a view only of the sky.

The next day each in turn was brought to a room where a woman in a dark skirt and jacket and a white blouse introduced herself as a judge and said, "Because of your noncompliance with the demands of the representatives of the authorities, you are hereby sentenced to fifteen days of administrative imprisonment." That category of imprisonment was more severe than the usual kind in a local jail. It meant the prisoner did not receive a sleeping mat, blankets, or a pillow. He or she was given hot food only every other day and could be put to work cleaning yards, shoveling snow from the streets. As a rule, however, Jews who were arrested were kept separated from the others and were not subjected to forced public labor.

The members of the sit-in were returned to their cells and began the hunger strike. All were aware of revolutionaries who, during the time of the tsars, had refused food. And they knew of Gandhi. They refused all food and only drank water.

Volodya had been placed in the same cell with one of his close friends, Victor Polsky, a physicist whom he had met at the Moscow Electro-Vacuum Factory. Tall, red-haired, well groomed, Polsky was always one step ahead of the others in the group: the first to purchase a boat, the first to acquire an automobile. "Commander," they called him. His father-in-law was a well-known professor of physics, a position that normally opened doors for Polsky but was of no avail now as he sat in the cell with Volodya, starving and counting the days.

Out of a scrap of paper they made a chessboard, coloring squares dark with burned matches. They molded chess pieces out of bread. They played all the time. Nights they tried to sleep, Volodya's resounding snores later described by Polsky as a torture far worse than hunger.

Polsky and most of the others gave up the strike. By the thirteenth day Volodya was one of two still striking.

Masha had not participated in the sit-in. She, together with the wives of other prisoners, went to government offices to demand the release of their husbands.

The authorities did not want anyone of the group to die in jail or to look wan and wasted upon release, and so the prison doctor visited the cells and warned that if they did not end the strike, they would be fed by force. The prisoners were brought into a room where the tools of forced feeding had been laid out on a table: tubes, funnels, a device to keep the jaws apart. "We have our orders," one of the militiamen told them. "Whether you want to or not, you will eat." It is part of the torture for the torturer to display the instruments of torture before the one about to be tortured.

They were taken back to their cells.

One of the leaders of the group was Michael Zand, a linguist with a knowledge of ancient and modern Persian, as well as Arabic, Hebrew, Aramaic, and Urdu, a strong-willed, determined man with a powerful look. On the thirteenth day of the hunger strike, he was strapped to a bed and held down by two men while bouillon was poured into a tube that had been inserted through his nose—not down his throat, because he could have bitten down on it—into his esophagus and stomach. Volodya was then told by the militia that Zand had voluntarily ceased striking, and he terminated his strike. The first food they gave him was a soup of grits and pork and beef; the sudden ingestion of fat after thirteen days of starvation permanently injured his liver and gallbladder. After two days of forced feeding, Michael Zand was put into a hospital. The others were sent home when they finished serving their prison sentence.

Volodya arrived home, weak, gaunt, joking that he had been to a rehabilitation clinic to lose his paunch. His young son Leonid remembers being proud of his father and, at the same time, feeling frightened. No one in his family had ever before had any serious conflict with the authorities. A new kind of life had begun for him and his parents.

The hunger strike and the sit-in—the latter, according to Volodya, used for the first time ever in the Soviet Union—were additional weapons in the visa war.

There was a collective weapon as well, one organized by the entire Jewish people.

About eight hundred delegates from thirty-eight countries and every continent arrived in Brussels on February 23, 1971, to attend the first conference of world Jewry on the issue of Jewish emigration from the Soviet Union. The idea for the Brussels conference appears to have originated in New York. Many who came were uncertain whether there even was an issue: Were there any Jewish communities or individuals left in the Soviet Union after the Stalin decades and the war?

In Brussels there were terrorist threats and rumors of bombing by KGB agents. Everywhere, heavily armed police. A recent arrival from the USSR, Vitaly Rubin, addressed the conference and told of the Soviet Jews who were seeking the community of fellow Jews. As he spoke, it became apparent that Soviet Jewry was not a distant, dying remnant without vital memory and surviving on echoes alone. A stunning realization: There were Jews who had come through the decades of terror and war! Even those sympathetic early on to the cause of Soviet Jewry had not really believed that knowing and committed Jews were still to be found in the USSR.

Also at the conference were David Ben-Gurion, old and frail, together with the scholar Gershom Scholem, the writers André Schwarz-Bart and Elie Wiesel, and a number of Soviet Jews from Israel who had suffered imprisonment in labor camps and incarceration in insane asylums before receiving their exit visas. Masha's ailing mother, Bertha Rashkovsky, was present as well.

On the second day of the conference, a sudden telephone call came from Moscow: Thirty Jews, Volodya among them, had gathered at the

Presidium of the Supreme Soviet, where they presented a petition requesting the right to emigrate. The conference, spurred on by that deed, set up five commissions to carry forward the struggle and explore how to influence governments, media, and university campuses throughout the Western world. There was the usual bureaucratic infighting, the recurring organizational squabbles. In the end no worldwide assembly was established, and there was no coordinated strategy for an international campaign. But the charged atmosphere of the three-day conference sent delegates home eager to continue their labors.

Nothing was said of the situation of those Soviet Jews who seemed content to remain in the Soviet Union and whose lives might be profoundly affected by the dire repercussions of a persistent international thrust for Jewish emigration.

With nearly a hundred journalists present, the Brussels conference had received much worldwide attention. Close upon the heels of the conference came an abrupt increase in Jewish emigration from the Soviet Union: 13,022 in 1971; 31,903 in 1972. Probably the Soviets were hoping to empty the country of its contentious Jews and thereby put an end to the emigration movement. But the reverse occurred. Visa requests increased. The movement grew stronger. In the last weeks of 1971 there were days when two planeloads of Soviet Jews left Vienna bound for Israel.

But the Soviet authorities were employing weapons of their own in the visa war. Suddenly, in August 1972, they levied an additional tax upon all emigrants, to cover all the costs incurred by the government for their higher education and advanced degrees. Anyone who had graduated from a university or an institute would now have to pay, in addition to all the prior fees and taxes, a further sum—a diploma tax, it came to be called—of from forty-five hundred to twelve thousand rubles.

Volodya and Masha were then earning less than two hundred rubles a month. A pair of shoes cost thirty to forty rubles; pants, twenty-five to forty rubles; a shirt, ten to fifteen rubles; a blouse, twenty to forty rubles. The diploma tax put an end to any hope they had of ever leaving the country. As it did to the hopes of the other refuseniks. Volodya knows the names of only three people—the artist Lev Sirkin and his wife, Larisa, and the surgeon Edward Shifrin—who, with the help of funds collected in the United States, were able to pay the tax and leave the USSR.

The Soviets had other weapons. It now appears that not all high government officials were of a single mind concerning the issue of Jewish emigration; some had begun to regard it as a situation that might have to be dealt with equitably. But the KGB continued its conventional strategy: surveillance, censorship of the mail, telephone monitoring, detention, interrogation, house arrest, conscription into the armed forces, blacklisting to prevent employment, menacing family members, beatings, accusations of spying for foreign powers, administrative imprisonment, exile, labor camp. Much of that arsenal was used by the KGB in the visa war against Volodya and Masha Slepak.

Sudden arrest and imprisonment were put into play in July 1974, when President Nixon visited Moscow in the aftermath of the 1973 Yom Kippur War in the Middle East and during the long debate then raging in the United States over the Jackson-Vanik Amendment to the Trade Reform Act. A frequent Soviet reaction to queries from the West about its treatment of the Jews inside its borders echoed an answer often given by the tsars: Our Jews are our business, entirely an internal matter; to presume to dictate to us how we ought deal with them is to violate our national sovereignty. Many in the West appeared satisfied with that response. In the early 1970s a similar rejoinder was introduced into the Cold War by the Americans, one involving a crucial trade agreement with the Soviets.

By 1972, with Richard Nixon in the White House and National Security Adviser Henry Kissinger a main force in the shaping of American foreign policy, détente had become the goal of the administration: a relaxation of the Cold War, an easing of the arms race, a hope that the Soviets might help in the negotiations that would end the American involvement in Vietnam. At the same time, détente looked good to the Soviets as well; they badly needed American help to energize their stagnant economy.

The two sides—President Nixon and Soviet Trade Minister Nikolai Patolichev—signed a trade agreement in October 1972. The Soviets would receive most-favored-nation status from the United States and afterward pay off their entire multibillion-dollar lend-lease debt from World War II.

That effort to diminish the tensions of the Cold War was abruptly upset by the issue of the emigration of Soviet Jewry. Earlier that same October, Senator Henry Jackson had proposed an amendment to the Trade Reform Act, stipulating that the USSR and other Communist countries would be eligible to receive most-favored-nation treatment and trade credits if their citizens were not denied "the right or opportunity to emigrate" and if their emigration were not impeded by taxes, fines, and other charges. In January 1973, Congressman Charles Vanik introduced a similar bill in the House of Representatives. Senator Jackson and his many supporters reasoned that if emigration was a domestic affair to the Soviets, then trade was a domestic matter to the Americans, who had a right to decide with whom they would deal and under what conditions.

It is not entirely clear why Senator Jackson put forth his amendment. When he broached the idea to his colleagues in the Senate, it received the support—at first reluctant and, because of the obvious plight of Soviet Jewry, in the end quite resolute—of Senators Jacob Javits and Abraham Ribicoff, who were Jews. Some conjecture that Senator Jackson was considering a run for the presidency in 1976 and believed the Soviet Jewry issue would gain him the support of American Jews and hard-line anti-Communists and take him to the White House. Whatever the reason, he introduced the amendment on October 4, 1972, and a bruising two-year-long debate followed.

The White House and the State Department opposed the amendment, as did American business groups. George Meany, head of the AFL-CIO and a strong anti-Communist, was in favor of it, together with many conservative organizations. Strange bedfellows were formed by that controversy. The government of Israel seemed vehement against the amendment; it wanted the dissident Russian Jews to let the diplomats do their quiet work. American Jews were divided: Much of the leadership opposed it; most Jews favored it.

It was the diploma tax—established by the Kremlin in August 1972 and published on December 27 and clearly aimed at the very heart of the Soviet Jew—that incensed American Jews and galvanized the majority into supporting the amendment. The conflict was joined, with the White House on one side and Congress and most of American Jewry on the other.

Into the controversy now entered more than one hundred Soviet Jewish dissidents. Responding to a statement made on February 12, 1973, by American Secretary of State William P. Rogers, who had urged quiet diplomacy as the only effective means to further the emigration of Soviet Jews, the activists sent a collective letter in which they appealed to American Jewish leaders to support the amendment. To permit the Soviet Union to select arbitrarily who could and could not emigrate "would have a tragic, irreparable effect and would mean a complete collapse of all hopes of repatriation for many thousands of Soviet Jews." Quiet diplomacy could work effectively, the letter said, only if it was supported by "loud diplomacy": meetings, demonstrations, open demands, official statements, campaigns in newspapers. Volodya was among those who signed the letter.

In March 1973 Soviet Jewish dissidents were informed through an unofficial channel—possibly a correspondent or a visitor who represented the Union of Councils for Soviet Jewry; Volodya cannot recall precisely—that if they wanted the Jackson-Vanik Amendment to pass Congress, they would have to send a letter insisting that they, the victims of human rights violations, firmly supported the amendment. The letter had to carry the signatures of several leaders of the Jewish movement.

The letter was written on April 10, 1973, and signed by Kirill Khenkin, Benjamin Levich, Victor Polsky, Vladimir Slepak, and Alexander Voronel, and it was sent through a tourist to Senator Jackson. On April 10, 1973, a special press conference was held by the dissidents in the apartment of Kirill Khenkin, a journalist and translator, who lived in a Stalinesque skyscraper on Kotelnicheskaya Naberezhnaya. Four of the Jewish dissidents were there, and three or four foreign correspondents. Copies of the letter to Senator Jackson were distributed to the correspondents. To write, mail, and distribute such a letter meant, in Volodya's words, "that, as we say in Russian, we took all the blows and all the fire on ourselves." But the KGB stayed silent; it was the time of détente, and apparently the authorities did not want trouble with foreign correspondents in the heart of Moscow.

From within the ranks of the Russian dissidents, Andrei Sakharov sent an open letter to the U.S. Congress, dated September 14, 1973, in which he urged passage of the amendment: "I am appealing to the Congress of the United States to give its support to the Jackson Amendment, which represents in my view and in the view of its sponsors an attempt to protect the right of emigration of citizens in countries that are entering into new and friendlier relations with the United States. . . . Adoption of the amendment . . . cannot be a threat to Soviet-American relations. Even less is it likely to imperil international détente."

Two months later there was an opposing response from the Soviet dissident historian Roy Medvedev: ". . . it would be unrealistic to presume that under pressure from the American Congress the Soviet government will adopt a special law permitting unrestricted emigration from the USSR for all who so desire. And if the American Congress should adopt the Jackson Amendment . . . on this account, and should refuse most-favored-nation status to the Soviet Union, this would probably not improve but only worsen prospects for resolution of the emigration problem in the near future. Also, Soviet-American relations would deteriorate."

Between those two letters came the sudden Yom Kippur War, which began on October 6, 1973, with a coordinated surprise attack by Egypt and Syria against Israel. In the apartment on Gorky Street, the Slepak family sat listening to Soviet radio broadcasts about Israeli provocations along the Suez Canal and the victorious attacks of the Egyptians and Syrians. Then: a day or so of silence, followed by announcements about the insidious Israelis being armed by Western imperialist powers, gaining the rear of the Egyptian Army, beginning to annihilate the civilian population. Over the shortwave radio given to the Slepaks by an overseas visitor came news of the surrounded Egyptian Third Army, of Israeli troops on the other side of the Suez Canal and within thirty miles of Cairo, of the Syrian withdrawal, of the maneuverings of diplomats.

In the United States the debate over the Jackson-Vanik Amendment grew hotter. The Israelis needed the support of the Nixon administration in the war; Nixon, willing to send arms, wondered if American Jews, desirous of his advocacy of Israel, might dampen their enthusiasm for the amendment. Kissinger, who was now secretary of state, reminded American Jews that an end to the war in the Middle East required the support of the Soviets, who would balk in view of the American Jewish support of the amendment. Caught in a classic conflict between the White House and Congress, American Jewry twisted and turned uncomfortably.

The diploma tax was quietly suspended—not rescinded—in March 1974. In June, Premier Brezhnev visited the United States, presented statistics on the numbers of Jews who had emigrated from the Soviet Union, gave his word that more would be leaving in the future, and lobbied for unconditional trade credits. Later that same month, President Nixon, engulfed and crippled by the Watergate scandal, traveled to Moscow. To avoid the possibility of demonstrations or other embarrassing public disturbances during his stay, the KGB, in advance of his arrival, arrested and imprisoned dozens of dissidents in Moscow, Leningrad, Kiev, and elsewhere—Volodya among them. Along with others, he was stripped and searched and taken to the town of Serpukhov, some sixty miles from Moscow, where he was put into a cell for fifteen days.

Two months later Nixon resigned the presidency, and Gerald Ford became president. On December 20 Congress passed the Trade Reform Act and the Jackson-Vanik Amendment. The Slepak family chronicles record, in Volodya's words, that "immediately afterward, Soviet Foreign Minister Gromyko issued a statement in the usual Soviet propagandistic tone: 'We will never let anyone dictate to us.' To save face," Volodya maintains, "they stopped the emigration."

But it was not the Jackson-Vanik Amendment that really angered the

Kremlin and brought defeat to Soviet Jews and Americans in this phase of the visa war—the Soviets might have been able to meet its stipulations and emigration provisos—but an amendment to the Import-Export Bank bill, proposed by Senator Adlai Stevenson III. The amendment limited credits to the USSR to three hundred million dollars a year for four years—credits the Kremlin desperately needed at the time to finance, at low interest rates, its purchases of American technology. That limitation, which insulted and infuriated the Kremlin, put an end to the trade debate, and on January 10, 1975, the Soviets abruptly canceled the agreement their trade minister had signed in October 1972 with President Nixon.

Inside the Soviet Union, KGB repression of dissidents intensified. Many young men who applied for exit visas were conscripted into the armed forces. There was an increase in trials of Jewish dissidents and a decrease in emigration: from 20,628 in 1974 to 13,221 in 1975. In Volodya's words, the Kremlin nullified its trade agreement with the United States because "the Soviets couldn't say that three hundred million dollars was too little in exchange for the Jews."

Still, the Kremlin needed most-favored-nation status. Also, Brezhnev wanted an arms agreement and probably felt it necessary to respond to Western criticism of his embarrassing 1976 Stalinesque crackdown against human rights activists. To the surprise of many, in that same year, 1976, the number of Jews granted permission to emigrate suddenly rose. And kept rising every year to 1979, when 51,320 left.

Volodya and Masha were not among them. Their visa war continued. But after the Jackson-Vanik Amendment it was a very different kind of war, because America was now involved.

Solomon Slepak, an old man with a bad heart and recent prostate surgery, had a weapon of his own in the visa war: silence.

His first wife, Volodya's mother, had died after a long battle with cancer. Sanya, the older of Volodya's two sons, adds to the family chronicles an account of how as a child he would come into the room of his grandparents, where his grandmother would be lying behind a screen, and hear her scream at him to leave because she could not bear visitors. Sometimes his grandfather would be seated at a table, reading a newspaper, the entire paper held high and open in front of him, concealing his face. Sanya remembers that his grandfather taught him to read by spreading the newspaper on the table and showing him how to put letters together to make words. Once, in another world and time, Solomon

Slepak, recently arrived in New York, had learned to read English from newspapers spread on the floor, taught by his sister's children. Often Sanya and his grandfather would go for a walk and Sanya would ask for a chocolate and they would wait on a line for an hour or longer at the candy store, and as they waited, his grandfather would tell him tales about legendary fighters for the cause of the Revolution, about stalwart workers, about young boys and their heroic deeds.

When his wife died, the Old Bolshevik married again and now lived in a small house with his second wife. From time to time he and Volodya and Masha continued to call one another and meet—until the complete separation that followed when they told him of their plans to emigrate to Israel. From then on, the Old Bolshevik would have nothing to do with his son and daughter-in-law. They would hear about him on occasion through Volodya's cousin Anatoly.

Masha's mother once remonstrated with Solomon Slepak. "Grandchildren shouldn't suffer because a father and a son have difficulties between them. The grandchildren have only one grandfather. How can you bear to deprive them of their grandfather?"

And so Sanya—at times alone, at times with his little brother, Leonid—traveled by Metro and tram three or four times a year to Solomon's house. The Old Bolshevik lived on Mashkova Street, a narrow side road in the center of old Moscow. The one-story house, inside a courtyard, was made of wood, a ramshackle affair, leaning walls, creaking floors, something out of Gogol. It had a small backyard, with flowers and bushes. A big German shepherd dog raced about, barking furiously. Redolent of poverty, the house looked shrunken and withdrawn from the outside world, forgotten by history, like the man who lived inside.

Almost always their grandfather's wife would let them in, and they would find their grandfather seated at a large round table, writing. She was much younger than Solomon, with little education, a typical Russian commoner, from the lowest rungs of society. Always seeming agitated when the children visited, she fussed about anxiously, worked too hard at her hostessing, talked endlessly, until Solomon would say, "It's enough, it's enough, calm down."

Sometimes their grandfather would meet them at the door, push the dog aside, and take their coats, happy to see them. Books and papers lay heaped on the table, together with large dictionaries, and it would take a few minutes for him to put everything away. The room was small, a couch on one side and the table in the center, and furnished in Russian peasant fashion: a clutter of ornamented pillows and a tablecloth and

shelf hangings and needlework on the walls. The boys and their grandfather would sit around the table and engage in small talk. He would ask
about the health of their parents. They knew not to say anything to their
grandfather about their father's activities. The old man's wife brought
them tea and preserves. In later years the boys learned that she was an alcoholic, that she often abused their grandfather, stole his money, beat him.

Leonid Slepak, slight of build, strikingly attractive, and seven years
younger than his brother, spent much of his childhood in neighborhood
child care centers. At times, if he was ill, his grandfather would come
over to the apartment on Gorky Street and stay with him. He would
bring along his work—he was always writing, translating—and sit at the
living room table with his books and papers. Once Leonid kept disturbing him, and Solomon put aside his work and read him an Italian fairy
tale, "Onionhead," translated into Russian and very popular then in the
Soviet Union. How the little vegetables—onions, radishes, leeks—made
a revolution and overthrew the oranges and tomatoes.

One time Solomon handed little Leonid a Russian rendering of *Alice
in Wonderland*. In his own hands he held another copy, in English. He
told Leonid to follow as he read and translated directly from English
into Russian and to see if he made any mistakes. With growing wonder
and delight, Leonid followed his grandfather's flawless translation. *Alice
in Wonderland* was the first book Leonid read in English.

The boys also went to visit Solomon in the hospital when he lay recovering from a heart attack in the fall of 1974. That time they came with
their father, who brought along a gift of fruits. It was early evening, cold
and rainy, no snow yet on the ground. Solomon Slepak lay in a small
room with only one other bed, which was empty. That was surprising;
most hospital rooms had six or ten or twelve beds. Clearly, he was in a
room reserved for Old Bolsheviks.

He lay in the far left corner, and as they entered, he looked up and
brusquely asked Volodya if he had changed his mind about emigrating
to Israel. Volodya said no. Solomon pointed to the fruits and then to a
small table and then to the door. Volodya put the fruits on the table and
left the room and stood outside in the hallway. The boys came over to
their grandfather and sat on his bed for a while, talking with him. Then
they said good-bye and joined their father and went home.

Because the Slepak apartment was in the heart of the city, it had become
by 1974 a collection point, a kind of lodgment area and operations cen-

ter, in the visa war. It was down the street from two major hotels, the National and the Intourist: 15 Gorky Street. You walked past the shops to the entrance archway. To the left of the entrance was a large bookstore; to the right, a dairy products store. You went beneath the archway and turned into the courtyard. All the entrances to the apartments were from the courtyard, and the way into the Slepaks' was through the first entrance, a wooden double door with waist-high glass panels, then another set of doors into a small foyer, where you saw the back of the elevator shaft, covered with wire mesh. You went left to the spiral staircase and up half a flight to the elevator, where you pulled open a heavy steel door and pushed through two swinging wooden doors into the tiny elevator. You pulled the steel door shut and stepped out of the way as the two doors swung back into place. Then you pushed the button to the eighth floor, rode up, opened the swinging doors and the steel door, and stepped out. You found yourself looking at two apartments, one in front, the other to the right. Number 77, the one to the right, with its brown wooden door, was the apartment of the Slepaks.

By 1974 Volodya's name had appeared several times in the newspapers: a dissident, an enemy of the people. Most of the dwellers in the building might say hello when passing by in the courtyard or on the street but otherwise avoided Volodya and Masha. The only friends they had in the building lived on the floor below theirs, a married couple, he an architect, she an editor. Leonid's classmates no longer visited. Sanya, now grown, lived elsewhere with a girlfriend.

Inside that communal apartment, in the room he shared with Masha—the other occupants were Leonid and a police sergeant and his wife, who lived behind their closed door and were often drunk—Volodya carefully prepared the means by which the lists of names, and the necessary accompanying data, of those requesting invitations to Israel were smuggled out to the West; tens of thousands of names went through his hands. First he bought Russian souvenir wooden dolls. He then cut the head off each doll, drilled a hole in the body, inserted the tightly rolled film negatives of the lists, glued the head back on, and gave the doll to a visitor who had been recommended by friends from abroad. The souvenir doll left the Soviet Union unconcealed in one's baggage, a tourist's memento. Among the Jewish dissidents, only three knew of the dolls, and only Volodya, and on occasion Leonid, handled the operation. None of the dolls was ever unmasked.

A tiny weapon, those dolls, and among the most effective.

A new weapon emerged: the Helsinki Accords Monitoring Group.

The Helsinki Accords were signed in 1975 by thirty-five nations, including the Soviet Union and the United States, the former, because it wanted the international recognition given by the accords to its theretofore provisional postwar borders; the latter, because it wanted the Soviet Union to commit itself to the 1948 Declaration of Human Rights, which called for universal freedom of expression and opinion. The agreement, three years in the making, carried no legal weight but was considered of great moral and political significance. The nations that signed the accords were to be "guided by the principle that such universal guarantees . . . should be firmly adhered to in their own country and elsewhere." Of special significance to Soviet Jewish dissidents was the commitment by participating nations to "respect human rights and fundamental freedoms, including freedom of thought, conscience, religion," and the promise to work for the reunification of families through emigration.

But the Soviets, who wanted the West to honor the fixed-border guarantees in the accords, had no intention of adhering to the human rights provisions, which they regarded as mere rhetoric. To counter that attitude and the possible sacrifice of human rights by the White House for the goal of détente, Representative Millicent Fenwick introduced a bill on March 23, 1976, to set up "a commission to monitor compliance with the Helsinki Accords." The bill passed. Congressman Dante Fascell became chairman of the commission.

At the time the bill was making its way through Congress and to the desk of President Ford, who signed it that June, Yuri Orlov, a Soviet physicist and longtime dissident, organized a group in Moscow to monitor Soviet compliance with the human rights agreements, which came to be known as the Helsinki Accords Monitoring Group.

Similar monitoring groups, stimulated by the Helsinki group but independent of it, then came into existence in other regions of the Soviet Union—the Ukraine, Lithuania, Armenia, Georgia. From those groups issued a steady stream of reports on arrests, on trials, on the persecution of Pentecostalists, Catholics, Crimean Tatars, on conditions in labor camps, on the use of drugs and psychiatric treatment against political prisoners—on a vast range of human rights abuses.

Among the earliest members recruited by Orlov for the Moscow group were Alexander Ginzburg, Anatoly Shcharansky, and Elena Bonner, Andrei Sakharov's wife. Orlov asked Shcharansky and Vitaly Rubin, the prominent Sinologist whose emigration requests had been turned down repeatedly since 1972, to serve as representatives of the Jewish emigration movement. That June, Rubin was suddenly granted his visa, and he departed for Israel. Volodya stepped into his place.

The monitoring groups became an indispensable weapon for Russian dissidents and Jewish refuseniks and the bane of the Soviet authorities. Yuri Orlov was told by the KGB that the Moscow group was illegal; he ignored orders to disband it. The KGB subjected the apartments of monitors to intensive searches. Orlov and Ginzburg were arrested in February 1977. Orlov was given the maximum sentence for anti-Soviet slander: seven years in a labor camp and five years of exile. Ginzburg, tried in July 1978—far beyond the nine-month limit for pretrial detention—was sentenced to eight years in the camps.

In a photograph taken some time in May 1978 outside the Lublino courthouse in Moscow, where the trial of Yuri Orlov was taking place— Orlov's wife had been made to strip and was searched by male guards before being permitted to enter the courthouse—one can see Andrei Sakharov in front of half a dozen uniformed guards. He seems to be walking past them in some hurry. Around that same time, Sakharov and his wife were photographed with Volodya. They are wearing leather jackets, and buds are growing on the bushes behind them. Volodya is sporting rather natty sunglasses. He was only days away from his own arrest.

The Helsinki Accords, which the Soviets had initially treated as the greatest moment in history since the crushing of Hitler—so elated had they been by the world's recognition of their war-acquired territories— was now beginning to be perceived by them as a major tactical blunder. The accords had placed on the international agenda certain basic issues that affected the lives of all people: freedom of movement, the open exchange of information, family reunification. Regarded as neither rhetoric nor platitudes by the Americans, by Soviet dissidents, even by Communist parties in the West, the terms set by the framers of the Helsinki Accords had unexpectedly become a weapon directed against the Kremlin. The incessant reporting by the monitoring groups placed Soviet infractions in full view of the world and paraded the torn and tormented nature of life in the Marxist-Leninist Soviet Union. Further complicating matters for the Kremlin was the fact that the direction of Jewish emigration had undergone a significant change over the years: Many were dropping out of the Israel pipeline near Vienna—to the great annoyance of the Israelis—and choosing instead to go to America. Thus many of the Soviet Union's best-educated Jews were now offering their services not only to the socialist Zionist state but also to the capitalist West. And perhaps the most ominous development of all: As if emulating the Jews, other national groups were embarking upon emigration campaigns. In 1974 Volga Germans demonstrated at party offices, where they displayed banners and placards, and staged sit-ins and hunger strikes.

In the apartment on Gorky Street, Volodya Slepak and Anatoly Shcharansky collected information on Soviet violations of human rights and sent it on to the Western countries that had signed the Helsinki Accords. Information came to them from everywhere, mostly by messenger—people traveling by train and plane, carrying lists of those harassed, searched, arrested, tried, sentenced.

Shcharansky was in his late twenties, a short, balding, feisty scientist and computer specialist, who had grown up knowing very little about being Jewish. He was bright, witty, life-loving. Anti-Semitism and the Six-Day War turned him into a dissident. He applied for an exit visa in the spring of 1973 and was refused. He married in 1974. Because his English was excellent, he served as Sakharov's interpreter at press conferences. He was among the first to understand the value of contacts with the foreign press and had already experienced numerous collisions with the KGB, whose agents were now openly following him, standing alongside him on buses, running behind him on the stairs of the Metro, even jumping after him into the taxis he hailed; Shcharansky always insisted that they pay part of the fare.

He and Volodya worked assiduously at their task on the Helsinki Monitoring Group. Each infraction involving a Jew which came to their attention was documented and carefully confirmed. An accumulation of such cases was presented to the entire group. After lengthy discussion and further investigation, a statement was prepared containing the names of those whose rights had been violated. The statement was reviewed by the group, and numerous copies were then made on a typewriter. Every copy was signed by all the members of the group. No statement was issued if there was any doubt as to the trustworthiness of the facts it contained. Then the copies were distributed through the regular mail to the Soviet government and to each of the other governments that had signed the accords; to the other signatories through channels considered more reliable than the mail, such as diplomats, correspondents, visitors from abroad; to *Khronika*, the dissident publication that had ceased appearing regularly in 1972 and was now being published intermittently; and to the archives of the Helsinki Monitoring Group. Usually the group published from two to four such statements every month.

Discussions and decisions concerning petitions, open letters, and demonstrations nearly always took place outdoors—in a forest or a park. If necessity at times dictated that such discussions be held inside, the spoken word was never used. They wrote on magic slates or on sheets of paper that, as soon as the discussions ended, were burned or torn to pieces and flushed down a toilet.

Some months before Volodya became seriously involved with the Helsinki Monitoring Group, he and Masha were divorced. Early that year, 1976, they were in difficult straits. No one among the hundreds of refuseniks in Moscow was receiving notification of a change in status. Everything seemed frozen for them, except the passage of time—especially frightening in a family with a boy who would soon come of age to be drafted into the army.

Of the two sons in the Slepak family, Sanya, the older one, knew that he would not be taken because of his defective vision. He had graduated from high school in 1969, could not gain admittance into a university— "You will never be allowed to have an education in this country; we are not training specialists for Israel," a KGB agent had bluntly told him— and he now worked at odd jobs—night watchman, restaurant waiter, train porter—unable to find permanent employment because as the son of a dissident and an active dissident himself, he was being dogged relentlessly by the KGB. But Leonid, the younger son, would soon be of draft age.

Volodya and Masha knew only too well how the Soviet Army treated the sons of those who had requested exit visas to Israel. And they were acquainted with young Jews who were refused visas for years after their army service because in response to questions by OVIR officials, they had admitted to remembering the names of their former commanding officers—a state secret, they were told, when informed that their visas would not be issued. Someone had suggested to Volodya that the entire family was being refused visas on account of his security status. In desperation, he and Masha decided, in January 1976, to try the maneuver of formal divorce as a possible means of disengaging her status, and that of their sons, from his.

They went through the divorce proceedings. Each submitted an application for divorce to a court. At a session of the court they stated that their decision had not been impulsive, had not come after a quarrel; that they had no financial claims against each other; that their only desire was to live separately; that their children were adults. The court made no effort to persuade them to change their minds and approved the divorce.

Masha then applied to OVIR with Leonid and separately from Volodya and Sanya. But they were quickly refused. An official informed her that OVIR did not believe the divorce was real, and that she would be allowed to emigrate only when permission was given to Volodya.

They remained divorced but went on living in the same apartment, hoping that OVIR might one day relent and permit Masha and Leonid to leave.

Into the apartment on Gorky Street came the news about the major counteroffensive begun by the Kremlin in its war against dissidents and visa-seekers. Early in March 1977 Volodya and Shcharansky read with astonishment an open letter in *Izvestia* that was a dangerous attack against the Moscow community of refuseniks. The letter had been written by Dr. Sanya Lipavsky, a man deeply respected and trusted by the refuseniks. The chronicles describe him through Masha's eyes as a man of average height, with a bushy brown mustache, brown eyes, short graying hair, and the self-assured smile of a cat. In the letter Dr. Lipavsky wrote that he was giving up his request for an exit visa; he admitted to having been an informer for the Central Intelligence Agency and denounced several major figures in the Jewish dissident movement—among them Vitaly Rubin, Professor Alexander Lerner, David Azbel, Vladimir Slepak, Anatoly Shcharansky, Mark Ya. Azbel, and some Americans—as spies in the pay of the CIA. Some on the list were no longer in the Soviet Union. The others might soon be facing a charge of treason, for which the penalty was death. On March 12 an article in *Pravda* claimed that the dissidents were "supported, paid, and praised by the West."

A few among the dissidents thought the Kremlin was giving expression to its anger over President Carter's recent meeting in the White House with Vladimir Bukovsky, the dissident who had arranged Volodya's initial contact with the foreign press, was soon afterward arrested and sentenced to seven years in a labor camp, and then released in 1976 in a prisoner exchange for the Chilean Communist leader Luis Corvalan Lepe. But most dissidents saw the linking of the dissident movement with the CIA as an ominous turn in Kremlin policy.

The family chronicles record that Masha was warned twice—once in their apartment by a friend of the family using the magic slate and a second time in a neighborhood park by an acquaintance—that there was a provocateur in their midst and that serious trouble awaited them all. Both times Masha informed Volodya, who said it was to be expected, there was nothing he could do about it. Masha said, "You must find out who it is." Volodya said, "I don't want to be bothered with that because this evil among us is unavoidable. Even if I find out and we expel him, tomorrow somebody else will take his place. That's the way it is, and that's the way it's going to be. I'm not going to deal with it." Masha said, "Suit yourself; let it be on your conscience. My job was to warn you, and I fulfilled my duty."

The serious trouble foretold by the friend now arrived. Though President Carter and the American State Department quickly denied the espionage charges, Lipavsky's letter and the vituperative article that accompanied it were chilling. The dissidents were shocked and dismayed by his accusation, utterly bewildered by his motives. It is now thought that he had offered his services to the security organs in 1962 to save the life of his father, an engineer sentenced to death for stealing large quantities of costly fabric from a textile factory; the sentence was altered to thirteen years in prison, and in the 1970s Lipavsky entered the refusenik world as a KGB informer and provocateur.

Jews in the pay of the CIA! Jews a threat to the security of the Motherland! That was how newspapers and journals began to report it throughout the USSR. Reading the news reports and appalled by the charges, Volodya and Masha sensed the venom in the air—under Stalin, Jews had been poisoners; now they were spies for the CIA—and heard echoes of old purges and the "Doctors' Plot." The Kremlin's objective was obvious: to sever all communication between the Soviet dissidents and the American government.

It was now clear that Brezhnev did not intend to let the dissidents prevail; the nettlesome Helsinki monitoring groups would be terminated. From everywhere came news of arrests and trials. It appeared to matter little to the Soviets that President Carter seemed personally concerned with human rights issues and that détente and strategic arms reduction treaties might be put in jeopardy, though as a possible gesture toward most-favored-nation status and the Jackson-Vanik Amendment, the Kremlin increased the number of nonrefusenik Jews leaving the Soviet Union in 1978 and 1979. There were disturbances in Poland, Czechoslovakia, Romania, and East Germany: Students and workers were pointing to the Helsinki Accords, demanding human rights. But in the Soviet heartland, the monitoring groups were being scythed and winnowed by arrests, trials, and harsh sentences. Near-annihilation of the human rights groups and a rise in Jewish emigration—simultaneously!

Inside and outside the Soviet Union, people watching and caught up in the visa war found the situation bewildering. David Shipler, *The New York Times* correspondent to the 1977–78 international Belgrade Conference, where the measure was taken of adherence to the Helsinki Accords, said, "Nobody knows all that goes into a decision to arrest and try one dissident, to let another emigrate, and to ignore a third. Unpredictability seems a hallmark of high policy, probably intended to keep activists off balance."

A photograph shows Shcharansky and Volodya seated next to each other. Nothing in the picture tells us where it was taken. The pitiless lens reveals the stress in their faces. Worry lines in Volodya's forehead are a weighty counterpoint to his rakish shock of thick, wavy hair and debonair graying beard; his friends had nicknamed him the Beard. In the straight, thin lines of their mouths one sees a heavy grimness and weariness. Deep shadows make caverns of their eyes. The picture was taken shortly before Shcharansky's arrest.

On March 15, 1977—eleven days after the publication in *Izvestia* of the letter by Lipavsky and the lengthy article accusing Shcharansky and other Jewish dissidents of being agents of the CIA and engaging in espionage against the Motherland—Shcharansky and Volodya and Masha were together in the Gorky Street apartment. Shcharansky, whose parents lived in a town about fifty miles from Moscow, on occasion, to avoid the trouble of travel, moved in with one of his refusenik friends in Moscow. His wife, Avital, had been granted an exit visa in 1975 and was in Israel. He was now living at the Slepaks' and could travel nowhere without the KGB all around him. His friends, aware that his arrest might be imminent, would not let him walk outside alone. It was six in the evening; he and Masha and Volodya were completing one of their weekly Hebrew lessons.

Two foreign correspondents, David Satter of the London *Financial Times* and Hal Piper of the *Baltimore Sun*, suddenly entered the apartment and announced that Mikhail Stern, a dissident Jewish physician serving a sentence in a labor camp since 1974, had been given his freedom for reasons of ill health. Shcharansky and the Slepaks, elated by the news of Stern's release, found it a cause for celebration. The only drink on hand was a bottle of cognac. Shcharansky, after downing a toast, which turned him immediately reckless because he could not tolerate liquor, was abruptly eager to relate the good news to other correspondents, and he and Volodya wrote out a short statement. But the telephone inside the apartment had long ago been disconnected by the KGB. Shcharansky scooped up some two-kopek coins for the public telephone on the street. Followed by Volodya and the correspondents, he dashed out the door—into the arms of two KGB agents, who had been waiting in the hallway.

The elevator could hold only four people, but five pushed themselves inside: the KGB agents, the correspondents, and Shcharansky. Volodya shouted, "I'll go downstairs on foot," and headed for the stairway. Squeezed tightly together inside the rickety elevator, the agents, the correspondents, and Shcharansky rode slowly down. The agents formed a phalanx with Shcharansky as he walked down the half flight of steps to the marble foyer and out into the courtyard and the street. Outside the building, numerous hands abruptly separated him from the correspondents, twisted his arms behind his back, and propelled him into the rear seat of a waiting Volga sedan, which sped away. He found himself seated between two KGB agents. The car brought him to Lefortovo Prison and the cruel cold midnight of the KGB penal system.

At about that time, a rabbi, Gerald Wolpe, who had flown from America to Eastern Europe and completed a mission to deliver vital medication to a seriously ill refusenik in Kiev, arrived with his wife, Elaine, in Moscow. There were certain people the Wolpes needed to meet, and because they knew that Volodya served as the refusenik central nervous system, the key to nearly everyone in the movement, they set out along Gorky Street, following the finger on the equestrian statue of Yuri Dolgoruky, founder of Moscow, which pointed to the Slepak apartment. And found themselves in the midst of turmoil.

Inside the apartment were a number of leading—by then nearly legendary—refuseniks, including the Slepaks, Ida Nudel, and Shcharansky's brother. Ida Nudel was furious, and when she saw the Wolpes, she shouted, "Why don't you Americans do something?"

Volodya tried to calm her.

It took a moment before the Wolpes realized what had transpired. The preliminary charges against Shcharansky had just been issued. Among other things, he would be tried for espionage. And quite possibly receive the death penalty. The conversation that then took place was conducted on magic slates; no voices.

The great fear among those in the apartment was that no one outside the Soviet Union would know what was happening to Shcharansky. It was vital that the documents containing the charges be brought to the United States and made available to certain individuals. Somehow Shcharansky's brother had obtained copies of the charges. Certain of the documents, many of which had already been translated into English, were given to Rabbi Wolpe, who spread them out one at a time on a deep windowsill and began to photograph them with his camera. There was no time to photograph all the documents. Volodya had rigged up a copier and was hurriedly making duplicates.

On the way to the airport, Rabbi Wolpe said to a non-Jewish woman in their tour group, "We're trying to help some people. Could you take this film out for us?" She said, without hesitation, "Yes." Elaine Wolpe had taped documents and copies to her underwear and skin and managed to get through customs without being searched. The film and the documents reached their intended destination in the United States.

Shcharansky spent sixteen months in solitary confinement, was tried in July 1978, and sentenced to three years in prison and ten in a labor camp.

The KGB had an especially malicious weapon in the visa war: the exit visa itself, which it used to break up dissident groups and families. In 1977 it wielded this weapon against the Slepaks.

Until he reached tenth grade in 1967, Sanya Slepak did not encounter anti-Semitism in his school. It was one of the best schools in Moscow; his grandfather, whom he loved deeply, had somehow persuaded the principal to admit him. Children and grandchildren of the Soviet elite sat in its classrooms, walked through its hallways, romped about its playground. His first sense of the abnormal in the world around him came not from contact with Jews but from the Russian friends of his parents. He remembers listening to discussions about the Stalin purges, unjustified bans on books, censorship of poets and novelists, matters cultural and intellectual rather than ethnic.

In those post-Stalin years the most gratifying aesthetic experience of many Muscovites was not the official theater or ballet but the companionship of friends: social gatherings, discussions about the latest books, about one's experience abroad; smoky rooms, barbecues, shish kebab, Georgian dinners, Russian folk songs, the guitar, wine. Not the same apartment always, but always the same group. Those were the early years of the Moscow intelligentsia, the time of the *kompanii*, vividly and scrupulously described by Russians who were there, the nascent years of the democratic movement. During his year in tenth grade Sanya on occasion attended such gatherings in the company of his parents and listened to the talk. In later years, he went on his own.

Among the Russians were Jews, most of whom at first felt entirely Russian. Then, with the impetus of the Six-Day War, some of the Jews began to concentrate upon Jewish issues. And that was the start of the Jewish movement. David and Goliath, Sanya remembers thinking when he learned of Israel's stunning victory, suddenly aware and proud of being a Jew. And for the first time he began to encounter the anti-Semitism in his country: in the newspapers, over the radio, in the streets.

His summer trips with his parents and their close Jewish friends began after that; before, he had spent vacations with his grandmother. Now, the sailing and hiking; the quiet talk around campfires; the study of Hebrew from the little vocabulary book *Elef Milim*; the ghostly voices from shortwave radios. And the slow opening out of himself to alternative worlds where Jews were not despised, slandered, maligned.

Never during all his years in high school was he called *zhid* to his face, but he had no close friends among the Russian students. He refused to take part in classes on Marxist-Leninist teachings. Still, because of the watchful stewardship of the principal and the teachers, no incidents marred his high school years. His classmates were polite, but aside from the cool hello, they shunned him.

He wanted to pursue studies in biology, but the KGB saw to it that no university or institute would accept him after he graduated from high school in 1969. A friend got him a job as a lab technician in a medical research institute in Moscow. He worked there for two years. The KGB arrested him for his dissident activities and kept him in prison for fifteen days, and he lost the job.

He worked at odd jobs, and for the dissident movement: liaison with foreign correspondents, demonstrations, protests, samizdat. His girlfriend, Alyona, who later became his wife, typed carbon copies of *Exodus* by Leon Uris; the novel, illegal in the Soviet Union, was a near-sacred text to Jewish dissidents. His entire life was now given over to dissident activity; life in Russia was a long, cold twilight of bleak waiting until they received their visas. The KGB harassed him regularly, picked him up, threatened him, at times beat him, warned him that he would never get his visa if he continued his activities. But youthful bravado pushed away fear and filled him with confidence: No harm would come to him or his family; the authorities would not dare. Too many knew about them; all the world was watching. Publicity would save them, no matter what Soviet regulations they might disobey.

He was twenty-five years old in 1977. Of medium height, with features remarkably like those of his mother: roundish face, full lips, weak eyes behind thick lenses. He led two separate lives, one with the Jewish dissidents, the other with Russians and Jews his age, the latter a purely social, nonideological group with whom he partied, got drunk. The Jewish dissidents were the wrong crowd for wildness.

In the early fall of that year the KGB called him in and offered him an exit visa. They would bring him in often, at times show him his exit visa, all filled in, his picture on it, put it on the desk in front of him, offer him the visa if he telephoned to cancel the next demonstration, agreed not to communicate with correspondents. He would refuse, and they would tear up the visa and sometimes beat him before sending him home.

In the fall of 1977 an international conference was to commence in Belgrade, where adherence to the Helsinki Accords would be evaluated. The Slepak case was scheduled to be brought before the conference by the representative from the United States. The KGB, wanting to forestall embarrassment to the Soviet Union and, at the same time, seeing a way to break up the Slepak family, brought Sanya in and informed him that he could leave for Israel on condition that he telephone the foreign correspondents and inform them he had been given permission to emigrate. He said no, he didn't trust the KGB; he would make the call, he said, and what would prevent them from then tearing up the visa? They sent him home.

The next morning they brought him back and said they were giving him the visa on his terms. He said he would first leave the country, and then the correspondents would be called by his father. They agreed, and gave him one week to get out.

Among the refuseniks the response to obtaining a visa was straightforward: Take it and leave. No matter the pain, the family circumstance, the cost of separation. Sanya spent part of the week lurching about in a drunken stupor. It was a very difficult time for him—difficult to say good-bye to his friends, to his family, to the apartment, to Moscow.

He called his grandfather, who said he did not want to see him. Sanya went anyway. When he entered the house, the old man was standing in front of the window, with his back to the room. Sanya sensed he did not want to be touched. He said he was leaving in a few days and was sure he would never see him again. The old man began to tremble and cry. He said, "I would understand if you were going to America. But to that fascist country! You are so stubborn."

Sanya turned to leave. The old man said, with his back still to his grandson, "Good luck." Sanya heard those words as his grandfather's blessing.

Hundreds of people were at the airport to see him off, most of them Jews, some his partygoing Russian friends. No elation, no dancing; a sober, quiet, sophisticated crowd. He embraced his parents. Leonid, his younger brother, was not present; a week earlier he had received his conscription notice and written a letter to the authorities saying he refused to serve in the armed forces of the Soviet Union. Then he had left the apartment and gone underground, first saying good-bye to his older brother. Sanya boarded the plane and flew to Vienna with one other Jewish family. Two days in the Vienna holding center: a Red Cross building, slanted roof, guard towers with Austrian police at the gates. In the morning a loudspeaker called out, *"Achtung! Achtung!"* An uncomfortable experience.

In Israel he was met by his grandmother and relatives and friends. He rented an apartment in Jerusalem, was asked by the Israeli Foreign Office to work on behalf of Russian Jewry, began to travel to conferences.

One day in June 1978 Sanya was listening to the English-language news broadcast over Radio Israel and heard that his parents had been arrested. He hurried to Tel Aviv and met with Nechemyah Levanon, an Israeli who had once played a major part in the secret Mossad operation that had brought Hebrew books into Stalin's Soviet Union. After some while Sanya was told that the Israeli government could do nothing about his parents. Sanya's dark sense of things was that the Israelis wanted his parents and certain other leading refuseniks to remain in the USSR because they were keeping alive the drive for emigration to Israel.

The international campaign to obtain exit visas for the Slepaks now changed direction and began to focus massively upon getting Volodya released from prison. About a year after his arrival in Israel, Sanya found himself needing to make a decision. His father had been sentenced to five years of exile in Siberia. His mother, given a suspended sentence, had gone to live with his father in a village near the Mongolian border. His brother was in hiding with friends in Moscow or elsewhere. Their lives were scattered, frozen. Sanya was twenty-six years old. The dissident years had stolen from him his university education; they had suspended and sundered his life. He was not sure what to do.

In telephone conversations with his father, he had talked about studying veterinary medicine and said there were no such schools in Israel. His father, disturbed by what he perceived to be the intent behind the words, said it would be wrong to leave Israel; Russian Jews should go to

Israel, look how long they had been struggling for exit visas. But in Israel the sunlight hurt Sanya's eyes, and the language was strange to his ears. He had begun to consider applying to universities in America.

On June 2, 1978, the Slepak apartment became a field of combat. It had been a battlefield of sorts since the early 1970s, a planning area, a headquarters, but never had there been an act of violence against people inside its rooms. During even the most heated of debates, hands were never raised. The bitterest of quarrels among the refuseniks had been settled without force inside the apartment.

The quarrel centered on the distribution of funds, and the man who helped resolve it was an American lawyer, one of the many hundreds of visitors who knocked on the door to apartment 77. Many came from Philadelphia, the hometown of the American: Leonard Shuster, Stuart and Enid Wurtman, Sheila and Dan Segal; Eileen Sussman. And from other American cities. And from Canada, France, Britain, Sweden, Denmark. And from as far away as Australia.

On a day in July 1974 the American and his wife, Joseph and Connie Smukler, came out of their hotel in the center of Moscow, walked along Gorky Street past apartment buildings and shops, turned left into number 15, and took the elevator up to the eighth floor. The wooden door to apartment 77, pieces of it jaggedly bolted together, had plainly suffered a recent smashing.

Joseph Smukler's knock was answered by Volodya. The Smuklers had not met him before and were immediately taken by the handsome man with the deep voice and thick shock of graying hair and luxuriant beard. To the right of the vestibule in which they stood was a doorway that led to the room once occupied by Volodya's parents and now the room in which Volodya and Masha lived; beyond were a hallway and the bathroom and water closet and kitchen, and the room of the couple with whom they shared the apartment, and that of their sons, where Leonid, then fifteen years old, lived by himself. As soon as they came through the doorway to their right, the Smuklers saw at the far side of the room a window covered with a lace curtain and, on the right-hand wall, to their astonishment, a small Israeli flag and a map of Israel. An Israeli flag and a map of Israel—in the heart of Soviet Russia!

Joseph Smukler had first heard of Volodya from the news stories of the dissidents who had signed the 1970 Letter of the 75 to U Thant requesting his support in their effort to emigrate from the Soviet Union. Volodya's name was prominent among the signatories.

A chance encounter with a newly arrived Russian couple in a restaurant in Israel during the summer of 1973 had plunged the Smuklers deep into the travail of Soviet Jewry. The man pleaded with them to help get his brother out of Leningrad. Back in Philadelphia the Smuklers became increasingly involved with a small circle of people who were attempting to establish an organization to serve as a disciplined instrument in the growing struggle for Jewish emigration from the Soviet Union. They decided to travel to Leningrad the following summer and meet the brother of the man they had happened upon in Israel. They were given a list of people to see in Moscow, and on that list were the names of Volodya and Masha Slepak.

They arrived in Moscow shortly after the visit of President Nixon. To deter possible demonstrations in Nixon's presence, the KGB had arrested many dissidents and scattered them to prisons dozens of miles from the city. Volodya, too, had been arrested, the door to the apartment smashed in by fifteen militiamen at eight o'clock in the morning, then the door to the bedroom broken, and Volodya hauled out of bed and taken away. Only recently released, many of the dissidents had joyfully reunited earlier that day in the apartment of Alexander Lunts, a noted mathematician and refusenik. Now some had assembled in the Slepak apartment and were quietly sitting and standing about as the Smuklers entered.

Also in the room at the time, and under the table, was Sanya's dog, a huge 145-pound, thirty-inch-high Russian black terrier named Akhbar, which Sanya had bought as a puppy. One of the men who had broken into the apartment had threatened to shoot the dog if it was not removed to another room. Leonid had tried to slip out to call foreign correspondents and been warned that if he went anywhere near the telephone on the street, they would break every one of his fingers and he would never be able to dial a telephone again.

Previous visitors had informed Volodya of the Smuklers' arrival: Joseph, then in his early forties; Connie, slender, quietly blond and strikingly lovely, possessed of a discerning intelligence and a sharp wit. Both were untutored in the ways of combat and survival in the visa war.

The furniture in the room was old and threadbare. Volodya directed Joseph Smukler to an overstuffed armchair. There were brief and muted introductions. Masha left the room and headed down the hallway to the kitchen. Using a magic slate, Smukler wrote, "We're friends from Philadelphia. How can we help you?" They drew up lists: books, goods. How to get money through to them: American Jews were in the habit of writing checks for their philanthropic causes, but don't send checks, urged the refuseniks, because the government takes 35 percent of every check. Bring in jeans instead. They were all so new at it in those early years of the visa war, before the time of organizations, movements, bureaucracies, the Helsinki Accords, the monitoring groups, the focus of the world on the issue of human rights. Quickly the warmest of friendships developed between the refuseniks and the Americans. Masha entered with tea and snacks. The dog suddenly rose, and the table shook. At one point Masha spoke quietly in Russian, and someone wrote down her words in English on a magic slate and showed them to the Smuklers: "We are doing this for the children. Not for ourselves but for the children. So they won't have to live here."

Back home the Smuklers became more deeply involved with the competing territories of the National Conference on Soviet Jewry, an establishment organization; the Union of Councils for Soviet Jews, a grassroots outfit; the Jewish Community Relations Council; the United Synagogue; and others.

From the Soviet Union there began to be heard disconcerting news of a rift in the ranks of Jewish activists.

Early in 1975 Robert Toth, the Moscow correspondent for the *Los Angeles Times*, who had written frequently about Jewish activists on the basis of material given him by Shcharansky, wrote a disturbing piece about internecine warfare between two groups of refuseniks: bitter accusations, abuses of funds, contending ideologies. A war inside a war.

The dissension was born of a deep ideological difference: Should the refuseniks spend precious money and energy building educational institutions in the Soviet Union and educating themselves and their children while waiting to get out, or should they concentrate all their efforts on emigration and make no attempt at all to establish a community while still there? Volodya sided with the latter group; he wanted nothing to do with any sort of possible communal life in the Soviet Union.

That summer the Smuklers returned to Moscow and the Slepak apartment. Nothing much had changed, except that the Israeli flag and map had been torn from the wall by the KGB, and pale outlines marked their haunting absence. At a meeting of refuseniks in the apartment, Joseph Smukler tried to smooth over the differences and, aided by Volodya, who turned out to be an adept negotiator, to some extent succeeded. With the help of the indispensable magic slates, the factions agreed not to issue damaging statements against each other and to set up a committee that would monitor and be accountable for the spending of funds collected from overseas. Smukler assured the refuseniks of the continued cooperation of the American Jewish community.

Participating in the meeting was Dr. Sanya Lipavsky.

From February 17 to 19, 1976, the Smuklers attended the second Brussels Conference: twelve hundred delegates from thirty-two countries. They met Masha's mother; she had been brought in from Israel to plead the cause of her daughter's family. "Please do something for them," she implored. "My children are dying."

There was more bureaucratic wrangling. Conflicts broke out between the establishment organizations and militant student groups. No overall goals were set by the conference; no international directions established. The movement to save Russian Jewry had pretty much begun as—and now looked to be remaining—a loose gathering of grass-roots organizations.

Connie Smukler traveled often to the Soviet Union during the 1970s, frequently saw the Slepaks. The apartment teemed with visitors from abroad. From Philadelphia alone, after briefings from the Smuklers and others, came a hundred or more people each year, at times four a week. They got off their planes, checked into their hotels, and walked up Gorky Street to the apartment. We're friends from Philadelphia, greetings from so-and-so, what can we do to help you? They brought jeans, goods, magazines, books, photographs, messages, good wishes, and information about strategies, demonstrations, conferences. Volodya sat smoking his pipe and listening patiently, at times dozing. Masha seemed always to be in the kitchen, preparing tea and cakes.

Joseph Smukler's name was among those listed as agents of the CIA in the letter by Lipavsky printed in *Izvestia*. The day the letter appeared was March 4, 1977, but the date on the newspaper was March 5, the anniversary of the death of Stalin. An error? An ominous warning of sorts? All on the list had attended the 1975 meeting in the Slepak apartment, when peace had been made between the warring refusenik factions.

Joseph Smukler applied for a tourist visa to the Soviet Union in 1977 and was refused. The reason given was that he was an agent of the CIA. He was turned down repeatedly until 1988.

A little more than a year after Shcharansky's arrest on March 15, 1977—he was still being held in Lefortovo Prison, still under interrogation, still awaiting trial—fighting broke out in the Slepak apartment between the Slepaks and the KGB as new and different weapons came into use in the visa war.

By the spring of 1978 the longest-standing and probably best-known refusenik not yet arrested was Volodya Slepak. His and Masha's refusal dated to 1970. He was now generally regarded as the leader of the Jewish dissident movement in the Soviet Union.

There were still many long-standing well-known refuseniks then, among them Ida Nudel, an economist. She was in her late forties, about five feet three inches in height, vigorous, with dark eyes and hair and a loud voice. She lived in the southern part of Moscow not far from Ryazansky Prospekt. Her sister had received an exit visa, but Ida Nudel had been refused since 1971 because of the claim by OVIR that she knew state secrets. She fought endlessly to aid dissidents who were in prison and to get herself out of the country. She was repeatedly harassed, arrested; her apartment, scoured; her body, searched. After the appearance of the Lipavsky letter in *Izvestia* and the arrest of Shcharansky, she had commented that Soviet Jews were now being accused of spying in the Soviet Union, "only because an accusation of having murdered a Christian boy would be completely ridiculous in a country of atheists."

In that spring of 1978 a NATO summit, a discussion concerning the Strategic Arms Limitation Treaty, was to take place in Washington. On May 26, some days before the summit, Masha Slepak and Ida Nudel and twenty-three other Jewish women signed and sent a letter to Premier Brezhnev in which they stated that they planned to stage a demonstration outside the Lenin Library on June 1, International Children's Day. They would be accompanied by seventeen children and intended to display banners decrying their illegal detention in the USSR.

On the first day of June the women assembled with their children in five apartments. All were immediately placed under house arrest by the watching KGB and prevented from leaving. The women proceeded to hang their banners over the balconies and displayed their placards from the windows. Suddenly there were militiamen and KGB agents everywhere, guarding rooftops, requisitioning adjacent apartments, forming a crowd in the street below each of the five buildings. In one of the apartments the women set up placards bearing the Star of David, with one displaying the clearly visible words VISAS TO ISRAEL. The KGB agents tried to smash down the door, but the women fought back and the KGB withdrew. From an adjoining apartment a KGB officer, swinging a long stick, tore down the VISAS TO ISRAEL placard. In other apartments KGB agents stormed the doors, fought their way through the women and children, used their fists and long poles with nails to rip the other placards away from the women.

At Ida Nudel's apartment KGB agents confronted a heavily barricaded door and a balcony covered with slogans. As quickly as their poles removed the slogans, Ida Nudel replaced them. They broke her windows with a wrench tied to a rope. She was still inside the apartment when they left at the end of the day.

That same morning, Masha Slepak, needing to walk her little dog, Chuka, discovered she could not open the apartment door. Olga, Leonid's girlfriend, was living in the apartment at the time. Her Russian father, a naval captain, had died when she was three; her Jewish mother had gone off somewhere, having abandoned three-year-old Olga and her little sister to their grandmother, who had raised them in a town outside Moscow. Olga banged on the door, shouting that she had to walk the dog and go to work. KGB agents opened the door—they had roped it to the stairway—and let her out. She walked the dog, returned, and left. The door was again roped shut. Masha locked it from the inside as well. Alone in the apartment now with Volodya, Masha said in a sudden flush of barely controlled anger, "I cannot endure this humiliation!" She wanted to go out to the balcony facing Gorky Street and demonstrate from there.

Volodya agreed.

They took a sheet, and with a pencil wrapped in cotton and dipped in paint, Volodya wrote on it, LET US GO TO OUR SON IN ISRAEL. They went through the hallway to their sons' room. Outside on the balcony each grasped a corner of the sheet. Together they lifted and suspended it over the ledge.

It was a warm, sunny day. The streets were crowded with Muscovites on their way to work. It did not take long for a large crowd to gather. KGB agents in the neighboring apartment tried to tear down the banner with a long pole, but Volodya seized the pole and broke it. The crowd began to number in the thousands, and traffic came to a halt.

From the apartment above, someone poured a kettle of boiling water on Volodya, scalding his head. KGB agents on the street below cheered as the water splashed Volodya. He wrapped a towel around his head, and he and Masha went on displaying the sheet. Shouts rose from the crowd: "Hit them!" "Call the executioners!"

In their eighth-floor apartment, Volodya and Masha heard pounding on the wooden door. Volodya rushed to lock the door to their sons' bedroom. KGB agents smashed the apartment door to pieces with axes and then hurried through the hallway and broke down the bedroom door and rushed inside and tore away the banner and quickly conveyed Volodya and Masha down the elevator to the courtyard and the street to a waiting prison van that brought them to a militia station in Moscow.

In the station they sat together for a while on a bench and then were separated. Volodya was taken to another militia station and put in an underground cell that measured about ten feet by seven feet. A small barred window at ground level, an iron door with a peephole, and a little door within the larger one through which food could be pushed into the cell. The floor was of wood, one section raised for a sleeping area. No pillow or mattress. Water and bread for food. On the third night he was put in a prison van with criminals. Inside the van were two round metal chambers, each with a single seat, that served as isolation areas, a jail within a jail. Volodya was ordered inside one of the chambers, and the curved door banged shut in his face. He was taken to Butyrskaya Prison, where he was told to remove his clothes. With the others, he was searched. Papers were then filled out for each man: name, date of birth, reason for arrest. Showered, dressed, they were taken to a room and each given a mattress, pillow, blanket. Volodya was delivered to a cell in which he found six others, one of whom was soon removed. Six iron plank beds in two levels; a table with two benches, all screwed into the floor; a sink; a lavatory pan in a corner. The men wanted to know why he was there. He said he had staged a demonstration. The men said, "On Gorky Street?" He said, "Yes." They said, "We heard all about it," and introduced themselves to Volodya.

Meanwhile, inside the militia station, Masha, now separated from Volodya, was asked to give up her internal passport and then interrogated. Your name, date and place of birth, where are your children? why did you go out to the balcony? At first she closed her eyes and refused to respond. By Soviet law the accused has the right not to answer. She was told, "Come with us," put into a van, and delivered to another militia station, where she was given a tin cup and placed in an empty cell. A concrete floor and a narrow wooden rise for a bed. No pillow or mattress. A small barred window, the glass painted white and barely letting in the last light of the day. Light shone in from the corridor through the small ventilating hole above the cell door. After a while she heard the sound of knocking and tapped her cup on the wall in response. She then put the mouth of her cup to the wall and her ear to the bottom of the cup and learned there were three men in the adjacent cell. They asked who she was and why she was there. She cupped her hands around her mouth as she directed her words to the wall and told about the demonstration on Gorky Street. She put her cup to the wall and heard them say that they already knew about it. The guard came to her cell and said in a kindly tone, "It is forbidden to knock on the walls and to speak to the other prisoners. Better for you not to do it."

The next day she began to experience pain in her stomach from the bread and water and sugar they fed her. The bread was black bread gone unsold in the shops and grown hard or moldy, then collected, ground into powder, sprinkled with water and yeast, and rebaked. She was interrogated twice each day during the next two days. Thinking she would make things easier for Volodya, she said it was all her idea to write the words on the sheet, to hang the sheet from the balcony. The pain in her stomach grew worse. A doctor was called. She was put into a van. It was night, and the van made several stops, each time loading and unloading prisoners. Masha, seated in an isolation chamber, listened to the two guards talking about her: She was wearing jeans, and they thought she was a lesbian. They stopped next to a van. Guards were shouting, "Faster, faster," and suddenly she heard the heavy, easily recognizable breathing of Volodya, who was being brought into her van, an especially egregious administrative error; people involved in the same crime were never to be transported in the same van. She cried out, "Volodya!" and heard her husband respond, "Yes, it's me." She said, "I took everything upon myself," and he shouted back, "You are foolish; don't say another word." The guards yelled, "Shut up! One more word and you'll be beaten!"

The van brought them both to Butyrskaya Prison. Volodya and the other men were taken inside. A moment or two later Masha followed, under guard. She found herself inside a hall as immense as a railroad station, with a domed ceiling and tall arched walls. Many doors led off the hall. In front of one door she saw a pile of men's shoes and immediately recognized Volodya's sandals among them. She was placed inside a tiny holding cell that had no light. Needlelike protrusions studded its concrete sides so one could not lean against the walls. After a half hour she was brought into a room with small benches and tables divided by glass partitions. Moments later, seated at one of the tables, with an interrogator behind the partition, Masha was again asked her name, place and date of birth, the reason she had staged the demonstration, who had put her up to it. She said she could not respond, the pain in her stomach was too severe. The interrogation continued. After some while the interrogator pointed to a large metal door in which there was a smaller door. Masha went out through the smaller door into a courtyard. From there a van took her to the militia station in her district, where she was asked to sign a statement that obligated her not to leave Moscow. She was then allowed to go home. They did not return her internal passport until some days later.

The following morning she went with her brother to see Sakharov and informed him of what had happened. Sakharov's mother-in-law, Ruth, Elena Bonner's mother, was there. She said she knew about the prison that was the size of a railroad station; she and others had been there before. Sakharov said he had no doubt Volodya would be put on trial. Masha asked, "What should I do?" Sakharov said, with infinite gentleness, "You must be strong."

Some days later, Ida Nudel was arrested in Trubnaya Square during a demonstration, and on June 21 was sentenced to four years of exile. On the very day of her trial Volodya was tried for malicious hooliganism in a different court. Walking along a corridor to the courtroom, he saw with surprise, through the windows, a crowd assembled outside. A huge crowd. Solidarity with him and Masha after their balcony demonstration.

He had been assigned an attorney, a man named Popov, who was a member of the Communist Party and seemed to be an honest person. At the start of the trial Volodya took the floor and said that he was grateful to attorney Popov, who had helped him prepare for the trial; then, addressing the judge, he asked permission to defend himself, in accordance with such and such paragraphs of the Judicial Code of Procedure. The judge granted his request.

The courtroom held about forty seats for the public, all of which had been taken early by KGB men in civilian clothes. There was a table for the prosecuting attorney and one for the defense, a large table for the judge, a small one for the secretary. Two guards stood near the defendant; a third guard, at the entrance door. Not one of Volodya's friends or family was permitted inside; they were told the courtroom was full.

Masha was not at the trial but in a hospital, undergoing treatment for a stomach ulcer.

Volodya, defending himself, argued that freedom of speech was guaranteed by the Soviet constitution. He talked about the Universal Declaration of Human Rights and the inviolability of the home.

The trial lasted one day. Found guilty of malicious hooliganism, he was sentenced to five years in exile.

Masha learned of the sentence as she lay in the hospital, listening to a small radio given her by a friend. She closed her eyes, feigning sleep, her temples throbbing and the words "five years" echoing inside her head. Through her terror and grief she wondered where Volodya would be sent and what would now happen to her. They were technically still divorced, and the authorities might not let her accompany him as his wife. But they might let her go as his companion, and perhaps if she, too, were sentenced to exile, they might send her to his place of exile. But that was so naive. The court never fulfilled the defendant's request for a place of exile.

Strange, how the patients in the room kept staring at her.

A young night nurse who was Jewish later whispered to Masha that everyone in the hospital had been told to keep an eye on her because she was an enemy of the people.

A man in a white coat, a doctor, a smirk on his face, suddenly bent over her. He said Volodya had received five years in exile.

The next morning she was told they were planning to do a serious invasive test on her, and she ate breakfast, making the test impossible. The head doctor summoned her and said brusquely that they intended to do all the necessary tests and she should make no further attempt to obstruct their efforts.

In the evening Masha's brother, Zalya, and Sanya's girlfriend, Alyona, came to visit. She asked them to bring her clothes the next day. Alyona arrived early, left the clothes in the room, and walked out. Masha donned them and started from the hospital. The woman in the next bed hurried out of the room toward the nurses' station. Alyona and Zalya stood waiting for Masha outside the hospital building. They made it through the front gate and took a taxi to the apartment.

Masha spent the following days going from one government office to another, trying to find out where Volodya was being exiled, without success.

She went to see him in Butyrskaya Prison. Huge stone walls covered with moss. An enclosed courtyard. Bushes, the lawn recently mown, no flowers. A sad medieval castle look. She carried a parcel containing a plastic coffee mug, butter, a loaf of white bread, sausage, cheese, cookies, cigarettes, onions, garlic cloves, tea, a few apples; a sports suit, cotton socks, a sweater, handkerchiefs, a pair of heavy shoes. The mug, the tea—removed by the guards with no explanation. The shoes and sweater—out. It's summer now, not time yet for winter clothes. Not before October.

She was given permission to speak with Volodya. They sat in a room with a glass partition between them and communicated through phones, a guard nearby. Volodya wore a blue jacket and looked pale, exhausted, his beard long, his hair graying. She said, "You need a haircut." He said, "No, it's all right; this way it's warmer." They talked about the appeals court, her coming trial, her intention, if she was sentenced to exile, to request that she be sent to wherever Volodya was going. They spoke about Leonid. The minutes flew by. The guard shouted, "The meeting is over!" Volodya stood, waved his hand, smiled, and walked out of the room.

The court of appeals upheld Volodya's sentence. Masha went to visit him again in Butyrskaya Prison and was told he had been sent the day before to the transit prison near the railroad tracks. He had begun his journey into exile.

For her trial in the last week of July, Masha wore a skirt and blouse and brought along a backpack containing a toothbrush, a bar of soap, a change of clothes, a coffee mug, some cheese. Friends helped her put together a statement to the judge in which she said that she knew the decision of the court had been predetermined and she would not participate in the hearing. She waived the right to be represented by a court lawyer. The small courtroom was crowded with strangers. The charges against Masha were read aloud. Malicious hooliganism. Masha asked for permission to read her statement and then came forward and placed the statement on the dais before the judge. In response to a question by the judge, Masha responded that she refused to participate in this court hearing. The judge told her to be seated. The prosecuting attorney, a blond-haired woman, gave Masha an odd look. To every question put to Masha by the judge, she gave the same response: "I refuse to participate in this court hearing." There were murmurs of annoyance from the audience in the court: "Who does she think she is?" "What way is that to show respect for a judge?" The people in the audience were militiamen dressed in civilian clothes; to Masha's eyes, thugs cut from the same mold. She noticed a familiar face, the woman from the apartment above the Slepaks who had poured boiling water on Volodya's head, who later testified that the demonstration had indeed blocked traffic on Gorky Street. The judge asked Masha if she agreed with that testimony. Masha said, "I refuse to participate in this court hearing." The hearing went on for more than an hour. To the judge's request that she make a statement, Masha responded by rising and saying, "I refuse to participate in this court hearing and waive the right to a final statement."

The court was then recessed for a half hour. When it resumed, the prosecuting attorney addressed the judge. Reading from a sheet of paper, she stated that all in the courtroom could clearly observe that Citizen Slepak had fully understood and denounced her act of hooliganism, and now, considering her wholehearted plea of guilt and her repentance for what she had done, it would be possible to sentence Citizen Slepak to three years in a labor camp—here a pause before continuing—and to place her on probation. The prosecuting attorney then sat down. Clearly, she had read a speech written for her before the trial by someone who had not anticipated Masha's silence.

The judge read the sentence: three years in a labor camp, with probation. The sentence could be appealed within seven days. The trial was over. Masha and her friends were overjoyed at the outcome.

Volodya and Masha believe that her sentence was suspended because of her poor health and also because there was nothing to be gained from imprisoning her; the Kremlin authorities had isolated Volodya and knew that Masha would want to follow him into exile.

Now Masha lived in the apartment with Olga, Leonid's girlfriend. The police sergeant and his wife had left two years before the balcony demonstration. In their room now were a middle-aged woman who was a postal clerk and her teenage son; they had been given a telephone of their own and warned not to let the Slepaks use it or it would be disconnected.

Masha's family was shattered. Leonid in hiding to avoid prison for refusing to be conscripted, moving from apartment to apartment in Moscow or journeying by train—not plane; you had to give your name and show your internal passport when you traveled by plane—to friends he could trust in Leningrad and Vilna and Armenia. Sanya in Israel and traveling often to Europe and England and the United States under the sponsorship of the Israeli Foreign Office and Jewish organizations, to meetings and conferences, where he spoke to small groups of influential people and large crowds, pleading his parents' cause, raising funds. And Volodya traveling by railroad with other prisoners under tight guard to his place of exile. None of the officials with whom Masha met could tell her his final destination.

At the end of August, Solomon Slepak, who had spent the summer in a small country house outside Moscow with his second wife, returned home. Astonishingly, he knew nothing of what had transpired with Volodya and Masha and was informed by his nephew Anatoly of Volodya's arrest and sentence. He suffered a heart attack.

Solomon's Russian wife later told Masha and Leonid that the old man spent the last days of his long life seated on the sofa with his hat on his head, swaying slowly back and forth and mumbling words in a language she could not understand. Masha thought the old man might have been praying in Hebrew.

Solomon Slepak was eighty-six years old when he died on September 2, 1978. Two days later he was buried in a Moscow cemetery reserved for party members only two ranks below those interred in the Kremlin wall. Volodya doesn't know and can't even conjecture who might have authorized his father's burial in that cemetery. Present at the funeral were relatives, a few friends, and a representative of the local Communist Party committee. The representative delivered a brief speech. KGB agents hovered in the background. The coffin was nailed shut.

After being petitioned by Masha some days before, a high official of the Interior Ministry, acting in compliance with Soviet law, had approved her request that Volodya be allowed to attend his father's funeral, on condition that while in Moscow he not visit with refuseniks or speak to correspondents or meet any foreigners.

Four days after arriving in his village of exile, Volodya received a telephone call from Masha: His father was dead. She added that she had obtained permission for Volodya to return to Moscow for the funeral. Volodya, shaken and profoundly sad, told himself: What a tragedy. He never understood me, and I'm not sure I ever understood him. His communism turned everything upside down. But he was my father. At the regional office of the militia, Volodya procured the necessary papers and returned by bus and plane to Moscow. He arrived in time for the funeral.

His father's Russian wife, mortified and outraged by Masha's arrest and by Volodya's arrest and exile, would have nothing to do with them. She regarded herself as a patriotic Soviet woman and refused to let Volodya have his father's personal papers. Years later, after her death, Volodya tried to obtain the papers through the children from her first marriage. But they had thrown everything away. Volodya was left with nothing of his father's library, nothing of the Old Bolshevik's letters, manuscripts, notebooks, the intimate record of his lifetime of work for the party.

Masha had requested and was granted leave to accompany Volodya into exile.

On September 8 they set out on a 5,000-mile journey to a village in Siberia that lay about 150 miles south of the city of Chita and some 200 miles from the region of China where Solomon Slepak, sixty years before, had fought as commander of a Bolshevik partisan division during the Civil War.

The Amulet

Before his trial Volodya was kept in Butyrskaya Prison for four weeks. Once, a week, a shower and change of underwear. Mornings each prisoner received six hundred grams of black bread and two cubes of sugar. Hot food three times a day.

After his trial and the rejection of his appeal, he was transferred to Krasnopresnenskaya Prison. The routine strip search. Guards poked through his bag of personal belongings and then put him into a cell with about thirty others. It was a transit prison; men constantly came and went. He spent four days there and was sent to another cell, strip-searched again, his bag turned inside out. The cell was called, in prison idiom, the accumulator.

One evening he was taken with others to a police van. Guards with machine guns loaded them inside. There was room in the back for at most twenty people standing solidly jammed together, but more than twenty-five needed transport. The surplus prisoners were stacked like sacks on the heads of those standing.

The van brought them to a railroad depot outside Moscow. A concrete platform, a web of tracks, sheds, empty railroad cars. Lights on tall poles illumined the tracks.

A second van pulled up, and out of it jumped guards with muzzled German shepherd dogs. The prisoners were herded onto the platform and ordered to squat with their hands clasped behind them. Each prisoner's small bag of personal belongings lay on the ground by his right foot. A guard pointed to a railroad car and announced that when he gave the signal, the prisoners were to run to the car and stop there. He said, "If while you are running, you take a single step to the left or to the right, it will be considered an escape attempt, and you will be shot." The muzzles were removed from the dogs.

Guards with a leash in the left hand, a weapon in the right; guards in front and on the sides; a guard in the rear with a long rubber truncheon for prisoners moving too slowly. Dogs and guards at their heels, the prisoners dashed across the ties and tracks and pebbled ground and came to a halt near the car, where they squatted and were counted and made to answer to their names and state the article of the penal code under which they had been sentenced. Then, again, they were strip-searched. And sent to their compartments.

Volodya found himself in a car with a long corridor where armed guards walked up and down. The corridor windows were painted white on the outside. Windowless compartments walled by thick chicken-wire grillwork lined the side of the corridor across from the translucent windows. The guards—Central Asians: Uzbeks, Yakuts, Buryats—knew hardly any Russian and were unable to communicate with the prisoners beyond the barking of basic commands. Each compartment, built to accommodate four passengers, contained at least ten prisoners, and on one of the many trains Volodya took on that long journey, one compartment held thirty, packed into the seats, the luggage bins, and standing. None of the men knew in which direction they were being ferried or what sort of fire or ice awaited them at their final destination.

Each prisoner received food to last until the end of the first leg of the journey: black bread, salted herring, and six lumps of sugar. Because they were normally given two lumps of sugar daily, they now knew they would be traveling in that car for three days. They felt the bump as the car was attached to a freight or passenger train. Soon the train started up. They rolled, creaking and clanking, away from Moscow.

Volodya was then fifty-one years old.

Siberia is a land so vast—about three million square miles—that its boundaries are often given as imprecise, roughly extending eastward from the Ural Mountains to the Pacific region until recently known as the Soviet Far East, and southward from the tundra world along the rim of the Arctic Ocean through a zone of vast forests to the near-lunar landscape of the nontillable, semidesert steppes of Central Asia and Mongolia.

Its use as a site for penal colonies and political exile began in the seventeenth century. The arduous journey, which originally took months, was made easier when the Trans-Siberian Railroad was completed in 1905. That was the railroad the young Bolshevik, Solomon Slepak, once took with his wife and daughter and infant son, Volodya, to a new life in China as a journalist and Comintern agent representing the then-nascent Soviet government. Now his son was riding it into exile as a prisoner of that government.

Always that journey—*etap*, the Russians called it, the transport under guard—from the initial transit prison to the final destination was the very worst of times for a prisoner. On the train you were allowed out of your cell twice a day to go to the toilet. And you had no idea where the train was heading unless it stopped in local towns and villages to pick up "transits," prisoners who were being brought to various district centers for trial. From those "transits" you would learn the direction the train was traveling.

During the first day of travel, the train Volodya was riding stopped briefly to pick up two lads. He watched as they were brought into the adjacent compartment. When the train was moving again, he called through the wall, "Boys, where are we traveling through?" and one of them answered, "Through the land of evergreen tomatoes," and the men in both compartments roared with laughter. Soon they were in a world of tall and broken hills, the train navigating their curving shoulders among dense forests. The Ural Mountains. Their first stop would be the city of Sverdlovsk.

At the end of each stage of the *etap*, the prisoners were directed off the train and made to squat and wait with their hands behind them, armed guards and killer dogs all around, until they were taken by van to a prison. There they stayed until the authorities organized the next leg of the journey, when they again received their food rations and went off on another train.

Beyond the Ural Mountains, the stops along the journey—Sverdlovsk, Novosibirsk, Krasnoyarsk, Irkutsk—were cities with prisons. They arrived in Sverdlovsk late at night, were counted, taken by van to a prison, strip-searched, and after showering put in a cell. The city served as a hub, as the gateway to the Gulag, the vast system of forced-labor prisons in the USSR. From Sverdlovsk the prisoners went off in different directions: to labor camps, to places of exile.

In Volodya's cell there were about one hundred beds and 150 prisoners: thieves, criminals, murderers, some making the journey a second or third time.

A "striper," a man whose striped prison garb indicated he was being sent to a maximum-security camp, seemed to be the acknowledged leader of the cell. He asked Volodya what crime he was being sent away for. Volodya told him about the demonstration. The man said, "Aha, a good kike!"

The prisoners' class system divided the world into good kikes and bad kikes. The bad kikes were Brezhnev, bureaucrats, members of the Communist Party; the good kikes, Sakharov, all other dissidents, and now Volodya.

Being a good kike earned Volodya respect and a bed for night sleeping; the shortage of beds necessitated their use during the day as well. When Volodya won second place in a chess contest organized among the prisoners, his standing in the eyes of the others rose considerably. A dissident, a political prisoner, a nice fellow, and also a splendid chess player. A good kike indeed!

He was in that cell fourteen days. Each morning they received their daily ration of bread and sugar; three times a day, hot food. There were two sinks and two lavatory pans in the cell. By the second week three-quarters of the prisoners had dysentery. Some lay about like dying men. They lit strips of blankets and burned pieces of bread and ate the charcoal to stop the diarrhea. No one said anything to the authorities. Telling the guards or doctors about the illness might have resulted in a two-week quarantine of the cell, possibly of the entire prison, an embarrassment to the officials administering the trains and prisons—they would have to answer to those above them for the unsanitary conditions of the cells—and brutal vengeance wreaked by prisoners and authorities upon the one who had dared say aloud what all knew but wanted kept silent. Volodya, too, fell ill.

One day a desperately ill Armenian asked the guards for a doctor. The striper had four prisoners beat him mercilessly; in prison language, they "unbuttoned his kidneys." When the doctor finally arrived, the Armenian said he needed something for a headache.

On the police van to the train that was to take him out of Sverdlovsk, Volodya discovered that the contents of his bag had been stolen and a large rag left inside it to simulate his possessions. The thief was no doubt one of the guards who had searched the bag; no one in the cell would have dared steal from another prisoner. Volodya was left with only the leather sandals and cotton jogging suit he was wearing. A disastrous turn. One of the men in the crowded van removed his jacket and gave it to Volodya. "You're going to freedom," he said. An exile was considered a free man by those who were headed to the labor camps. "It's cold there; take it."

On the train to Novosibirsk, Volodya was in constant pain from the dysentery and cold in his sandals and jogging outfit and one jacket. Next to him a sick old man who could not control his bladder used one of his own high boots as a latrine bucket, which he emptied during his evening trips to the toilet.

The train halted briefly at one point, and two young women prisoners were brought on board and placed alone in a separate compartment. They were on their way to a labor camp. From their compartment came the sweet sounds of their voices as they sang duets. Russian folk songs. There were eight guards in the car, all Asians. From time to time the singing would stop as guards entered the compartment and raped the women. A normal activity in Gulag life; no woman would think of resisting or complaining.

Normal, too, was the way the prisoners were given water on the train. Twice a day a tank was attached to the outside of the chicken-wire wall of each compartment, and a tap pushed through to the inside. One cup for all in the compartment; it went from mouth to mouth. Near Irkutsk there was a camp for prisoners with tuberculosis. On board the train were many who carried that disease.

It was near the end of August. In Irkutsk, Volodya saw light frost in the early mornings and thin ice on puddles.

One month and two days after he left Moscow, Volodya arrived in the Siberian city of Chita. His father had once had a girlfriend there, during his years as a Bolshevik commander. Volodya spent four days in the prison in Chita. A police van brought him to Aginskoye; he remembers a punishing ride of more than seven hours along a narrow road that wound through mountains and valleys and steppes. In the van were Russians, one very sad-looking man who had killed someone in a labor camp and was returning from his court hearing, and Buryats, who shared their goat cheese and cured lard with Volodya. It turned out that the man had good reason to be sad: This was the second time he had committed murder, and he was sure he would now receive the death penalty.

After a weekend stay in the prison in Aginskoye, Volodya was taken by the deputy chief of police in a jeep the twenty miles to the village of Tsokto-Khangil. It was August 28, 1978.

Volodya thought that he had been assigned originally to Tsokto-Khangil, but months later he discovered that by law, he could have chosen to stay in Aginskoye, a fairly large town with a sizable Russian population. He had not been informed that exile meant only that he could not vote or leave the district and had to appear once a week to register in the local militia station. Probably the KGB had told the militia of Aginskoye that they didn't want him living among so many Russians and to send him to the village.

It was early afternoon and turning cool when they arrived in Tsokto-Khangil. The entire village was actually a kolkhoz, a collective farm. The deputy chief of police brought Volodya to the one cafeteria in the village and treated him to a full meal. Then he took him to the office of the head bookkeeper of the kolkhoz, who was expecting him.

Volodya had no clothes, no money. The bookkeeper led him to the only hotel in the village; the dirt road that ran parallel to the village went on to Mongolia, and truckers used the cafeteria and the hotel for food and rest stops. The one-story hotel had four rooms. Slanting floors. A sink in the corridor. The water closet, with no running water, outdoors. He was given a small room with a bed. The bookkeeper advanced him one ruble against his future earnings and told him to report the following morning to the kolkhoz office.

The chronicles record Volodya's initial response to his village of exile, to its dirt roads, enormous sky, the rush and hiss of wind across the endless steppes. He felt, in his words, "bewitched by the purity of the air and the songs of the birds." The sensation did not last long.

He had traveled about five thousand miles, during which he had been entirely cut off from the world beyond *etap*. He asked if he could send a cable to his wife from the post office. He had no money for the cable and borrowed ten rubles against his future earnings. In Moscow neither the Interior Ministry nor the KGB had informed Masha of Volodya's final destination. Hearing nothing from him for so many weeks, she had begun to fear he might be dead. He cabled that he was in the village of Tsokto-Khangil, Aginskoye District, Chitinskaya Province, and asked that she send him some money. Shortly afterward she called and told him about her trial and sentence.

Later that day, with the money he had borrowed, he bought a pair of heavy work boots, strips of white cotton cloth to use as socks, two sets of underwear, a flannel shirt, cotton pants, and a cotton-padded jacket. He was now dressed warmly enough to withstand moderately cold weather.

He reported to the kolkhoz chairman, a Mongolian who happened also to be a deputy to the Supreme Soviet. He was not pleased to have

an enemy of the people on his kolkhoz and lectured Volodya sternly
about his behavior as an exile: He expected him to work hard and not
cause trouble. He assigned Volodya to a job in the granary. Months later
Volodya discovered that according to law, he could have chosen his job
and changed it at will. But no one had informed him of his rights as an
exile, and there were no lawbooks available in prison.

The next day two hundred rubles arrived from Masha. Two days later
she phoned again to tell him that his father had died.

All her life, as far back as she could remember, Masha had a sense of herself as an amulet; others used her for their own good luck. Often her
mother had called Masha "my amulet," "my good-luck charm," and in
1976 Bertha purchased a red, blue, and yellow enamel amulet in a shop
in Jerusalem, had the back of its metal case engraved with the Hebrew
words *le-masha me-ima* ("To Masha from Mother"), and asked an American tourist to deliver it to Masha in Moscow. Near and distant friends
would beg Masha to accompany them to the OVIR office when they
went to submit their applications for exit visas. More often than not
their visas were granted, and they were certain it was because of Masha's
presence. She accepted as her destiny the uncanny probability that she
was alive to serve as the good fortune of others, but not her own.

In September 1978, some days after the funeral of Solomon Slepak,
she and Volodya—aided by impatient KGB agents who had grown
weary of watching them wait in endless lines in the crowded Moscow
airport—managed to buy tickets for one of the usually sold-out direct
flights to Chita. They arrived before sunrise and took a cab to the bus
station, which was closed.

It had been hot in Moscow when they left, but it was quite cold in
Chita. Buryats stood around in silence. The bus arrived: old, rickety,
twenty-five seats. Chita lay in an enormous valley surrounded by forest-
covered mountains. A river, the Chitinka, ran through the city. Masha
saw small houses, fences. On the seat beside her, Volodya slept.

The bus, swaying and rattling, left the city and began to climb. Tall
evergreens lined the narrow asphalt road. Huge, polished boulders lay
among the trees. They kept climbing, the road now chiseled out of the
side of a cliff. A broad valley below and mountains like a theater back-
drop stretching to the horizon. The sun rose, bathing one side of the
valley in a pale light and leaving the other in blue-green shadows. A river
snaked through the valley, houses and fields along its banks. Masha

thought it all a beautiful sight and remembered that Chekhov, in his account of his travels to the island of Sakhalin, had described the region as "Russia's Switzerland."

Gradually the road turned narrow, rocky, dangerous. It dropped to a dusty valley. They rode through a silent village of wooden houses covered with gray dust and stopped briefly at a coffeehouse in a valley burned by the sun. Along the horizon lay forested hills. After four hours of travel they reached the Trans-Siberian Railroad crossing just as a train was passing. A sign on the side of each car: MOSCOW–PEKING. The railroad Volodya and his family had once taken on their way to China and back. No villages on these steppes, no people. Short, thin, stunted trees, with few branches. Six hours on the road and now, along the horizon, houses on the hills and the town of Aginskoye. A bus station at the edge of the town, a well-lighted waiting room.

Masha and Volodya recovered their belongings and stood on the ticket line for the bus to Tsokto-Khangil. The bus was due in from the south in two hours. In that region Aginskoye was the last town with a large presence of Russians. Southward extended the land of the Buryats—Asian people of the steppes, nomads, Buddhists.

The bus to Tsokto-Khangil was older than the one from Chita. The road, unpaved and rutted; the terrain, an infinite desolation. The doors on the bus couldn't be closed entirely; dust powdered the driver and passengers. The Buryats in the bus gazed curiously at Masha and Volodya; they did not often see Russians traveling this far south. Trembling like an old horse, the bus made its way up and down hills, and on what seemed the highest hill it stopped, and the Buryats climbed out to pray. They offered money as bribes to evil spirits and candies and cookies to good spirits. Twenty minutes of prayers and offerings. They climbed back on the bus, and now along the road ran a dry riverbed in which grew scrawny birch trees with crooked trunks the thickness of an arm and bent to the ground as if permanently overwhelmed, defeated.

The village of Tsokto-Khangil sat in the middle of a valley that was about thirty miles long and seven miles wide. Low hills fenced in the valley; the sun rose, burned its way across the valley, and set. About three thousand men, women, and children lived in the one-story wooden houses of the village. There were nearly two hundred houses, each with a backyard in which nothing grew.

In the village square stood the administrative buildings of the kolkhoz: the kolkhoz office, on the first floor of which was the village telephone center; the House of Culture, with a concert hall; the post office, with a telegraph, an international telephone line, and a bookshop. Nearby were a medical aid station staffed with a Russian nurse; a maternity ward; a veterinary aid station; a machine and tractor station; the hotel where Masha and Volodya first stayed; a department store; a restaurant; a child care center; a boarding school for the children of Buryat shepherds; a yard for agricultural machinery; another food shop; a greenhouse; a bathhouse; sheds for cows. The entire village was a collective farm that raised pigs and cows and was domesticating the Buryats, attempting to get them to sever their ties to the seminomadic traditions of their ancestors, who had lived off sheep, and to settle into the life of sedentary shepherds bound to a Soviet kolkhoz.

Masha and Volodya arrived on an evening in the second week of September, in weather that had been warm during the day but was brushed with a strange dry cold when they came down off the bus. No one greeted them; no one spoke to them. A wind blew from the north down toward Mongolia and the Gobi Desert.

The hotel was a shabby one-story building. At the far end of its single corridor were two faucets, only one of which had a sink beneath it. The water from the other faucet ran directly onto the floor and through the semirotted boards to the ground below. The room they were given had two iron beds, a table, chairs; a lightbulb hung from the ceiling by a wire. There was electricity only in the morning and evening. The window was without curtains. Gazing out into the darkness, Masha felt she was on a planet burned to dead charcoal by a merciless sun. Five hundred thousand square miles of dull, unfruitful earth, and the Gobi Desert only a few hundred miles away. Still, people live here, she thought that first night. It is possible to survive here.

Volodya woke early to go to his job. They had brought with them a one-burner stove, on which Masha cooked their breakfast. Volodya worked unloading the grain trucks that arrived from the combines. At one point during the day the chairman of the kolkhoz said to him that he knew all about Zionism: The Zionists were evil people who wanted to conquer the world.

Toward the end of September, with the start of the very cold weather, Volodya was given a job as a stoker in the boiler room that heated the kolkhoz garage, in which were trucks and jeeps. There was no antifreeze on the kolkhoz, and frozen water lines could spell disaster for the vehicles. His salary was 120 to 140 rubles a month. He and Masha could not have survived on that, but assistance came from the special fund established by the refuseniks. The money that entered the fund through the sale of tape recorders, radios, cameras, and clothing left behind by overseas visitors was allotted to impoverished refusenik families whose wage earners had lost their jobs and could not find work, and to prisoners and the families of prisoners.

In October winter descended swiftly and cruelly upon the village. Volodya worked in the boiler room of the kolkhoz garage. His labors began at 8:00 A.M. Stripped to the waist in the blistering heat, he stoked the furnace for twenty-four hours and then had forty-eight hours free. He toiled week after week. Twenty-four hours of labor in that boiler room; forty-eight hours off.

In the beginning all the villagers appeared alike to Masha. But Volodya, who had spent his childhood in China, distinguished easily among the various Asian faces: Buryats, Tatars, Yakuts. He began to talk at length to Masha about his years in China. He had never done that before, talked to anyone about those years. Life in Peking and Mukden. His Chinese nanny. The day he and his sister saw the wildcat in the garden. His exile returned him in memory to the warmth and innocence of his beginnings.

At first there was no place where they could live other than in that wretched hotel, its heating system erratic, its walls pocked with holes, its toilets in the yard outside. It was a stop for truck drivers who hauled goods from Chita to Mongolia, which lay a few dozen miles to the south. An old Buryat woman would open the door for them at all hours of the day or night. She would give each a room with a bed, food, and a bottle of vodka, and they would drink until they dropped.

Masha grew fearful of remaining alone in the hotel. At times, when Volodya worked nights, drivers who had discovered there were exiles living in the hotel would yell drunkenly through the door, "Open up! Open the door!" and Masha would say, "Go away or I'll call the police."

One night a Buryat driver, drunk to near-unconsciousness, tore the door off its hinges and stood there, staring into the room, swaying. Masha said in a calm voice, "Why are you behaving so badly?" The driver, seeming to sober up a little at her composed, reprimanding tone, pulled himself up and said, "I wanted to open the door and look." She said, "Well, you looked. Now you can go back to your room, or I'll call the police."

Volodya told the chairman of the kolkhoz that he and Masha could not go on living in the hotel. Why couldn't they settle in nearby Aginskoye, only twenty miles away? But the KGB authorities didn't want the Slepaks in Aginskoye and suggested to the kolkhoz chairman that he give them one of the apartments in the two-story brick building nearing completion in Tsokto-Khangil. The chairman of the kolkhoz called Volodya in and said, "I intended to give that apartment to the best worker in the kolkhoz, and instead I have to give it to an outlaw, to an anti-Soviet element."

Volodya said, "You aren't giving me that apartment. You were ordered to do so. Why are you complaining to me? If you don't like it, you should complain to them." And he left.

The apartment was one room in a two-story brick building near the dirt road and dry riverbed that ran to the west of the village. The room measured twenty feet by ten. There was a ten-by-seven kitchen and a bathroom, a toilet, a balcony. In the toilet and bathroom were sinks and a tub and a lavatory pan—entirely unusable because there was no running water in the village. From the window and balcony they had a clear view of the unpaved road to Mongolia and the riverbed and the steppes beyond, numbing with monotony, barren save for brownish, brittle, rain-starved grass, and empty of people. Wolves and foxes roamed about, and packs of wild dogs. In the farthest distance were hills, tall climbing mounds of gray rock, without trees, without vegetation.

The building had been constructed by a crew of Armenians from blueprints drawn up for apartment projects in the more moderate climate of Moldavia: hollow plywood doors, thin outer walls with no insulation against the cold. Because it was among the last to have been completed, the apartment was built of whatever pieces of lumber had been left. The result was a nightmarish dwelling: buckling, shabbily painted walls, ill-fitting doors, warped windows, cracks between the floor planks. Cold air blew in through the doors and windows, and the floor was difficult to walk on because of the uneven length and thickness of the boards.

Masha and Volodya began to transform the apartment. They repainted the walls, doors, and floors. With the planking of discarded packing crates, Volodya built shelves and a table for the kitchen. In a garbage dump he found a junked bed, which he brought to the apartment and repaired. He built bookshelves, shoe racks, benches, a sofa. He had brought tools with him from Moscow; the nails he found along the sides of the road that ran through the village. Once, out on the steppes, he came upon a new wrench. Often the Buryats, after repairing broken machinery or equipment, carelessly left the hardware behind. They didn't care. None of it really belonged to them; it was all the property of the Communist state.

One night in early November it began to snow, tiny flakes thickly falling. The wind picked up the dust and sand of the steppes, mixed it with the snow, and pelted the village. In the dry air of the morning the snow vanished quickly, but the village stood pallid and dust-covered. Everywhere, sand—in one's clothes, eyes, mouth, food. Toward the end of the month Masha and Volodya moved into the apartment.

In the evenings the uncovered windows seemed menacing black holes to Masha, and she bought fabric and made curtains. She and Volodya went to the department store and brought back cartons, which they laid out on the uneven planks of the floor and then covered with plastic; the floor was even now, and insulated. She stuffed rags into the hollows of the plywood doors, and when the frost deepened and the winds grew stronger, she bought the thick felt used by the Buryats for their yurtas— the tepeelike structures in which they lived during the periods they grazed sheep on the steppes—and hung it over the doors for further insulation.

The Buryats had never before lived with an exile in their midst, indeed had been informed by the authorities that these Russians were enemies of the people and were to be shunned. But Masha invited the Buryats who lived in their building to join them for tea and cookies, and finally, after repeated invitations, some came and sat in silence, looking around the apartment, sipping the tea, nibbling on the cookies. Volodya had earlier explained to her that Buryats were of Mongolian stock and were called Buryats on this side of the border and Mongols on the Mongolian side. Mongolia, Masha of course knew, was a puppet client state of the Soviet Union. The Buryats invited by Masha into the Slepak apartment later invited the Slepaks into their apartments. Masha and Volodya noticed they had covered their windows with curtains, and their floors with cartons and plastic, and their doors with felt.

Volodya built a lamp for the kitchen and a wall desk and a desk lamp for himself. On the wall over the desk he hung photographs of Andrei Sakharov, Natan Shcharansky, Ida Nudel, Iosif Begun, and Yuri Orlov. Near their bed were photographs of Sanya and Leonid.

To his delight, Volodya discovered that the bookstore in Tsokto-Khangil—stocked with the usual pens, pencils, maps, notebooks, periodicals, children's books, and adult books—also had on its shelves volumes difficult to obtain even in Moscow. Masha began to buy children's books, intending to send them to her grandchildren abroad so they could read and not forget the Russian language. The family chronicles offer Volodya's attempt to clarify the odd presence there of those books: "It was one of the paradoxes of the socialist system that when a book was published, copies would be distributed to bookstores in the Soviet Union, not on the basis of demand but according to population."

They had brought with them from Moscow a small shortwave radio. But in Tsokto-Khangil the Voice of America was being successfully jammed. They were able to buy a small television set, but the satellite signal gave them only three or four hours a day of watching. The isolation they felt was nearly overwhelming.

Their difficulties with the people of the village did not involve language—all spoke Russian—but culture: They were sophisticated urbanites in the midst of a world of erstwhile seminomads, core Muscovites among border Buryats, Jews who dreamed of distant Israel living with Asians whose homeland was nearby Mongolia. Even had the KGB not insisted that they be separated from any sort of communal life in their place of exile, they would still have felt thrice imprisoned: exile, Jew, Russian. In a prison state called the Soviet Union.

Slowly they came to know some of the villagers. A chance encounter here, an affable greeting there. Word spread: The Moscow couple didn't seem so menacing, indeed were friendly, helpful; the man an engineer, the woman a doctor. Why are you here? We are Jews and we want to go to Israel, and they won't let us. No one in the village had ever seen a Jew, though many knew of Israel. Twice over the years they were asked to Buryat weddings. Party bosses came from Aginskoye and scolded the Buryats for hosting enemies of the people. The Buryats listened quietly with impassive faces. One day one of the Buryat men said to Masha and Volodya, "Why do you want to go to Israel? It's so far away. You're good people. Stay here with us. We'll give you a dozen sheep, two dozen, if you want." Another said later in a confiding tone to Volodya, "Listen, your wife is too old. If you want, we'll find you two young ones."

The dirt roads and lifeless steppes froze to the hardness of iron as the temperature dropped to forty degrees below zero Fahrenheit. At night the cows and pigs fell silent and the air was still save for the occasional barking of dogs in different corners of the village. The sky cloudless, myriad stars would shine coldly and clearly. During the day Masha and Volodya took frequent walks through the village and along the steppes. The winds were harsh. On the steppes a herd of horses roamed freely, and sheep grazed on the winter grass.

One day every family in the apartment building abruptly left to join their relatives in the wooden houses throughout the village. A fierce storm was coming, they said. Masha and Volodya had no place to go. The village became very quiet. A haze covered the sun. The wind began to rise, a sound like someone blowing through a pipe, high-pitched, then howling. The sun, hidden by the haze, grew darker. Wind blowing and whistling and howling shrilly outside. Snow mixed with sand striking the windows and the balcony door. The door and the metal roof of the apartment house rattling. Very dark outside and the storm growing more fierce and suddenly no electricity and cold in the apartment. They put on heavy clothes. Colder and colder. Volodya lit the kerosene lamp, a small, shuddering flame. They wrapped blankets around themselves, but it was impossible to fall asleep; something kept clanging and banging outside.

The storm lasted fifteen hours. When day came, they saw a vast landscape of snow, and electric poles down in the snow amid a tangle of wires, and the barely visible roofs of nearby houses, and on the steppes little mounds where sheep had died. It took bulldozers five days to clear the road from Aginskoye to the village, which remained all that time without water, telephone, mail. Masha and Volodya lived off the food and water they had stored in the apartment.

That February, Leonid, still avoiding conscription and living on the run, decided to fly from Moscow to Siberia to see his parents. By flying, he risked discovery, but his parents desperately needed certain foods and medicines and the heavy parkas brought to Moscow as gifts by visitors from Canada.

Direct flights from Moscow to Chita were booked far in advance, mostly by army officers and government officials; Chita was a large military center. Leonid used a plastic shopping bag full of pens, chewing gum, and women's stockings to persuade one of the high-level Moscow airport personnel to get him a ticket at least as far as Irkutsk. From there he got on a local flight to Chita, an old commuter plane with about twenty passengers. One of its windows, warped and not fully closed, let in arctic air. A man tried to shove a rag into the crack, with no success. The propeller-driven aircraft lurched and bounced in the gusting Siberian winds. Someone had taken a goat on board; there were other animals as well. People vomited. Leonid had with him a large backpack and two enormous bags of food, medicines, and other necessities. In Chita he was told that the bus to Aginskoye had departed and the next bus was in the morning. He spent the night on the floor of the bus station and left the following day. Six hours on that winding road in an old bus with almost no shock absorbers. It was nearing dark in Aginskoye when he arrived. None of the cabdrivers wanted to take him to Tsokto-Khangil. He offered money to some men who were standing around. They didn't want money. They had plenty of money; there was nothing to buy with it. He held up two packs of Marlboro cigarettes, and a fight nearly erupted over who would take him. On the road to the village in the pitch-dark night, the driver asked where exactly he was going, and Leonid told him, and the driver said, "Ah, that couple from Moscow. The word is they're nice people." He knew precisely where Masha and Volodya lived and left Leonid off at their door.

His parents had not seen him in months, did not know he was coming, and greeted him with excitement and disbelief. He was able to stay only briefly and flew back to Moscow with his mother.

In order for Masha to retain her Moscow residence permit—Volodya's lapsed during his exile—and the registration for the apartment, it was necessary that she return regularly, be seen in the apartment building by neighbors, and keep her air tickets as proof that she had traveled back to the city.

One of the regulations printed on the last page of every Soviet citizen's internal passport stipulated that a citizen could be absent from a place of residence no longer than six months. After that the apartment could be taken back by the government—on the grounds that there was insufficient living space for the people, and that a person who doesn't use an apartment doesn't need it. A lawyer friend in Moscow had advised Masha that it was best she not remain away longer than four months because sometimes apartments were taken away after an absence of five months.

So in mid-February 1979, about four and a half months after she had arrived in Tsokto-Khangil, Masha together with Leonid took the bus to Aginskoye and a second bus to Chita, and a plane from Chita to Irkutsk, and another plane from Irkutsk to Novosibirsk, and finally a plane to Moscow. Frigid weather, uncertain travel, irregular flight schedules, crowded airports, lengthy delays, jostling and pleading and bribing clerks for tickets—a hellish journey Masha repeated every three or four months throughout the five years they lived in exile. In Moscow she saw her relatives, greeted friends, did some necessary shopping—for herself and Volodya and also for the Buryat women she came to know, who sent her with lists of goods to buy: clothes, winter boots, candy; she spent hours on long lines in Moscow stores and brought back everything they asked for; she wanted to live with them in peace—and then returned to Tsokto-Khangil.

That first year of exile she remained in Moscow two and a half months, waiting with Leonid and Olga for the arrival of their first child, born in early April, a son, whom they named Eugene, after Olga's father.

That same April came the joyful news that five of the men imprisoned for their involvement with the 1970 "Leningrad Hijacking Plot" had been released. And about one week later the Kremlin traded five religious and political dissidents for two Soviet spies imprisoned in the United States. Shcharansky, however, languished on in a prison camp, and Ida Nudel in a distant exile.

In late April, Leonid returned to Tsokto-Khangil to say good-bye to his parents; he had been notified by OVIR that his request for an exit visa was approved. He spent five days with his parents. Talking with his mother. Playing chess with his father. Nights, sleeping on the floor. Just being with them in their exile.

He was twenty years old. One day, at the age of four, he had come running in tears to his mother from the courtyard of the apartment building on Gorky Street where he was playing with friends. One of the children had called him a *zhid*, a Jew, a kike.

"But you are a Jew," said his mother.

"No, I'm not," Leonid cried.

"Well, what do you think you are?"

"I'm a Muscovite."

An odd reply from a four-year-old, who might have been expected to respond with the more traditional answer that he was Russian or Soviet.

His mother told Leonid to calm himself. Then she said, "I am Jewish; your father is Jewish; both your grandparents are Jewish. That makes you Jewish."

Leonid replied stubbornly, "You can be anything you want. I am a Muscovite."

That was the first and only time in his entire childhood that Leonid experienced anti-Semitism. But he did not grow up in an ordinary Russian neighborhood or attend a commonplace Russian school. Together with his older brother, Sanya, he was raised among the very elite of the Soviet system. He lived in an apartment with three rooms, in one of which was a family of strangers only because Grandfather Solomon could not bear the notion of living in such luxury while so many in Moscow needed a roof over their heads. He knew nothing of his father's work. He was of course aware that his father traveled often by train or plane to testing grounds and to various factories in Minsk in White Russia. On the day he was admitted into the Pioneers, at the age of ten, he ran home and proudly showed his red scarf to his father, who at that moment was deep in conversation with a man from Riga. His father sat listening to his son's bubbling words, an odd dismissive smile on his face. The man from Riga drew from a pocket a postcard with a stamp from Israel and showed it to Volodya and then to Leonid. The boy was a passionate collector of foreign stamps, his sole source for acquisitions the bookstore on their street, which sold stamps only from socialist countries. And now suddenly, in the hands of this stranger, a truly foreign stamp! And from Israel! The man from Riga let Leonid steam the stamp from the card and put it into his album. His father warned him never to show the stamp in school.

Early recollections.

He knew almost nothing about Israel but sensed there was something different about his parents and their friends and that the difference had to do with Israel. Anything foreign was forbidden fruit to a Russian and exciting. And it was clear to Leonid by the age of eleven that his family was in the process of going to Israel; they were emigrating, this year, next year. There was nothing religious about their act of emigration; they were simply one family among others, a community of ethnics, united by blood and waiting to leave for a Jewish country. But they didn't leave. And the years dragged on.

As enthusiastic as Leonid was about foreign stamps so was his older brother, Sanya, passionate about living creatures. In their room, with its balcony overlooking Gorky Street—once their parents' room, when the grandparents Solomon and Fanya had lived in the apartment—Sanya had built a terrarium for hedgehogs, lizards, a viper, and had a cage with fifteen birds, and raised to full size an eagle, given to him during a trip in the Crimea, where it had fallen out of its nest; it sat on a glass shelf in that small room: a beady-eyed, hook-mouthed presence, defecating fiercely against the walls and double doors of the balcony. They left it in the Moscow Zoo one day, thrusting it clandestinely through the narrow bars of the aviary after the zoo officials had refused to take it because they had enough eagles. Sanya subscribed to a magazine called *Young Naturalist*, and some of its exquisite color photographs of birds and fish adorned the walls of the room.

Leonid spent a year in a Moscow institute of construction engineering, passed his first semester with ease, and, just before he was to take his final exams, was informed by one of the professors that he would not pass, that it would be best if he left. Since he was doing well in his studies, it was clear that the school was responding to an order from the KGB that he be dropped from its rolls. He took the exams that June of 1977, failed them, and was expelled. That now left him open to immediate conscription into the armed forces.

On a Thursday in October a postcard came, notifying him that he was to report the following Monday to the local draft board. He and his parents spent the weekend drafting a letter to the minister of defense, in which he stated that he refused to serve in the armed forces of the Soviet Union for two reasons. First, he had been trying to leave the country since the age of ten. If he was now drafted for two, perhaps three years, he would afterward be told that he was a security risk and couldn't leave for five more years; he would then have waited a total of fifteen years to leave the country, an absurd situation. And second, he had become a citizen of Israel at the age of thirteen and could not pledge his loyalty to the USSR, where he was being held against his will. The letter was mailed to the office of the minister of defense, and a copy sent to the local draft board. Copies were circulated among foreign correspondents.

That Monday night Leonid packed a bag and left the Gorky Street apartment. On Thursday of that same week, October 27, Sanya departed for Israel. Leonid, in hiding, could not go to the airport to bid farewell to his brother. From the end of October to the end of November, Leonid remained inside the Moscow apartment of a friend, keeping away from the windows and listening to records of classical music. He met his parents one night in December in Pushkin Square and told them he was getting out of Moscow and going to Vilna to live with friends he had met during one of his summer trips to the Crimea, when he had been introduced to and become part of a *kompaniya*—young people from well-to-do families, most of them not Jews: painters, actors, "free" professionals, people who could get away with not working for a while because they could claim they were between projects and would therefore not be accused by the authorities of being economic parasites, a criminal offense.

He took a train to Vilna, first making certain to shake off any possible KGB tail, something he had been doing since the age of thirteen. He did not have time to purchase a train ticket. On the train he paid the conductor, who pocketed the money and let Leonid sleep in his compartment.

In the early spring of 1978 he returned to Moscow from Vilna with a high fever and in near-delirium. Clearly in need of a physician, he went directly to the apartment on Gorky Street, where his mother tended to him. As soon as he was well, he left.

That was a tense period. The KGB was closing down the entire

Helsinki Accords Monitoring Group. Orlov had been arrested. Shcharansky was in prison. Leonid's father, spearheading a worldwide campaign to free Shcharansky, was a prime KGB target. Leonid went to friends in Armenia. Later that spring he was back in Moscow, staying in the apartment of close friends. His girlfriend, Olga, whom he loved, showed up to tell him that his parents had been arrested for staging a demonstration from his and Sanya's balcony. Leonid, nineteen years old, suddenly aware that he was alone and might have no one to care for him were he to be arrested and exiled, asked Olga to marry him. She agreed. At considerable personal peril, he visited his mother in the hospital where she was undergoing tests and treatment for her ulcer. To apply for the marriage license, he needed his internal passport, which she was keeping for him. Masha was appalled when she saw him; the hospital was full of KGB informers. She gave him the passport, and he fled.

He and Olga applied for their marriage license in her grandmother's little town outside Moscow, and were married. When his father was sentenced to exile, Leonid reasoned that the danger to his own person had lessened considerably. The international furor over his father's sentence was enormous; the KGB would not want to add to it by arresting the son as well. Besides, he, Leonid, was really not much of a dissident; until turning eighteen, he had never participated in petitions or demonstrations because he was a minor, and since eighteen he had been on the run. It made no sense for the KGB to arrest him now.

He returned to the apartment with Olga. From there he went to see his parents in February 1979, and he flew back with his mother to await the birth of his child, which occurred on April 2. On April 8 Leonid went to the hospital to bring home his wife and infant son. Later, on the way into the apartment with his new family, he checked the mailbox and saw the postcard from OVIR: He was to appear at the OVIR office on April 16 to pick up his exit visa.

When you reported to receive your exit visa, you yielded up your internal passport to the authorities. But Leonid needed his internal passport to get on a flight to Chita; he wanted to see his father one final time before he departed. The April 16 deadline for the exit visa was too soon.

Masha accompanied him to OVIR the next day; he remembers she wore the amulet purchased by her mother in Jerusalem. He informed the official that he had come for his exit visa. But, he added, there had been a change in his status since the time of his original application: He had a wife now, and an infant son. And his father was in exile. He would have to write a new application.

The official gave him the necessary papers to fill out and said his visa would be extended only until May 12.

The following day Masha was informed that Volodya had been taken seriously ill. She left immediately for Chita. It seemed that after one of his twenty-four-hour shifts at the furnace, Volodya, drenched with sweat, had walked out into a freezing April morning and was soon in the hospital in Aginskoye with double pneumonia.

By the end of April, with Masha present, his condition had improved, and he returned to the village. When Leonid arrived in Tsokto-Khangil in the last week of April, his father looked pale and was breathing with difficulty. He spent five days with his parents in their apartment, kept Volodya company during his boiler room shifts, slept nights on the floor in a fleece-lined bag, which he left behind when he departed.

He and Volodya talked at length about Israel. Leonid had warm feelings about Israel, but his second language, which he could read and speak fluently, was American English. Since the age of twelve he had been meeting five to fifteen visiting Americans every day in the Gorky Street apartment, translating their conversations with his mother. He knew American movies and pop music, had spent time with American girls, au pairs in the apartments of American diplomatic personnel. Yes, he liked Israel, but he wanted to live in the United States.

Volodya said, "You must go to Israel; otherwise you will damage the image of the movement and my image in particular. I am sure you will go on tour, campaigning in America, to raise money for the movement. Then you can choose where you want to live. Why are you choosing now? You don't know about Israel. Maybe you'll like it. Go to Israel, be there awhile, do the campaign, everything will settle down, and then you'll decide where you want to live."

Leonid listened in silence. That was their only serious conversation during those days in Tsokto-Khangil. He would normally never talk about matters somber or sentimental with his father. With his mother, yes, but with his father—much rather discuss the nail in the wall, play chess, just be in each other's presence. Leonid and Volodya parted with the hope that they would meet each other after the exile. He and Masha boarded the morning bus to Aginskoye. Volodya stood on the side of the road, watching them leave.

That was the first of May. There followed frantic days in Moscow: document-collecting, farewell parties, packing. On the evening of May 9 the Gorky Street apartment witnessed a large, joyous crowd. Leonid's friends, his parents' friends: Jews, Russians, dissidents, refuseniks, journalists. The next evening was quiet, with a small and intimate family gathering.

On Friday, May 11, Masha accompanied Leonid and his wife and infant son to the Moscow airport and watched them take off for Vienna. Leonid and Olga and little Eugene stayed in the transit camp in Vienna over the weekend and on Monday, May 14, arrived in Israel. A week after being reunited with his grandmother and other relatives there, Leonid found himself in the United States, traveling with an Israeli passport given him by Nechemyah Levanon, talking about the plight of his parents, seeking political support and raising funds for the cause of Soviet Jewry. Sanya had met him on his arrival at Kennedy Airport in New York and then returned to the University of California in Santa Cruz, where he was attending veterinary school.

By the time Leonid arrived in Israel, Masha was hurrying back to Tsokto-Khangil. A week after she and Leonid had left for Moscow, Volodya had suffered a relapse of the pneumonia. In the hospital in Aginskoye the illness would not respond to penicillin, and his fever was dangerously high. Zalya, Masha's brother, came to visit him, but could do nothing. The doctor said to Zalya, "If the penicillin can't help him, it may be cancer." Zalya put in an emergency call to a family friend in Moscow, Dr. Eugenia Gural, who had just received permission to leave for Israel. Instead of getting her exit visa, she bought a ticket to Chita and arrived at Volodya's bedside in the Aginskoye hospital with a new British antibiotic. She remained for three days, administering the antibiotic to Volodya and at the same time saving the life of a senior nurse who was allergic to a different antibiotic, with which she was being treated by her colleagues. A week later Volodya was able to return to the village. In the meantime Dr. Gural had flown back to Moscow and shortly afterward left for Israel, where she now lives and practices medicine in Jerusalem.

Years later, once again engaged in the visa war, Masha would fly from Moscow to Siberia to help save the life of a fellow refusenik, Yuli Edelshtein, who lay near death in a labor camp. Keeping one another alive was another weapon in that war.

There is a photograph of Masha and Volodya taken sometime in 1979, in Tsokto-Khangil. Volodya looks like a somber patriarchal figure, streaks of gray in his thick beard and wavy hair, two deep creases between his brows, a grim line to his lips, and dark sadness in his eyes.

Masha's smile is pallid, a brave display of courage. Suspended from a chain around her neck is the amulet purchased for her in Jerusalem by her mother.

Masha brought packets of seed back from Moscow. Tatars in the village gave her a small plot of land, and she planted carrots, squash, and potatoes. In the boxes of earth on the balcony of their apartment, she cultivated onions, lettuce, dill, oregano, and garlic, and she and Volodya had greens during the early summer.

At the height of the summer, with the wind blowing oven heat from the Gobi Desert and the stench of the raw sewage that flowed from the apartment house, it became impossible to open the door to the balcony. Flies swarmed over the clots and coils of putrescence. The walls of the apartment turned black with flies. Masha and Volodya hung nets over the doors and windows. The Buryats who visited them gazed thoughtfully at the nets, noting the way they kept out the flies, and did the same in their apartments.

After the summer the air grew cool, and the earth given them by the Tatars and planted by Masha yielded potatoes and vegetables, which Masha and Volodya ate for months.

In the early fall the local electrician, a Buryat, paid them a visit. He sat for a while, gazing expressionlessly at the doors to the balcony. Finally he said, "So you're going to use the balcony? I saw you out there the other day."

Volodya nodded amiably.

"A great view," said the Buryat. "You can see very far. And from any hill around this valley people can see you. It would take no effort at all to shoot you with a rifle from any hill. And they'll never find out who shot. We have lots of people being killed here. Difficult to find who shoots from the hills."

After a moment of silence Volodya said evenly, "If they want to kill me, they'll kill me. I'm not going to hide." The word "they" resonated quietly in the still air.

The Buryat said nothing and soon left. On occasion Masha and Volodya encountered him in the village and offered polite greetings. He never visited them again.

Because of his ill health, Volodya could no longer walk the mile to the kolkhoz boiler room and was given the job of stoker in the boiler room of the apartment building in which he and Masha lived. He came down with periodontal disease and lost some teeth.

Every morning that summer and early fall they took the short walk to the post office in the village square. Many seemed to know their address in exile; they were receiving letters and postcards from America, Australia, Europe. People they didn't know, telling them that they were not forgotten, that many thousands were now joined to their cause. And there were letters from the family in Israel. How strange that was! In Moscow there had been almost a complete absence of mail; the KGB had intercepted and read everything. Here, mail from every corner of the world. For some reason the authorities had neglected to inform the local post office to hold their mail, and no one in the post office seemed to care enough to do that on his own.

Masha began to hang the color postcards they received on the walls of the kitchen. Soon the walls began to fill with photographs of the great cities of America, Britain, Holland, Belgium, France, Sweden, Switzerland. On the wall near their bed she placed the postcards from Israel. Over the years the walls became completely covered. She would ask Volodya if it was realistic to think that they might ever see any of those cities, and he would say in his deep voice, "Of course! I have no doubt. We must believe in that." She spent many hours gazing at those picture postcards, went off at times in her reveries to the worlds on her walls. She felt intrigued, often mesmerized, by the postcards from Israel. Photographs of Tel Aviv. People on the beaches. The waves. Dark as pitch and twenty degrees below zero outside her window. And the longing for the warm beaches of Tel Aviv.

In November of that year, 1979, she was back in Moscow, holding a press conference in the apartment of Professor Alexander Lerner, a renowned mathematician and a refusenik. She had by then become Volodya's voice to the world. In a room crowded with dozens of reporters and refuseniks sitting or standing around a large dark wood dining table, Lerner's oil paintings on the walls, she talked about the horror of what had happened to her husband, his punishing isolation in a cruel land at the far end of the world.

By chance, in the apartment that day was Sister Gloria Coleman, a nun from the United States who, through her friend Sister Ann Gillen, had become involved in the movement for Soviet Jewry. She stood there listening to Masha's calmly delivered words. She was awed by her outspokenness in an apartment near the very center of the Soviet empire. Masha spoke slowly, in Russian, and someone translated. None of the people in this movement, she said—aloud, without a magic slate—had committed any crimes against the Soviet Union. They simply wanted exit visas. They wanted to do what all free people are able to do: emigrate to the country of their choice. The stories published in *Izvestia* that claimed they were involved in espionage were untrue. They did not wish to harm the Soviet Union; they wanted only to leave it.

She completed her remarks. Questions were directed to her by the reporters—spoken, without the use of magic slates. Sister Gloria remembers Masha's poised and dignified presence, an eminently civilized woman, her answers delivered in a tone of self-possession and then translated. The press conference came to an end. Masha traveled back to Tsokto-Khangil.

In a letter she wrote that autumn, she opened her heart, sharing the despair that often came upon the refuseniks: their nearly unendurable inner torment and stress: stripped of home, community, and country; the leaders suddenly exiled, jailed; the families fractured; the burden of unbounded waiting borne by parents and children who felt themselves belonging nowhere. "Our sons are free," she wrote. "Our dream has come true. If it is God's will, we'll see them again. If not, then . . . After so many years, the pain has deadened. Ten years of refusals and stress have told on us both.

"Here in Siberia, our daily life consists of waiting for the 5:00 p.m. radio news broadcast. Every morning we visit the post office; letters are the main link with the world. . . . Our life here resembles science fiction. We are so far away, more than 8,000 km from Moscow. We two are so alien to the environment here. . . .

"Time slips away. Heat, dust, stuffy air, flies, foul smells. . . . In the winter the sewer pipe fell off. . . . After it thawed out, the stuff flowed to a pit through the gutter.

"In front of our apartment is a 'public convenience,' which hasn't been cleaned since last September. . . . No water. Forty-one months are left to go for us without a water supply. We'll have to carry it in buckets from a source 300 meters from our building."

Masha's poignant locution about God's will was her way of expressing hope in the language of her pious grandmother. She believed deeply in an all-knowing, all-powerful Being who was beyond humankind's ability to describe, as did Leonid, though neither of them was formally religious. Volodya, uncertain, was the agnostic.

In the warm weather of the following year Volodya was a watchman in the kolkhoz greenhouse, and then for three months he worked in the international telephone station at the post office, talking at times with people in Moscow and elsewhere. The KGB got wind of that and had him fired. Aware of the law on that matter, he sued the KGB in a local court; a worker could not be arbitrarily dismissed from a job he or she had worked on for three months or longer. While the lawsuit wound its way through the bureaucracy of the legal system, he did not have to work, according to the law. Astonishingly, he won the case and was compensated for all the time he hadn't worked—to the fury of the KGB. He returned to his job as stoker in the boiler room of the building where Masha and he lived.

As the 1970s drew to a close, Masha and Volodya were among the seventy Jews in the Soviet Union who had been in refusal for more than ten years. In all, there were about 4,800 refuseniks in the USSR, 221 of them for five years or more. One Muscovite, Benjamin Bogomolny, had been refused a visa since his first application in 1966 and would not be allowed to leave until October 1986.

In the last week of December 1979 Volodya and Masha were in their apartment in Tsokto-Khangil when they heard over the radio that the Soviet Union had invaded Afghanistan. They understood immediately that the era of détente was over.

The months went slowly by. The two of them were often ill. The horrid desert climate, the unsanitary conditions in the village. And their improper diet. Food distribution to the village was erratic. There was rice, pasta, frozen fish. Few vegetables. The Buryats would not sell their meat in the winter, when they froze and stored it, and the meat they sold in the summer was often unfit to eat. Every three days there was a shipment of bread from Aginskoye, quickly snapped up by the old women and children who waited hours on line for its arrival. Once, astonishingly, a sack of flour from Belgium found its way to the village, and Masha bought it. At about the same time a bag of yeast arrived for them through the mail from a friend in Sweden. For weeks afterward Masha, still able to recall her grandmother's recipes, baked breads and challahs.

Alcoholism, arthritis, cirrhosis of the liver, syphilis, gonorrhea, were endemic among the villagers. Requested by the authorities in a nearby village to accept a well-paying job as a doctor in a new clinic, Masha refused, offering instead to work without pay as a volunteer, a proposal they turned down. She was fearful that if someone in her care were to complain to the authorities of maltreatment, it would be used as grounds to have her arrested and separated from Volodya. She practiced medicine only on her husband, to keep him alive.

Traveling back and forth every three or four months between Tsokto-Khangil and Moscow, she repeatedly experienced the cruelties of winter in Siberia. Her ulcer became a recurrent distress; her legs, exposed to the cold, were once dangerously frostbitten. She practiced medicine on herself as well.

She was in the apartment on the day in February 1980 when her brother telephoned from Moscow. He had just heard from their sister, Gera, who lived in Beersheba, that their mother had died. In a hospital in Beersheba, in the wilderness of Judea. "I will heal and be a bridge for you," her mother had promised before leaving nine years ago. But even God seemed powerless to build a bridge between the deserts of Judea and Gobi.

News of the world beyond Tsokto-Khangil reached Masha and Volodya over the radio and the small television set, for which Volodya had managed to rig up an antenna that now enabled them to receive the local television station in Chita and a Moscow station via satellite. And news came from the relatives and friends who visited them. Thus they learned that in 1980 the number of Jews who received exit visas was 60 percent less than in previous years; in the next year the number was again cut by 50 percent. It seemed that with the end of détente the Kremlin no longer had anything to gain by letting the Jews leave.

They learned, too, that Ida Nudel, released from exile in March 1982, was finding it impossible to acquire a new Moscow residence permit—her old one had lapsed during her years in exile—and therefore could not reapply for an exit visa. Lost in a Soviet-style bureaucratic nightmare, she was eventually ordered out of Moscow by the KGB and permitted to register in the Moldavian Republic near the Black Sea, where she lived in misery and isolation until she was allowed to emigrate in October 1987.

By the time the Slepaks returned to Moscow in December 1982, Leonid Brezhnev was dead and Yuri Andropov—a former head of the KGB who had once referred to Volodya and other refuseniks as a menace that should be exterminated—now ruled in his place. Ronald Reagan was the president of the United States. The 100,000 Soviet troops in Afghanistan were mired in a war grimly reminiscent of America's Vietnam involvement. The Cold War had heated up, and serious talk about disarmament had cooled. Between 1983 and 1986 only about 1,000 Jews a year left (896 in 1984 and 1,140 in 1985); emigration had averaged more

than 25,000 a year during the 1970s. Jewish mass emigration had come
to a halt. When my wife and I met the Slepaks in January 1985, they were
staring grimly at the bitter prospect of living out the remainder of their
lives in the Soviet Union.

In Siberia, Volodya had counted the days with care. He knew precisely
how long he had served in exile and how much time he had left. You
counted from the day of your arrest, knowing that according to Soviet
law, one day in prison or in a prison railway car was equal to three days
of exile. He knew, too, that after his exile he would lose his Moscow residency permit and might be ordered by the authorities to live beyond the
100-kilometer (62.5-mile) city limit. Technically he and Masha were still
divorced; they had hoped all the years that the divorce might have
gained Masha an exit visa—vainly, as it turned out. In January 1982, at
the beginning of their last year of exile, they went to the village soviet
and were remarried. It was now possible for Volodya to apply for and obtain a Moscow residency permit.

Later that winter there was a violent snowstorm that melted too
quickly in a sudden thaw. A powerful stream tore through the houses,
and for four days much of the village lay deep in water. Houses collapsed. Pigs, dogs, calves, sheep perished.

With the spring rain the steppes returned to life: pink, yellow, and
white blossoms, poppies, tulips, grasshoppers, birds, butterflies. It was a
brief life, lasting about one month. The summer came, and with it winds
from the Gobi Desert carrying blast furnace heat. And dust. The moisture in one's eyes dried. And in one's mouth and nostrils. The humidity
was 10 percent. Volodya began to cough. Masha wet down bedsheets and
hung them about the apartment.

Fall and winter came. Masha marked the time on the wall calendar,
every morning crossing out a day. They began to sell off some of their
possessions, gave some away; they packed and sent things to Moscow.

Volodya's appointed day of release was December 2, 1982. Several days
before, he called the airport in Chita and booked two tickets on a flight
to Moscow.

On the day of his release he and Masha took the bus to Aginskoye. In
the militia station he picked up his internal passport and all the documents he needed. They spent the night in a hotel in Aginskoye and took
the morning bus to Chita. Masha gazed out the dusty window at the
steppes, the hills, the forests, the valleys. Five years of their lives, gone.

Because of a balcony demonstration. For a postcard from OVIR. On the seat beside her Volodya slept.

It was dark when they arrived in Chita, and they stayed that night in the airport hotel. At about four o'clock the next morning, in freezing air, they boarded the flight to Moscow and arrived early Sunday morning, December 4.

When Volodya emerged from the Moscow airport terminal, he had the eerie sensation that he had never left the city. Five years, and nothing seemed to have changed. Streets, buildings, trams, traffic, clothes, shops. Dirty snow on the streets, an icy wind. Moscow frozen in time.

In the apartment on Gorky Street the woman who occupied the third room appeared genuinely happy to see him. Everything about the apartment—the walls, the furniture, the floors, the windows—was the same as when he had departed. Except the front door. The old, broken door, smashed during one of the many KGB searches of the apartment, had been replaced by a new wooden door, painted the identical brown as the previous one. Masha called relatives and friends. Volodya was home! Yes, home. Safe. Excitement, joy.

Volodya wanted to reapply immediately for an exit visa but couldn't, because he no longer had a Moscow residence permit. Masha went with him to the local militia station to apply for the permit, and the officer in charge of residence permits said it would be necessary for them to turn in their internal passports while the application was processed. They handed him their passports.

Weeks went by. Volodya repeatedly called the officer, who said he could do nothing for them; he had sent on the application to his chiefs and was himself waiting for their decision. Eleven months after Volodya turned in the application, it was approved. Residence permit in hand, he applied to OVIR for an exit visa. The answer came one month later. Refused. The reason: "Secrecy."

On the day he received the residence permit, indeed at the same time it was being stamped into his internal passport at the local militia station, Volodya was told to see another officer in that station. The officer warned him that because he hadn't worked in months, he was about to be indicted and brought to trial as a parasite; he had two weeks to find a job. Volodya said that he hadn't even been able to look for a job because he hadn't had his internal passport, which had been taken from him in that same militia station. The officer said that was no affair of his, it was a different department.

His friends helped him find a job as an elevator operator in a hospital. Working nights, he discovered that if he halted the elevator between certain floors, he was able to penetrate the Soviet jamming of overseas radio broadcasts. He began to listen again to the voices of the West, in that way keeping himself aware of the worldwide activities of the movement: demonstrations wherever high Soviet officials appeared, at political meetings, cultural events, scientific conferences, conventions of judges and lawyers. There was continuing unrest because of the refuseniks.

At the Geneva Summit conference in December 1985—in the wake of the sudden deaths of Soviet Premiers Andropov in 1984 and Chernenko in 1985—the plight of Soviet Jewry was mentioned to the new Soviet premier, Mikhail Gorbachev, by President Ronald Reagan. Demonstrators hoisted placards and marched through downtown streets. Avital Shcharansky displayed a photograph of her imprisoned husband, and Jesse Jackson asked the Soviet premier about the Jews and was informed that the "so-called problem of Jews in the Soviet Union does not exist." Such events were widely reported by the media; they filtered out of the small radio Volodya held to his ear when he stopped the elevator during the quiet moments of the night and went searching for cracks in the wall of Soviet jamming.

After a year as an elevator operator, he was promoted to the job of controller. From behind a desk in a small office, he ran the hospital's electricity, water supply, sewage, and heating systems. Problems in those systems were directed to him; he called the electricians, plumbers, repair crews.

In February 1986 Shcharansky was released, to everyone's joy and surprise. He flew off to a tumultuous welcome in Israel.

Between 1968 and 1986, nearly 270,000 Jews, 12.5 percent of Soviet Jewry, had emigrated. But there were about 10,000 refuseniks in the USSR in 1986, among them Masha and Volodya, whose names and long struggle were by then legendary. Elie Wiesel talked about them often—to American senators, to men and women in the House of Representatives, to government officials in France, to Gorbachev.

The likelihood of freedom for the refuseniks seemed dim. Some for whom hope of release was now dead had decided to turn their efforts at emigration inward, to create for themselves and their children a new Jewish culture inside the Soviet Union, in defiance of Soviet law. Secret religious schools for children; clandestine places of prayer and study for adults; illegal lectures on Jewish history and customs; furtive Purim and Hanukkah parties; covert Hebrew songfests in forests—all in place of the efforts previously expended on petitions, sit-ins, demonstrations, hunger strikes, now regarded as futile.

The Israelis did not take kindly to such activities, thought them a yielding to the Soviet effort to stifle Jewish emigration, a waning of the refuseniks' Zionist enthusiasm. On this matter Volodya tended to agree with the Israelis, who regarded him as one of their greatest assets.

In March 1986 he and Masha exchanged their single large communal apartment on Gorky Street for two small apartments. They moved into a six-story building on Vesnina Street, about a twenty-minute walk to the Kremlin. The woman and her son, their Gorky Street neighbors, went willingly into the second apartment in a different section of Moscow. Quite small, the apartments, but unshared, private. The Slepak apartment had two rooms, one with a balcony. And a telephone, which the KGB for some reason had not thought to shut down. On the first floor of the building were a bookstore and a hairdresser's shop. Soon visitors were finding their way to the new lodgings, Vesnina Street 8/10, apartment 52. Volodya again sat listening, smoking his pipe, talking. And Masha served tea and sugar cookies, hovered in the background, and worried about her husband's health.

Volodya applied again for an exit visa and was refused. The KGB tailed him constantly, arrested him several times for participating in demonstrations or for planning an action or to prevent trouble at official events like an international festival or a congress. Each time they held him for one day and sent him home.

In March 1987 a number of members of Congress met with Gorbachev in the Kremlin. One of the congressmen, James Scheuer, asked for the release of the Slepaks. Gorbachev replied, "Slepak will never leave the Soviet Union. Let's not discuss his case." Congressman Scheuer informed Masha and Voldya about the conversation.

One month later, in April, Masha and Volodya went on a seventeen-day hunger strike to commemorate their seventeen years of refusal. One day for each year, no food, only tap or mineral water, the strike announced in advance to the foreign press. They appeared in front of the Moscow "White House," the parliament building, wearing placards that read LET US GO TO OUR CHILDREN AND GRANDCHILDREN. Many refuseniks and KGB agents watched in silence. On the fourth day they were arrested by the KGB. They thought they might be detained for ten to fifteen days; it would have been Volodya's sixteenth such arrest in thirteen years. Instead they were brought back to their apartment and warned not to demonstrate again. Masha ended her strike that day; her health would not permit her to continue. Volodya kept at it through the seventeenth day. When he returned to his job after the strike, he learned that he had been fired. He never worked again in the Soviet Union.

That April about fifty refuseniks received invitations to a Passover Seder to be held in the Moscow residence of the American ambassador to the Soviet Union. The arrangements had been scrupulously attended to by several American Jewish women led by Sara Inick, wife of the American cultural attaché. The matzah and wine were flown in from Israel. In a large ballroom stood a dozen tables, all meticulously arranged for Passover. At each table sat a number of Americans: diplomats, press people. Ambassador Arthur Hartman and his wife greeted each person who entered. When everyone had arrived, the ambassador and his wife came over to Masha and Volodya, who had only the day before ended his hunger strike. They sat together at the same table. The ambassador put on a skullcap, and the Seder began. The refuseniks took turns reading from the Haggadah.

In the middle of the reading, George Shultz, the American secretary of state, entered the hall wearing a skullcap. He went slowly from one table of refuseniks to another, shaking hands, exchanging words, handing each person a book or memento. He recognized all the refuseniks, knew them by name, seemed awed and reverential in their presence. These activists—their names and photographs by now mythic symbols of defiance against tyranny, displayed everywhere, on placards, in books, schools, at demonstrations—were men and women who had for years defied, paid a terrible price, and were continuing to defy, a pitiless empire. Alexander Lerner was there that evening. Masha and Volodya Slepak. Viktor Brailovsky. Nahum Meiman. Iosif Begun. And many others. When George Shultz approached Masha and Volodya, he shook their hands and said he had a gift for them. His assistant handed him a photograph, which he gave to Masha and Volodya: a picture of Sanya and Leonid and the grandchildren taken at the time of the two brothers' hunger strike in front of the Capitol building in Washington, D.C., to commemorate their parents' seventeenth year in refusal. Shultz then briefly addressed the refuseniks. He said he and the American administration would never cease fighting for the freedom of Soviet Jewry. Then he introduced the new American ambassador; Ambassador Hartman was soon to retire. The reading of the Haggadah continued. At the conclusion of the Seder every family was presented with a box of Israeli matzos and every woman there received a red rose. Then all but a half dozen guests left.

In another room of the embassy, the half dozen guests who had remained, Volodya and Masha among them, spoke at some length with Richard Schifter, George Shultz's aide in human rights issues. He had accompanied Shultz into the hall, and the refuseniks in the room knew him well; it was his third or fourth visit to Moscow. Later, as the refuseniks left the protected grounds of the embassy and returned to Soviet soil, they passed under the scrutiny of many KGB eyes.

Congressman Scheuer was back in Moscow that August and again asked Gorbachev to release the Slepaks. Gorbachev said that if the Americans and Soviets signed an arms agreement, the Slepaks might be released. When Masha heard that, she thought: We are being sold like slaves, one by one, children and parents separately, each kept behind for a possible higher bid.

Suddenly, in September, one of the long-term refuseniks received permission to leave. Then others. And then Iosif Begun and Ida Nudel. For all the friends of the Slepaks, the card from OVIR, the exit visa. Only Masha, Volodya, Alexander Lerner, and a very few others were left. Masha thought she and Volodya were deliberately being separated from their old friends. To be alone in Moscow. Another exile. Interminable.

On October 13, 1987, at 2:00 p.m., the telephone rang in the Slepak apartment on Vesnina Street. Volodya wasn't home. Masha lifted the receiver.

A man's voice asked, "Is Vladimir Semyonovich at home?"

"No," said Masha.

"Is this Maria Isaakovna?"

"Yes."

"This is Deputy Chief of Moscow OVIR ———." He gave Masha his name, but she has since forgotten it and it is therefore absent from these chronicles. "You are granted permission to leave the USSR. Please come tomorrow to the OVIR office to get the card with the list of documents you must bring with you in order to obtain your visas."

Masha had the presence of mind to say, "But tomorrow is Wednesday; it is not a reception day at OVIR."

"It will be for you. When you arrive, ring the bell. A militiaman will open the door. Tell him your name, and say that Major [another forgotten name] is waiting for you. The major will give you the card with the list of the documents you must bring when you come for your exit visas."

Masha, stunned and disoriented, hung up the telephone. After eighteen years of waiting—that was it? A telephone call instead of the usual postcard! She had expected the heavens to part, the earth to tremble. This was so . . . ordinary. She sat waiting and after a while began to think she had imagined it all, had dreamed it; there had been no call.

Volodya returned. She told him about the telephone call. He refused to believe it. Finally he said, "Tomorrow we'll go to OVIR. If they give us the card, we'll know it's real."

The next day they went to OVIR. A guard let them inside. The empty building echoed with their footsteps. They felt like sleepwalkers. An official handed them the card with the list of documents they would need to bring in order to receive exit visas. Masha held the card. What they had endured for this little piece of paper!

They went over to the restaurant where a farewell party was in progress for Ida Nudel. Masha followed behind Volodya, who entered holding the card high over his head and announcing that they had received permission to leave. There was a large crowd—friends, correspondents. Pandemonium erupted. Joy. Tears. Exhilaration. If Slepak is getting out, we'll all get out! The correspondents wanted interviews.

There was much to do. They collected the many papers they needed, paid for the visas and for the loss of their Soviet citizenship. With the papers and a bank receipt in hand, they came to OVIR and got their visas. Showing the visas, they were able to book seats on a flight to Vienna. Then they went to the embassy of the Netherlands, which at the time represented Israel in the USSR, and received their visas to Israel. Their Austrian transit visas they obtained in the Austrian Embassy. All those visas enabled them finally to purchase the plane tickets they had booked.

In the meantime they were saying good-bye to all their relatives. They visited the graves of Masha's father and Volodya's mother. And stood in silence awhile before the grave of Solomon Slepak. They sold some of their furniture and gave away many of their possessions to relatives and to fellow refuseniks. About 150 people showed up at the farewell party in the apartment, among them Richard Schifter, aide to Secretary of State George Shultz.

Once again, by sheerest chance, in the apartment that evening was Sister Gloria Coleman, the Catholic nun from the United States who had become involved in the Soviet Jewry movement. Unaware that they had received permission to leave, she came with others to visit the Slepaks and stumbled upon the celebration. She recalls a crowded apartment filled with laughter and joy and remembers seeing Volodya, "an amazing-looking man, wonderfully well-looking, considering what he had been through, sitting there amid the reverence and respect being shown him by the refuseniks and the press. He was effusive. The whole room radiated with excitement, elation." She went over to Volodya and introduced herself. He took her hand in both of his. She was warmed by the way he immediately engaged her, brought her into the celebration, indeed by the way the refuseniks made all who were there, including the press, part of the evening's happiness. They did not play to the press; they involved the press as people in the drama of their lives.

The day before their departure Volodya and Masha brought their baggage to customs in the airport. Seven suitcases. They waited five hours and then stood watching as the customs agents picked everything apart. It was four in the morning when the agents were done. They had, they told Masha and Volodya, no blank forms for the baggage receipts. "But don't worry, when you come tomorrow to check in, the receipts will be there for you."

About two dozen people—relatives and very close friends—were at the airport to see them off. It was late afternoon of October 25, 1987. In an odd juncture of events, their son Sanya had left the Soviet Union precisely ten years before. The clerk at the counter who went through their tickets and documents could not find the baggage receipts; they would be unable to claim their baggage. To the devil with all the baggage, thought Masha, frantic. Let's just get out of this place! The chronicles record that it was a wet, cloudy day, the air filled with a mixture of snow and rain. The Soviet aircraft was a TU-154, and the flight number was SU-263. It departed for Vienna at 8:15 p.m.

During the flight an attendant came over to Masha and Volodya and handed them their baggage receipts. They had been found on the floor of the aircraft, she said. The final knife thrust of the KGB, thought Masha.

When she and Volodya descended the stairway and stepped onto the tarmac in the Vienna airport, they were met by Ambassador Max Kampelman, head of the American delegation to the Soviet-American Disarmament Conference in Vienna. Inside the terminal waited Sanya; Senator John and Teresa Heinz of Pennsylvania; the American ambassador to Austria; Marion Wiesel, wife of Elie Wiesel; a representative of the Jewish Agency, which was responsible for the settlement of Soviet immigrants in Israel; and the Slepaks' close friends Kirill and Irina Khenkin, who had come from Munich, where they worked for Radio Liberty, one of the stations Volodya used to bring in on his radio during his years in the forests outside Moscow, on camping trips in the Ukraine, in the apartment on Gorky Street, and as he navigated the hospital elevator through the waves of noise thrown up by the Kremlin against the outside world.

There were many journalists in the terminal. The press conference lasted about twenty minutes. As soon as it was over, the American ambassador asked Masha and Volodya to join him at his residence for dinner. They could spend the night there, in a room already prepared for them.

The next day Masha and Volodya and Sanya flew to Israel in a Learjet chartered by Senator Heinz, Elie Wiesel, and Patti and John Thompson, a Christian couple from Nashville. When the pilot announced that they were above Israeli waters, Volodya opened a bottle of champagne. They gazed out the windows at the blue glitter of the sea, and Masha saw the beaches of Tel Aviv below. The jet landed, and Masha and Volodya came out the door and down the stairs and stepped onto the soil of Israel. It was a warm, sunny October day. A huge crowd of relatives, friends, and reporters greeted them in the terminal. Leonid, involved at the time in a controversy with Israeli authorities over his passport and not wanting to touch down in Israel lest he be obliged to serve in the army, was not present. Volodya opened the press conference. "Finally we are here. . . ."

The chronicles record that Masha was wearing her amulet.

Three days later they celebrated Volodya's sixtieth birthday in the Jerusalem residence of Chaim Herzog, president of Israel. From the residence Volodya telephoned Moscow and talked with Alexander Lerner, who, some weeks later, received his exit visa and went to Israel. When the festivities at the residence of the president ended, Volodya and Masha made their way to a more private party arranged by some of their closest friends, immigrants from the Soviet Union, one of whom owned the Jerusalem discotheque where the second party went on and on until the very early hours of the morning.

The chronicles further record that Volodya and Masha flew to the United States that November and were greeted at Kennedy Airport by the five grandchildren they had never seen; three of the children were Leo's, and two Sanya's. They then traveled about for two months, pleading the cause of other refuseniks and raising funds for the Soviet Jewry movement. They were looked upon as valiant figures and listened to with profound regard as they spoke about the thousands of refuseniks still remaining in the USSR, their fate uncertain even in the days of perestroika and glasnost. Not until the dissolution of Communist power in 1991 would the word "refusenik" begin to fade from the world's agenda.

Finally the chronicles tell us that in June 1988 Masha and Volodya set out with a number of other refuseniks on a goodwill and fund-raising mission to London, Los Angeles, Australia, and New Zealand under the auspices of the World Jewish Congress. In Australia, at the request of Isi Liebler, then vice-president of the congress, they all were to meet and express their gratitude to Prime Minister Bob Hawke, one of the most noted figures in the struggle for Soviet Jewry.

During the night that Masha and Volodya stayed in Los Angeles, someone entered their second-floor hotel room through the balcony, whose doors they had neglected to lock, and stole every object of value that lay in view: their watches and camera, Volodya's wallet and credit cards, and all of Masha's jewelry, including the amulet. Fortunately they had placed their passports, traveler's checks, and airline tickets in a suitcase. They flew on to Australia for appearances before admiring audiences and the meeting with the prime minister. The mission over, they returned to Israel.

A few months later Volodya and Masha found suitable jobs in Israel. Their sons were by then permanently settled in the United States.

Here the chronicles come to an end.

Telephone Calls

Today, as Volodya approaches his seventieth birthday, his hair is entirely gray, his beard short and snowy white, growing in two roundish clumps from his smooth pink cheeks. He carries the same paunch, which he is still trying to lose, and his voice, somewhat huskier than before, remains deep and resonant and exuberant. And Masha is smooth-faced, plump, her intelligent eyes bright behind their thick glasses, her short, straight hair russet-colored, youthful, her voice lilting, musical. They seem to hide their scars well, though I am told that Masha has moments of dark moods, and that Volodya's boisterousness will suddenly evaporate when certain people and experiences come up in conversation.

In the summer of 1995 my wife and I visited them in the Pocono Mountains of Pennsylvania. They were spending a month in a house rented by Leonid. Deep inside a dense green world of oaks and white birches and elms and maples and evergreens, beneath a glittering blue sky, and in air so clear it seemed an intoxicating miracle each time one breathed, there, on the front deck, reclining on a chaise, was Volodya, reading a Russian book Leonid had brought back from a recent business trip to Moscow: *Polygons of Satan: Crimes of the Communist Party* by Igor Bunich, published in 1994 in Rostov-on-Don. On the cover was a picture of the young, bearded, aggressive Trotsky.

Volodya and Masha, looking remarkably robust, were cheerful, relaxed, given easily to hearty laughter. But I knew he had suffered a mild heart attack some months before and she was losing vision in one eye. Leonid had once told me that his father referred lightly to their various illnesses as "telephone calls from the other world."

Did their neighbors know who they were, these strangers in this Pennsylvania mountain village? To look at them—Volodya in a white polo shirt and baggy chinos and padding about in his bare feet; Masha in a dark blue linen skirt and a gauzy light pink sleeveless blouse and wearing clogs—who would think that once they had been among the leaders of a movement that had hurled itself against, and helped bring down, the Soviet colossus?

Masha prepared a green salad and cooked a pot of rice after a recipe taught her by an Israeli American visitor to their apartment in Israel. Outside, two deer emerged from the bluish green shadows of the woods and nibbled at the grass in front of the house.

We sat around a table, and they talked of their lives in apartment 7, Rivka Guber Street, Kfar Saba, the municipality near Tel Aviv where they now lived. Masha's Hebrew is now quite good; Volodya is more comfortable with English. In Kfar Saba, they said, there were new lights in the park near the apartment house, and on warm nights one could hear the high-pitched voices of children playing on the grass. Yes, the elementary school and home for the aged were still there, and nothing had changed in the bus station on the boulevard; it was the same busy, dusty place. In the apartment building lived people from America, Russia, Iraq, Iran, Yemen, Poland, Argentina, England, as well as native-born Israelis. A school principal, engineers, teachers, a retired professor of physiology, a fax machine technician, an IBM department head, an architect, a pharmacist, a physician, a tourist bus driver, the owner of a picture-framing shop, an accountant. The apartment house was a sprawl of connected tall white buildings with separate entrances; on warm days voices spilled from the open windows and mixed with the sounds of traffic on the boulevard and the voices of children in the park. Most of their family now lived in Israel—siblings, nieces, nephews, cousins—and the telephone in the apartment was often busy.

As the conversation ebbed and flowed around the subject of their family, one sensed in Volodya and Masha a subdued bewilderment and pain. They seemed unable to comprehend how it had happened: the separation between them and their sons. After all they had endured, now to be connected to their sons for most of the year only by telephone. And unable to call at a mere whim. Overseas telephone calls were costly. Their lives now brushed the borders of indigence, and they needed to be careful with their expenses. The Kremlin had robbed them of their most productive years. They came to Israel too late in life to have worked the minimum ten years necessary for a retirement pension. Nor could they have resumed their professions. Volodya had fallen behind nearly two decades in his field of engineering; when he tried to return to it in Israel, at the age of sixty, he found himself in a stupefying new world of technology, the disparity made even greater by the more rigorous requirements of Western engineering. Utterly futile to start training again at that age. The same was true of Masha. He obtained an engineering position in a laboratory at Tel Aviv University; she found work as a radiologist in the Kfar Saba hospital. Upon their retirement, neither will have worked the necessary ten years in Israel to qualify for a full Social Security pension, and Volodya will receive a small Prisoner of Zion pension. Not enough for them to live on, let alone make frequent telephone calls to their sons in America.

I asked: Did they regret having left the Soviet Union, seeing that the regime had collapsed?

Without hesitation, they answered: Not for a moment.

Volodya saw no immediate good future for the people of Russia; it would take forty years to create the beginnings of a worthwhile society there. And there was no hope at all for the Jews, who would ultimately vanish through assimilation. "The cultural buildup of Jews in Russia today is temporary and unnatural," he said. "It will be good until the first pogrom." And Masha added, "If we had not made the effort to leave, our children would have assimilated and disappeared as Jews."

Back in the 1960s they had talked at some length about the possibility of leaving the Soviet Union, long before that fateful December night, in 1968, when Masha prevailed upon Volodya to choose with her the dangerous path of emigration. They knew what they wanted: to have the same possibilities as everyone else for a job and a place in society; to be able to speak freely; to educate their children in the best schools; not to be stopped in one's tracks because one was a Jew. They did not want their sons to live in a society where a lifetime of achievement and gain could be destroyed in an instant by anti-Semitism. Why invest one's energy and creativity in such a society? Yes, while in refusal they had looked upon Israel as a perfect society, as one single harmonious family. Now they saw it as flawed, unified only in times of extreme crisis. True, it was a democracy, an open society; and yes, the entire world entered their sunny apartment through their radio and cable television. But they were concerned about the peace process, the terrorist attacks, the divisive politics, were appalled by what seemed to them a prevailing prejudice among some Israelis against Russian immigrants, who were at times accused of bringing criminals and prostitutes into the country, causing an increase in the number of road accidents, engaging in child abuse and acts of incest. A nasty business, all that bigotry. And in Israel! But no, they did not want to live in America. They had family in Israel. And many friends. They loved the informality of the country, the intimacies, the way people dropped in on one another, met and talked in each other's kitchens. They were suspicious of the government, the parliament, the authorities; they liked the people. Their dream? To live nine months of each year in Israel and three months in America, where they could be with their children and grandchildren. And, for a long time in the future, to receive no telephone calls from the other world.

They accompanied us to our car, Volodya still barefoot, walking easily on rough pebbles and grass. I warned him about deer ticks and Lyme disease, and he answered cheerfully in his loud and husky voice that he knew about it. They stood in the driveway, watching and waving, as we backed out onto the paved road and drove away.

Many things come to mind as I near the end of this work, things omitted and included. The long hesitation with which I approached it: How write it once the subject of the refuseniks dissolved? All the worthy people left out: impossible to include them all. Should I have written about Alexander Lavout, the mathematician in Moscow who monitored what he claimed were the Soviet psychiatric hospitals where dissidents were drugged and silenced? And Natasha Khassin of Moscow, who took it upon herself to care for prisoners in far-off regions of the Soviet Union? And Yuli Kosharovsky of Moscow, the clandestine teacher of Hebrew? And Arkady Mai of Moscow, the historian? And Elena Seidel of Moscow, teacher of English? And Misha Beizer of Leningrad, the historian? And Leonid Zeliger and Aba Taratuta, both of Leningrad, the former a teacher of Hebrew, the latter an engineer and a teacher of Hebrew? And Iosif Zisels, the physicist from Chernovtsy, who helped prisoners improve their tormented lives? And—well, in truth, the many omissions are painful to contemplate. But an end has to be made.

I consider the things included. The central mystery of Solomon Slepak's life: his repeated escapes from the clutches of Stalin. There has been no success in obtaining his KGB files, though many attempts were made before and during the writing of this work.

Recently a letter arrived from the KGB addressed to the grandmother of Olga, Leonid's wife. The grandmother, a woman in her eighties who resides in Moscow, was terrified by the return address and immediately telephoned Leonid in New York. It turned out he had forgotten to tell her that while in Moscow some weeks before, he had made out an application to see the KGB files on his father and grandfather and given her name as an in-care-of local address.

The letter, dated June 27, 1995, reads:

> Your application regarding Slepak, Vladimir Semyonovich, was reviewed.
>
> In accordance with Article No. 5 of the Legal Code of the Russian Federation, "On Search Activity in the Russian Federation," materials in connection with Slepak, V. S., as an individual whose guilt in committing a crime was not proved in an established manner, were destroyed.
>
> At the same time, we also inform you that, in accordance with the above-mentioned article, the right to demand from the authorities of the Federal Service of Security the data about the nature of the received information in regard to that person is available only to the person himself, whose guilt in committing a crime was not proved according to the procedures established by law.
>
> A. V. Tsarenko
Deputy Chief

It is not much of a consolation for Volodya and Masha to be told now by the KGB that Volodya's sentence to five years of exile was illegal. Volodya has decided to pursue the matter of his KGB files and will address his request directly to President Boris Yeltsin.

There is no mention in the letter about Leonid's request to see the KGB files on his grandfather, the Old Bolshevik, Solomon Slepak.

I consider, too, my fascination with Volodya's story, the way it held me in its grasp for years after its proximate appeal evaporated. Why did interest linger? What was there about it that was so beguiling? Perhaps the writer as amanuensis, as one watching from the sidelines and recording in safety the savage struggles of the activist, and wishing he had that courage, that boldness, to plunge into the foulness of existence, engage its cruelties, chance the scars of flesh and mind, face the possibility of annihilation? The individual who crosses the boundary from bystander to activist and hazards his or her life to change the world—an eternal mystery how that choice is made, that moment of crossing, the wonder of that transfiguration. The writer gazes upon it with awe, is mesmerized by its large daring, its radiance.

I have thought often about the exile of the Slepaks compared with the years in prisons and labor camps meted out to so many others. Torture, we know, leaves permanent psychic scars. Refusal is a condition of torture, crueler perhaps than exile, for there is a terminus to exile, and none to refusal. And surely exile is torture. During their five years in Siberia, Volodya and Masha experienced physical and mental subjugation, torture of an explicit and violating sort, and an initiation into the indifferent cruelty of despotism. But it was not the horror experienced, for example, by Gregory Steshenko in a psychiatric hospital, or by Natan Shcharansky and Alexander Solzhenitsyn in prisons and camps. In this regard, Volodya and Masha appear to have been more fortunate than some. Still, what point can there be in comparing pain and punishment? Do we know what scars they bear, what dreams wake them, what echoes of that cruel corner of Siberia haunt their sleep?

And finally, I write with the sobering impression that there is a cautionary tale in the Slepak chronicles; it waves a flag of danger at us in the sullen atmosphere of the early third century of the American Republic. Are there American variations of Solomon Slepak, those rendered so rigid by ideas that all reason fails them? Prudence, a cautious awareness of nuances, of complexities, of consequences, a perception of the unity of the American experience, and a saving sense of irony and humor—pervasive in the Founding Fathers and lacking in contemporary ideologues. Can we learn something from these chronicles about iron righteousness and rigid doctrine, about the stony heart, the sealed mind, the capricious use of law, and the tragedies that often result when theories are not adjusted to realities? Do the chronicles seem to reveal a glaring and almost obvious truth: the larger the nation, the more tumultuous its demise? Are we approaching the finale now to the bright possibilities once inherent in this land? Is that old America forever gone? Indeed, did it ever exist? Were we seduced as schoolchildren into a vision of a land green and golden from sea to shining sea, a land as illusory for many Americans as the Motherland of Solomon Slepak was for Volodya · and Masha? Perhaps the more sensible question is not about what we once were but about what we intend ourselves to be one day. Things are happening to us today that we don't seem able to explain. Can we enter the uncertain future without the corrosive cynicism, the clutching greed, the divisive self-interests—the beasts that destroyed the world of Solomon Slepak and rendered it uninhabitable to his family?

In December 1989 Volodya flew to Moscow to speak at a meeting of representatives of all the Jewish organizations in the former USSR. He arrived on the day Andrei Sakharov was laid to rest but too late to attend the funeral.

In Moscow's Cinema Center, rented for the conference, he addressed a crowd of about four hundred participants: young people, refuseniks, rabbis, Americans, Israelis. He told them how good it felt to be free, wished the refuseniks good luck, related some anecdotes about his life in Israel, and announced that in his opinion, the Jewish Agency, the body responsible for the settlement of immigrants in Israel, was not doing a proper job. Distrustful as ever of bureaucrats, ministers, and governments, Volodya rarely wasted an opportunity to make his views on that subject known. The head of the Jewish Agency, Simcha Dinitz, was present. There was a row.

The following day Volodya visited Andrei Sakharov's widow, Elena Bonner, and afterward went with members of the Israeli delegation to Sakharov's grave in the Vostriakovskoe Cemetery. They placed flowers on the grave and stood in silence in the gathering darkness.

One day that week Volodya traveled alone to his old apartment on Gorky Street, bearing a bouquet of flowers. A cold winter day, the streets of Moscow dirty with snow. He went past the bookstore and beneath the archway and through the courtyard and the entrance door and into the small foyer and climbed the half-flight of stairs to the narrow elevator. Then the rickety ride up. Apartment 77. The brown wooden door.

They were still there, the family with whom he and Masha had exchanged apartments back in March 1986: a married couple in their thirties, with a little girl; the woman's maternal grandmother, and her paternal grandmother's sister—that is, her father's aunt. Only the paternal grandmother's sister was Jewish. The other two women, the maternal grandmother and the young wife, were Russian; the young husband, half Russian, one-quarter Uzbek, one-quarter Ukrainian.

They were delighted to see Volodya. The man opened a bottle of cognac. They asked about life in Israel. Were Volodya and Masha happy there? And how were the boys? Volodya remained for two hours, talking.

Afterward he walked down one flight to the apartment of his old friends, a man and woman in their sixties. The man, Leonid, was an architect and the son of the Russian composer Reinhold Moritzovich Glière. His wife, Tamara, was an editor in a major children's publishing house; her father, once a member of the Moscow City Council. Their daughter had been in Sanya's class all through high school.

The woman hugged Volodya. She asked about Masha and the boys. They sat there talking. She was a large woman, the same height as Volodya but wider in build, her eyes deep blue, her blond hair going gray. An emotional person, she gave voice easily to her heart. She asked, "Why did you leave? You were born here; you have good friends here."

Volodya said, "You know, it was because of the anti-Semitism. We wanted a good future."

"But now the anti-Semitism is going down."

"It's like waves. Soon it will go up."

"But it's difficult to leave the place where one is born. How could you tear up your roots?" she asked.

To which Volodya responded, "Sometimes that's necessary."

He stayed two hours. The next day, he returned to Israel.

Two and a half years later, in June 1991, he was back in Moscow to deliver a talk at another conference. He found the city dirtier than ever, but otherwise the same, save for the foreign stores in its center: boutiques, French perfume shops, and a McDonald's in Pushkin Square, where, in December 1965, some two hundred people had assembled near the statue of the poet and unfurled placards with the words RESPECT THE SOVIET CONSTITUTION—the first human rights action with placards in Soviet history.

Masha did not accompany him on either trip. She refused to return to the scenes of her bitter memories in that sorrowful land.

He sensed the freedom in the city, the openness of talk and action. His father's Russia no longer existed. He asked himself: Where would he be now, my father, if he were still alive? And he answered: On the streets, demonstrating with the old Communists, trying for yet another chance at his old dream.

For the Jews in Moscow there were more schools, more synagogues. And summer camps and seminaries. Volodya met with old friends, told them that he saw no future for Jews in Russia. First get them out, he insisted; then strengthen their identity.

On the final day of the conference, he addressed the crowd—about three hundred delegates from Europe, Canada, Israel—at the Sabbath morning service in the Moscow synagogue across the street from the school he had attended as a child.

He had no opportunity on that trip to visit the apartment, but he telephoned the family to give them his good wishes. The young woman answered. How good it was to hear from him! Yes, they were all well. Except for her paternal grandmother's sister, the Jewish sister: She had died.

Volodya expressed his sorrow, offered his condolences. They talked for a while longer, and Volodya said good-bye and hung up. It was not lost on him that there were no more Jews left in the apartment on Gorky Street.

ᴙᴙᴙ *Bibliography* ᴙᴙᴙᴙᴙᴙᴙᴙᴙᴙᴙᴙᴙᴙᴙᴙ

Anyone familiar with this subject will recognize the debt I owe to those listed here. I want to acknowledge with special appreciation the work of Richard Pipes, Leonard Schapiro, Zvi Gitelman, Nora Levin, Nicholas V. Riasanovsky, Alan Bullock, Robert Conquest, Walter Laqueur, Arkady Vaksberg, and James H. Billington. Their writings were both loran and theodolite to my stumblings and constructions.

Adler, Nancy. *Victims of Soviet Terror*. Westport, Conn.: Praeger, 1993.

Alexandra, Victor. *The Kremlin*. New York: St. Martin's, 1963.

Alexeyeva, Ludmilla. *Soviet Dissent*. Middletown, Conn.: Wesleyan University Press, 1985.

Alexeyeva, Ludmilla, and Paul Goldberg. *The Thaw Generation*. Boston: Little, Brown, 1990.

Alter, Robert. *The Invention of Hebrew Prose*. Seattle: University of Washington Press, 1988.

Ammende, Ewald. *Human Life In Russia*. London: George Allen & Unwin, 1936. Reprinted in Cleveland: John T. Zubal, 1984.

Anti-Semitism in the Soviet Union. Proceedings of the Seminar on Soviet Anti-Semitism Held in Jerusalem, on April 7–8, 1978. Jerusalem: Hebrew University, 1979. 3 vols.

Antonov-Ovseyenko, Anton. *The Time of Stalin*. Harper & Row, 1983.

Arendt, Hannah. *Men in Dark Times*. New York: Harcourt, Brace, Jovanovich, 1968.

———. *The Origins of Totalitarianism*. New York: Harcourt, Brace & World, 1958.

Azbel, Mark Ya. *Refusenik*. New York: Paragon House, 1987.

Beizer, Mikhail. *The Jews of St. Petersburg*. Philadelphia: Jewish Publication Society, 1989.

Ben Ami (pseud. of Lova Eliav). *Between Hammer and Sickle*. Philadelphia: Jewish Publication Society, 1967.

Berlin, Isaiah. *Russian Thinkers*. New York: Viking, 1978.

Billington, James H. *The Icon and the Axe*. New York: Alfred A. Knopf, 1966.

Bonner, Elena. *Alone Together*. New York: Alfred A. Knopf, 1986.

Brachman, Edward R. *Challenging the Kremlin*. New York: Paragon House, 1992.

Brooks, Jeffrey. *When Russia Learned to Read*. Princeton, N.J.: Princeton University Press, 1985.

Brym, Robert J. *The Jewish Intelligentsia and Russian Marxism*. New York: Schocken Books, 1978.

Bukovsky, Vladimir. *To Build a Castle—My Life as a Dissenter*. New York: Viking, 1979.

Bullock, Alan. *Hitler and Stalin*. New York: Alfred A. Knopf, 1992.

Carr, Edward Hallett. *The Bolshevik Revolution 1917–1923*. New York: W. W. Norton, 1985. 3 vols.

————. *Twilight of the Comintern, 1930–1935*. New York: Pantheon, 1982.

Clubb, O. Edmund. *20th Century China*. New York: Columbia University Press, 1978.

Cohen, Stephen F. *Rethinking the Soviet Experience*. New York: Oxford University Press, 1985.

Conquest, Robert. *The Great Terror*. New York: Oxford University Press, 1990.

————. *The Harvest of Sorrow*. New York: Oxford University Press, 1986.

————. "Reds." *The New York Review of Books* (July 14, 1994).

————. *Stalin and the Kirov Murder*. New York: Oxford University Press, 1989.

Custine, Marquis de. *Empire of the Czar*. New York: Doubleday, 1989.

Daniels, Robert V. *A Documentary History of Communism*, vol. I, *Communism in Russia*. Hanover, N.H.: University Press of New England, 1984.

————. *Russia, the Roots of Confrontation*. Cambridge, Mass.: Harvard University Press, 1985.

————. *The Stalin Revolution*. Lexington, Mass.: D. C. Heath, 1972.

de Jonge, Alex. *Stalin and the Shaping of the Soviet Union*. New York: William Morrow, 1986.

Dobroszycki, Lucjan, and Jeffrey S. Gurock, eds. *The Holocaust in the Soviet Union*. Armonk, N.Y.: M. E. Sharpe, 1993.

Doder, Dusko. *Shadows and Whispers*. New York: Random House, 1986.

Drachman, Edward R. *Challenging the Kremlin*. New York: Paragon House, 1991.

Dubnow, Simon. *History of the Jews in Russia and Poland*. Philadelphia: Jewish Publication Society, 1935.

Dunlap, John B. *The Faces of Contemporary Russian Nationalism*. Princeton, N.J.: Princeton University Press, 1983.

Eckman, Lester Samuel. *Soviet Policy Toward Jews and Israel, 1917–1974*. New York: Shengold, 1974.

Eliav, Lova. See Ben Ami.

Emiot, Israel. *The Birobidzhan Affair*. Philadelphia: Jewish Publication Society, 1981.

Erman, Adolf. *Travels in Siberia*. Philadelphia: Lea & Blanchard, 1850.

Fairbank, John King. *The United States and China*. Cambridge, Mass.: Harvard University Press, 1973.

Fischer, Louis. *The Life of Lenin*. New York: Harper & Row, 1964.

Fitzpatrick, Sheila. *Stalin's Peasants*. New York: Oxford University Press, 1994.

Frankel, Jonathan. *Prophecy and Politics*. Cambridge, England: Cambridge University Press, 1981.

Fraser, John Foster. *The Real Siberia*. London: Cassell and Company, 1902.

Freedman, Robert O., ed. *Soviet Jewry in the Decisive Decade, 1971–1980*. Durham, N.C.: Duke University Press, 1984.

Garrison, Mark, and Abbott Gleason, eds. *Shared Destiny: Fifty Years of Soviet-American Relations*. Boston: Beacon Press, 1985.

Gilbert, Martin. *Atlas of Russian History*. New York: Dorset, 1972.

————. *The First World War*. New York: Henry Holt, 1994.

Gitelman, Zvi Y. *A Century of Ambivalence*. New York: Yivo, 1988.

————. *Jewish Nationality and Soviet Politics*. Princeton, N.J.: Princeton University Press, 1972.

Goldberg, Lea. *Russian Literature in the Nineteenth Century*. Jerusalem: Magnes Press, Hebrew University, 1976.

Goralski, Robert. *World War II Almanac*. New York: Putnam, 1981.

Gorky, Maxim. *Untimely Thoughts*. New Haven, Conn.: Yale University Press, 1995.

Goulden, Joseph C. *The Best Years: 1945–1950*. New York: Atheneum, 1976.

Hansson, Carola, and Karin Liden. *Moscow Women*. New York: Pantheon Books, 1983.

Heaps, Willard A. *The Story of Ellis Island*. New York: Seabury Press, 1967.

Heller, Mikhail, and Aleksandr Nekrich. *Utopia in Power*. New York: Summit Books, 1986.

Hingley, Ronald. *Russian Writers and Soviet Society 1917–1978*. London: Weidenfeld & Nicolson, 1979.

Hook, Brian, ed. *The Cambridge Encyclopedia of China*. New York: Cambridge University Press, 1982.

Howe, Irving. *Leon Trotsky*. New York: Viking, 1978.

———. *World of Our Fathers*. New York: Harcourt, Brace, Jovanovich, 1976.

Israel, Gerard. *The Jews in Russia*. New York: St. Martin's Press, 1975.

Ilyin, Olega. *White Road*. New York: Holt, Rinehart, Winston, 1984.

Kennan, George. *Siberia and the Exile System*. New York: Century Co., 1891. 2 vols.

Klehr, Harvey. *The Heyday of American Communism*. New York: Basic Books, 1984.

Klier, John Doyle. *Imperial Russia's Jewish Question, 1855–1881*. Cambridge, England: Cambridge University Press, 1995.

Knight, Amy. *Beria*. Princeton, N.J.: Princeton University Press, 1993.

Kochan, Lionel. *The Jews in Soviet Russia Since 1917*. New York: Oxford University Press, 1972.

Koenker, Diane. *Moscow Workers and the 1917 Revolution*. Princeton, N.J.: Princeton University Press, 1981.

Krasno, Rena. *Strangers Always*. Berkeley, Calif.: Pacific View Press, 1992.

Kublin, Hyman, ed. *Studies of the Chinese Jews*. New York: Paragon, 1971.

Laqueur, Walter. *The Dream That Failed*. New York: Oxford University Press, 1994.

———. "The Long Goodbye." *The New Republic* (April 11, 1994).

———. *The Long Road to Freedom*. New York: Collier Books, 1989.

———. *Stalin*. New York: Charles Scribner's Sons, 1990.

Lasch, Christopher. *The New Radicalism in America, 1889–1963*. New York: Alfred A. Knopf, 1965.

Lederhendler, Eli. *The Road to Modern Jewish Politics*. New York: Oxford University Press, 1989.

Levin, Nora. *The Jews in the Soviet Union Since 1917*. New York: New York University Press, 1990. 2 vols.

Levitas, Isaac. *The Jewish Community in Russia, 1844–1917*. Jerusalem: Posner and Sons, 1981.

Lewin, Moshe. *The Making of the Soviet System*. New York: Pantheon Books, 1985.

Lewis, Jonathan, and Philip Whitehead. *Stalin: A Time for Judgment*. New York: Pantheon, 1990.

Lih, Larst; Oleg V. Naumon, and Oleg V. Khlevniuk, eds. *Stalin's Letters to Molotov*. New Haven, Conn.: Yale University Press, 1995.

Lord, Walter. *The Good Years*. New York: Harper, 1960.

Lourie, Richard. *Russia Speaks*. New York: Edward Burlingame Books, 1991.

Lozansky, Edward D., ed. *Andrei Sakharov and Peace*. New York: Avon Books, 1985.

Lutz, Jessie Gregory. *China and the Christian Colleges, 1850–1950*. Ithaca, N.Y.: Cornell University Press, 1971.

Malia, Martin. *The Soviet Tragedy: A History of Socialism in Russia, 1917–1991*. New York: Free Press, 1994.

McCullough, David W. *Brooklyn—and How It Got That Way*. Photographs by Jim Kalett. New York: Dial Press, 1983.

McNeal, Robert H. *Stalin: Man and Ruler*. New York: New York University Press, 1990.

Medvedev, Roy A. *Let History Judge*. New York: Alfred A. Knopf, 1971.

———. *On Soviet Dissent*. New York: Columbia University Press, 1985.

Mehnert, Klaus. *The Russians & Their Favorite Books*. Stanford, Calif.: Hoover Institution Press, 1983.

Milner-Guland, Robin, and Nikolai Dejevsky. *Cultural Atlas of Russia and the Soviet Union*. New York: Facts on File, 1989.

Moore, Frederick F. *Siberia Today*. New York: D. Appleton and Company, 1919.

Moynahan, Brian, and Yevgeny Yevtushenko. *The Russian Century: A Photographic History of Russia's 100 Years*. New York: Random House, 1994.

Nakhimovsky, Alice Stone. *Russian-Jewish Literature and Identity*. Baltimore: Johns Hopkins University Press, 1992.

Nedava, Joseph. *Trotsky and the Jews*. Philadelphia: Jewish Publication Society, 1978.

Pethybridge, Roger, ed. *Witness to the Russian Revolution*. Secaucus, N.J.: Citadel Press, 1964.

Pinkus, Benjamin. *The Soviet Government and the Jews 1948–1967*. Cambridge, England: Cambridge University Press, 1984.

Pipes, Richard. *Russia Under the Bolshevik Regime*. New York: Alfred A. Knopf, 1993.

———. *Russia Under the Old Regime*. New York: Charles Scribner's Sons, 1974.

Powell, David E. *Anti-Religious Propaganda in the Soviet Union*. Cambridge, Mass.: MIT Press, 1975.

Prital, David, ed. *In Search of Self: The Soviet Jewish Intelligentsia and the Exodus*. Jerusalem: Mount Scopus Publications, 1983.

Pye, Lucian W. *Asian Power and Politics*. Cambridge, Mass.: Harvard University Press, 1985.

Radzinsky, Edvard. *The Last Tsar*. New York: Doubleday, 1992.

Raeff, Marc. *Understanding Imperial Russia*. New York: Columbia University Press, 1984.

Rapoport, Louis. *Stalin's War Against the Jews*. New York: Free Press, 1990.

Redlich, Shimon. *Propaganda and Nationalism in Wartime Russia*. New York: East European Quarterly, 1982.

Remnick, David. *Lenin's Tomb*. New York: Random House, 1993.

———. "The Exile Returns." *The New Yorker* (February 14, 1994).

Riasonovsky, Nicholas, V. *A History of Russia*. New York: Oxford University Press, 1984.

———. *The Image of Peter the Great in Russian History and Thought*. New York: Oxford University Press, 1985.

Ro'i, Yaacov, and Avi Becker, eds. *Jewish Culture and Identity in the Soviet Union*. New York: New York University Press, 1991.

Rubenstein, Joshua. *Soviet Dissidents: Their Struggle for Human Rights*. Boston: Beacon Press, 1985.

Sablinsky, Walter. *The Road to Bloody Sunday*. Princeton, N.J.: Princeton University Press, 1976.

Sakharov, Andrei. *Memoirs*. New York: Alfred A. Knopf, 1990.

Salisbury, Harrison E. *Black Night, White Snow: Russia's Revolutions, 1905–1917*. New York: Doubleday, 1978.

———. *China: One Hundred Years of Revolution*. New York: Holt, Rinehart & Winston, 1983.

———. *The New Emperors*. Boston: Little, Brown, 1992.

Sarna, Jonathan D. "The Myth of No Return: Jewish Return Migration to Eastern Europe, 1881–1914." *American Jewish History* (December 1981).

Schapiro, Leonard. *The Communist Party of the Soviet Union*. London: Methuen, 1970.

————. *The Russian Revolutions of 1917*. New York: Basic Books, 1984.

————. *Russian Studies*, ed. Ellen Dahrendorf. New York: Viking, 1986.

Schrecker, Ellen W. *No Ivory Tower*. New York: Oxford University Press, 1986.

Schroeter, Leonard. *The Last Exodus*. Seattle: University of Washington Press, 1979.

Schwarz, Solomon M., *The Jews in the Soviet Union*. Syracuse, N.Y.: Syracuse University Press, 1951.

Serge, Victor. *Memoirs of a Revolutionary*. London: Writers and Readers, 1963.

Shcharansky, Anatoly. *Fear No Evil*. New York: Random House, 1988.

Shindler, Colin. *Exit Visas*. London: Bachman and Turner, 1978.

Shipler, David K. "Dateline USSR: On the Human Rights Track." *Foreign Policy*, no. 75 (Summer 1989).

Shultz, George P. *Turmoil and Triumph*. New York: Charles Scribner's Sons, 1993.

Simon, Gerhard. *Church, State and Opposition in the U.S.S.R.* Berkeley and Los Angeles: University of California Press, 1974.

Solzhenitsyn, Alexander I. *The Gulag Archipelago*. New York: Harper, 1979. 3 vols.

Spence, Jonathan. *The Search for Modern China*. New York: W. W. Norton, 1990.

Stanislowski, Michael. *Tsar Nicholas I and the Jews*. Philadelphia: Jewish Publication Society, 1983.

Tolstaya, Tatyana. "Boris the First." *The New York Review of Books* (June 23, 1994).

————. "Undialectical Materialism." *The New Republic* (April 11, 1994).

Tuchman, Barbara W. *Stilwell and the American Experience in China, 1911–45*. New York: Macmillan Co., 1971.

Ulam, Adam B. *The Bolsheviks*. New York: Collier Books, 1965.

————. *The Communists*. New York: Charles Scribner's Sons, 1992.

Vaksberg, Arkady. *Stalin Against the Jews*. New York: Alfred A. Knopf, 1994.

Vasilieva, Larissa. *Kremlin Wives*. New York: Arcade Publishing, 1994.

Voinovich, Vladimir. *The Anti-Soviet Soviet Union*. New York: Harcourt, Brace, Jovanovich, 1985.

Volkogonov, Dmitri. *Lenin*. New York: Free Press, 1994.

Vudka, Aryeh, ed. "Caught in a Trap . . . Letters from Behind the Iron Curtain." (75 pp., stapled, 8½″ x 11″). Israel, July 1985.

Werth, Alexander. *Russia at War 1941–1945*. New York: E. P. Dutton, 1964. Reprinted in New York: Carroll & Graf, 1984.

Wettlin, Margaret. *Fifty Russian Winters*. New York: Pharos Books, 1992.

Wiesel, Elie. *The Jews of Silence*. New York: Henry Holt, 1966.

Willensky, Elliot. *When Brooklyn Was the World, 1920–1957*. New York: Harmony Books, 1986.

Winter, J. M. *The Experience of World War I*. New York: Oxford University Press, 1989.

Wyden, Peter. *The Passionate War*. New York: Simon and Schuster, 1983.